HOMEWARD
BOUND

To Maureen, David.
and Alfie its really
nice knowing you
Best Wishes
Bill van Romand

http://www.fast-print.net/bookshop

HOMEWARD BOUND

A catalogue record for this book is available from the British Library

ISBN 978-178456-211-3

First published 2015 by
FASTPRINT PUBLISHING
Peterborough, England.

PREFACE

"You should write a book about it!" they said. This was much easier said than done, but eventually I had to agree that it was a good idea and with that started the most daunting task of my life. I had to dig out 40 years' worth of sailing logs and numerous notes on the life I have lived and the places I have seen. I then began to appreciate what a privileged life I have been given. It certainly hasn't all been "plain sailing"; on the contrary, there were dangerous, life-threatening moments when I wondered what had possessed me to agree to take on a particular task and had prayed for guidance in getting me home safely.

I started my working life in 1959 as an apprentice in a steel window & door construction factory in The Hague but hated working in such unbelievably noisy and dirty conditions and craved the outdoor life. A year later, I decided to go to sea and, without encouragement from my parents (my Dad thought I would only last six months), I signed on as deck-boy on a Dutch cargo ship of the "Koninklijke Rotterdamsche Lloyd" later known as the P&O - Nedlloyd Line. Here I encountered my first taste of seeing the world from east to west stopping in almost all the countries near the equator belt.

These deep-sea days lasted just over 8 years, then I tried to live a life ashore but the sea was, by now, in my veins. Luckily I was given the opportunity of delivering motor boats across the sea and extensive inland waterways of Europe, reaching Finland in the north and Lebanon in the east. This was a totally new concept in boat deliveries. During this time, I also became known for testing newly-designed craft for several well-known boat builders. In 1986 I organised and executed the commissioning, hand-over and delivery of over 185 newly-built motor cruisers made in Taiwan and 10 years later I accepted the post of setting up, advising and running a boatbuilding facility in Egypt for a well-known UK boatyard.

Then in 2006, five years before retiring, I became the manager of a marina on the Thames, where I often amused my customers with my vast repertoire of sea-faring stories and was encouraged by them to write a book. So now, after seven years in the making, here is a small selection. I hope you enjoy reading them.

Acknowledgements

I would like to thank firstly my Grandmother, who encouraged me to go to sea and my girls, who were without me for most of the time; numerous boat builders and their agents, who believed in me; my customers who entrusted me with their vessels and June Ward who helped to unravel the mix of my Dutch and English grammar. Without them none of this would have been possible and I thank them all profusely for letting me pursue the making of this book.

B.v.B

Sailing Log

Total registered voyages:	761
With a total distance of:(645,580nm)	*1,196,259km*
Equivalent to going around the world	29 times
Longest voyages around the world	3 times
Longest non-stop voyage: Le Havre (France) - Bluff (New Zealand)	11,612nm
Longest held service: "Calypso II"	68 months
Second longest service: "Smit Lloyd 3"	14 months
Third longest held service on one vessel: STS "Ameland" (Shell tanker)	13½ months
New small craft commissioned: *from Taiwan-*	181
Longest small craft delivery: Gt Yarmouth - Beirut	3,600nm
Second longest small craft delivery: Düsseldorf - Bibione	3,400nm
Total voyages sailed single-handed:	129
Total distance covered single-handed:	57,650nm
Longest single-handed voyage: Düsseldorf - Gogolin (S of France)	3,010nm
Second longest single-handed voyage: Nice - Port Solent	2,649nm
Smallest craft delivery: Rapallo- Aranci nr Olbia	21 feet
Bay of Biscay crossings:	19
Passages through the French canals: *- of which 52 voyages single handed*	70
Fastest passage through the French Canals: *(October 1971 Burnham on Crouch – Antibes)*	10 days 16hrs
Passages through the German canals & rivers: *(Other than the river Rhine)*	36

River Rhine with various destinations: 78
-Emmerich-Dusseldorf-Colon- Frankfurt-Karlsruhe
-Strasbourg-Mulhouse.
Passages through the Dutch canals & rivers: 71
Passages through the Panama Canal: Quartermaster   6
Passages through the Suez Canal: Quartermaster   6

Regular Quartermaster on the navigable rivers & canals around the world: Maas, Schelde, Seine, Elbe, Weser, North-Ostsee canal, Noordzee Kanaal, Nieuwe Waterweg, Thames, Humber, Mersey, Buffalo Bayou to Houston, Mississippi, Alabama, Hudson, Rio de la Plata, Lake of Maracaibo, Shat-al-Arab waterway, Ganges to Calcutta, Chao Phraya and Mea Nam Nan.

Contents

HOMEWARD BOUND

Saint Jean Cap Ferrat - Port Solent

Duration:	35 days
Distance:	2649nm
Sailing hours:	340
Engine hours:	347
Fuel in Litres:	7341

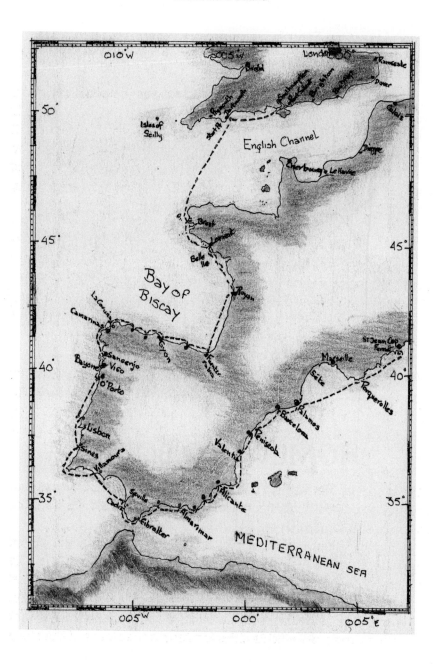

Saint Jean Cap Ferrat

Having been based in the south of France for the past three years on a 60 foot Classic Motor Yacht as skipper/engineer, I finally received the orders that we were going back to the UK. Of course it was fun and adventurous being here in this glorious location; anyone would have grasped at the opportunity to live in the most beautiful part of the south of France. Nevertheless I was glad to be on my way home soon.

We were situated in the little picturesque port of St Jean, which is strategically placed between Nice and Monaco on the lush, green hilled peninsular of Cap Ferrat with its red roofed villas. Sir Winston Churchill used to frequently visit a villa on the east side of the peninsular during the war, where he would relax and paint the most stunning scenery.

The owners and I had travelled the past three years extensively from here to numerous ports and bays including San Remo, Porto Fino, Elba, Capri, Amalfi, Positano, Sardinia, Corsica and the Balearics, but all this fantastic travelling around could not compare to going home.

My time spent in the Mediterranean was an experience I would not like to have missed and it was certainly a way of life quite different from the one to which I was normally accustomed.
If I was asked what was the most outstanding memory of this period in my life, then the first thing that would come to mind would be the way in which we explored the various coastlines, with the vessel travelling at a leisurely 8½ knots (nm), *a nautical mile =1853 metres*, which enabled us to hug the coast frequently, seeing views of rock formations, cliffs, old hillside cities located on the slopes of the steep

13

hills, dropping down to the water's edge, and sometimes just taking in the breathtaking, snow-capped mountain ranges in the background. Other times we sailed through very shallow, crystal clear, turquoise water with white foamed waves breaking onto pure white sandy beaches, but the greatest treat of all was that along many of the rugged coast lines we often came across beaches only accessible from the sea, where there was not a soul to be found - *like a desert island.* We would anchor and soak up the sun cooling ourselves in those warm crystal clear waters of the Mediterranean.

So, the conversation in September, was 'shall we, or shall we not?' and at the end of long discussions I suggested that if we were taking the boat back to the UK it would be better to do it now rather than later when winter was upon us, but due to circumstances beyond anyone's control, this was not to be.

Preparing for the Long Voyage Home

I started to prepare the boat for the long voyage home and as I had made this voyage three years earlier, I was able to dig out my paper work and refresh my memory as to what could be in store for me. It must be said that this little ship was extremely seaworthy but I still needed to be sure that all the safety equipment was up to date, and in doing my routine checks, I found that two of our three automatic bilge pump switches had to be replaced. The other thing I remembered from the last voyage was that the wheelhouse sliding doors had let in water badly; although this was more of a nuisance rather than being dangerous, I had already made a special water board for both the doors and hoped that these would work for me on my way home.

As part of the preparations I needed to take the boat out into the bay of St Hospice, which was conveniently just outside our harbour. For this, it needed to be a calm day so that I would be able to dive down to check the bottom of the boat, to clean the propellers, shafts and rudders from the build-up of barnacles, as it was during the summer period, with the sea temperature at an average 28 degrees Celsius that barnacles cling onto the boat for dear life. I certainly wasn't a diver and had slight claustrophobia but I ventured under the boat to scrape the propellers and rudders clean, taking me well over an hour.

Bay St Hospice with Monaco in the distance

The decision on the departure date was finally made but unfortunately for me, this was to be the end of November - *so much for the suggestion of doing the voyage earlier rather than later in the year!*

While making our plans, I had suggested tackling the voyage in two stages; the first stage would be single-handed as far as Gibraltar, to arrive in time for the festive season; the second stage would be with a crew and would commence in early spring when the weather was more predictable in the Atlantic. At this time, no decision was made on the final destination but it would be near the waters of the Solent between the British mainland and the Isle of Wight.

This would not be the first time I had taken a boat single-handed and the real beauty for me on this occasion was that I would be able to take my time; in fact, I was really looking forward to this voyage and to enjoying the time spent alone.

Walking path along St Hospice peninsular

There was no particular hurry in getting the boat to Gibraltar, except to be there in time to spend Christmas with the family. I didn't want to miss out on this as, like most families, Christmas is the only time of year when everyone is gathered together.

The day was nearly upon me and after all my preparations I was ready for my departure from St Jean Cap Ferrat. St Jean was only a 20 minute walk away along the sea front to Beaulieu sur Mer which lies at the bottom of a mountain range protecting the town -and us- from the severe weather conditions normally encountered when the Mistral wind blows from the Alps - *like a south facing garden wall at home, well sheltered and warm.*

This reminds me of a time long ago, when this high coast line was a blessing in disguise (Page 19) and taught a valuable lesson which gave me a wealth of additional experience.

It was in the very early days of the motor yacht boom (1969 - 1970) that I was introduced by a friend of mine to this totally novice idea of delivering motor cruisers by sea for a living, and I happened to be "in the right place at the right time".

In those days, luxury motor cruisers were in their infancy and very ill equipped, with little navigation equipment; radar and autopilots were mostly only used on commercial vessels. They were also rather small and the average 36 foot motor cruiser in the early seventies is now the 53 foot cruiser of today!

My experience in sailing small craft was just beginning, but this doesn't excuse me from getting into difficult situations like this, and others, that I have encountered.

Perhaps, some of the blame can be palmed off on my Merchant Navy days, where I was part of a team and was totally unaware of certain dangers, which were not my responsibility, and in particular the weather. Although I didn't really play a large role on the big ships, I soon learned that not paying enough attention to the weather was presenting me with unnecessary anxiety and it was only after a life-threatening experience later, in the Bay of Biscay, that weather forecasting and the possession of technical and mechanical knowledge became the most important part in my motor yacht deliveries. Unfortunately for me, it took several "instant shock treatments" to appreciate the need to respect the sea, especially in a small craft...

Anyway, it was time to say goodbye to all of my friends and some of them asked,

'Are you not going to miss being here?'

'No, I don't think so.'

I was so involved in getting the boat ready that I hadn't given it a thought, but I didn't think I would miss St Jean because we were heading towards winter and many people had gone home or stayed away from the harbour, leaving only a few others and me looking at a harbour without life, and to be honest, by now I was really looking forward to getting home myself.

Blessing in Disguise
Brundall, November 1971.

I had been given the task of delivering a 36 foot Motor yacht from Brundall on the river Yare in Norfolk, England to Athens, Greece via the French canals.

You could say that the boat and the voyage were almost doomed from the start. It all began with the building of this craft. The boatyard fitted her out with the then new, and unproven, up-rated engines. The owner, until now, a very patient Greek gentleman was getting quite anxious about receiving his boat; he had already waited since last summer and was told the delay was because of the engines.

This voyage through the French Canals was going to be my sixth since my start in boat deliveries and I was beginning to feel quite familiar and confident in navigating these great rivers of France. Of course, I was in possession of the proper navigation charts for the rivers and had made notes of importance at the side of the charts, for use every time I was passing through France.

I must say, November was not the best time in the year to be setting off on a 2500nm voyage from Brundall to Klyfada Athens.

First stop, Ramsgate. This stop was my last point of departure from the UK, where I would carry out my final check on the boat's mechanics, then fill her to the brim with fuel, which should carry me to Rouen - about 100km inland from Le Havre. *I found it easier to run straight up the river Seine rather than stopping in Le Havre and to get the "Permit de Circulation" custom clearance and fuel at the commercial port in Rouen.*

I refuelled the boat and found, to my horror, that she was consuming a lot more diesel than the average boat of this type and she did not perform accordingly; this meant that I could not do the intended distances between the Mediterranean ports without the support of two large oil drums to carry the extra fuel needed.

After leaving Ramsgate I set my heading across the channel, non-stop to Rouen, passing Le Havre on the way. From Rouen the plan was to sail on the river Seine, via Paris, onto the River Marne which I had recently discovered has the highest headroom, then through the beautiful canal system into the river Saône, where this particular story took place.

Canal de la Marne a la Saône

Thick fog had already hampered the voyage several times, but luckily I was able to continue, all-be-it at a slow pace. This slow progress was not appreciated by the owner who did not seem to understand the seriousness of fog. Personally, I thought I was doing rather well, and sailed through the canals at record speed. Finally I came out into the river Saône just above the town of Auxerre.

The River Saône runs through the Saône valley and often traps the fog, which is known to hang around for days.

By now it was December and I just happened to encounter a time of prolonged fog. I wouldn't say that I was totally confident in sailing through the fog on these rivers, but I had begun to gather enough experience of navigating in the mist by slowly following the river banks and using the kilometre signs, which kept me in navigable waters.

The first day on the river went well; although it was foggy, the river was narrow enough to allow me to see at least one side of the riverbank, and after a while I began to gain my confidence in sailing under these difficult conditions. The second day I followed the same procedure, however this was short lived...

07:00 - I woke-up and looked out of the saloon window but noticed that the fog was too thick and thought it better to stay put. In those days we did not have the luxury of radar nor autopilot, so the departure had to be postponed until the thick fog became less dense.

River Saône upstream Saint Jean de Losne

We had moored overnight just outside the lock, at km123, nearly 13km upstream from the ancient city of Tournus.

10:30 - at last, the fog had lifted enough to leave the lock. The current was carrying me downstream, which saved me putting on too much power.

Everything went well and the visibility was clear enough so that I was able to count the km posts one by one, but at km119 I began to lose visibility again, and I also had to navigate from one side of the river to the other in order stay in the main channel and avoid an island located in the middle of the river.

I felt a slight panic setting in, because the river had become much wider and I had lost sight of both riverbanks momentarily. I knew that somewhere in front of me now was the island. I slowed down to a mere drift, then... to my horror, I heard several loud crunches, banging and slamming noises, and the constant scraping of metal on the stern gear and propellers and I felt the boat being lifted several times as if going over road speed humps; the boat swung violently sideways and, after having thrown the dishes from the sink onto the floor, the boat finally came to a complete standstill.

I was shocked and perplexed and the only words I could say were 'I think we are aground!' Whilst uttering these words, I looked over the starboard side of the boat into the water and noticed leafless bushes sticking up out of the water close to the boat.

I took a deep breath and could feel my heart thumping fast and thought, what in heaven's name am I to do now? I left the boat where she was, lit up a cigarette, made myself a cup of tea and said, 'We won't be going anywhere' Rather an obvious statement, as there was no way that I was going to make any attempt to rescue the boat from its precarious position and, worse still, I couldn't possibly make an attempt until this thick fog had lifted.

My next job was to check that the boat had not received any

structural damage, like to the hull, and I also needed to inspect the fuel tank which was part of the bottom of the saloon. Thank God! The diesel tank was still intact, so at least we were safe for the time being.

I had come to the horrific conclusion that whilst trying to cross the river towards the other riverbank, I had struck the Digue (training wall).

Training walls are extensive, and used to regulate the flow of water in order to maintain a certain depth in the river and prevent corroding of the riverbanks when in flood.

A great amount of uncertainty entered my head and I must admit that I had become slightly nervous in attempting to salvage the boat without causing any further damage to her hull or underwater gear.

On the one hand, I knew that I couldn't stay here for long as the river level was high for now, but it could drop at any time and that would leave the boat stuck forever behind this training wall; on the other hand, I couldn't move until the fog had cleared.

The fog remained for the rest of the day and I told my crew we would keep 2 hourly watches through the night, just in case the fog lifted or the water level dropped dramatically.

The following morning the fog started to lift little by little, and by eleven o'clock I began to see the island ahead of us and, just as it said on the chart, it was preceded by a trail of tall grass neatly marking the line and direction of the training wall below the waterline.

I now had the additional problem in that the cargo barges had begun to make their way up and down the river and their wash was hitting and moving the boat about and, with the underwater gear still touching the ground occasionally, this could jeopardise the mobility of the boat.

Now I had no other choice than to try to get the boat back over the wall, preferably the same way as she had come!

I started the engines and checked whether we still had a set of propellers under the boat - thank God we did!

I gently swung the boat around and slowly moved her upstream towards the training wall and, with our hearts in our throats - not making a sound, we waited anxiously for her to hit the wall and hoped that she would hop over in the same way as she had been thrown over in the first place, and then... to my great surprise, the boat lifted herself straight over the wall and back into the river with a single bump! What a relief!

I didn't have time to analyse the situation but I think that the river level had risen overnight enough for the boat to clear the wall. Now that we were back into the navigable river again I tried to turn the boat to face downstream, but how stupid of me if I thought we had escaped disaster.

The boat began to sail in a full circle like a dog looking for its tail and I couldn't straighten her up. Now what?

The town of Tournus was only 6km downstream and once more we were lucky because I found out that we could drift, stern first, downstream and the boat would hold her steerage by means of counter-propeller, a tactic normally used when mooring stern first in a marina berth.

I am not sure how long it took, but sometime later I moored the boat safely alongside some empty sand barges, which were conveniently moored outside a Builders Merchant at the lower end of Tournus town.

So far, so good!

It was now Thursday afternoon and here we were with a boat which couldn't be moved until we could assess the damage and repair whatever was wrong with the underwater gear.

24

I went ashore to the Builders Merchant's office to see whether they would be able to help us in our hour of need.

I walked into the reception and asked the lady whether we could hire a crane locally, but before she could answer, her boss came out of his office and replied, in English, that he knew of a diver in Mâcon, 40km away, who would be able to dive but not before next Monday.

This left us with a peaceful weekend and, incidentally, the fog had returned once more and we couldn't see across the river for days.

The diver arrived on the Monday and, after a prolonged investigation, he stuck his head above the water, took his breather piece out of his mouth and said,

'I can't get the propellers off, but I will be able to take the rudders out without the boat being lifted from the water.'

That was a great relief, because there wasn't a crane or any other facility for lifting a boat around here, so I decided to go ahead with the project.

The diver finally came up with the rudders, or what remained of them! However, he optimistically stated that he could get them repaired locally.

It took a full ten days for the rudders to be returned and once the diver had fitted them we were on our way again.

The voyage down river was going well, except for the damaged propellers which gave us a bumpy ride; however, we were able to maintain a reasonable speed and reached the port of Marseille several days later.

In Marseille, I went to the local Chandlery and was told that they would be able to repair our propellers, and within the hour a diver came and dismantled them. They were in such a state they were unrecognisable, and I thought, if they can repair these, then they are real magicians!

However, being just before the festive season, we were unable to find anyone to do the job until the New Year. Now, with our mobility removed, we had no alternative than to wait for the New Year here in Marseille – not exactly a hardship.

Pierre, the Chandlery's manager, had promised me that once the festive season had passed, he would have the propellers back under the boat and would send us on our way again. In the meantime, I hadn't told a soul in the UK, not even my wife, about the incident and thought it was only fair that I pay for the repair myself as I felt that this was totally my fault - at least I had learned a valuable lesson from this affair.

Pierre kept his promise and on the 6th January we refuelled the boat, near the Marseille's pilot boat station, and took the opportunity of scrounging two fifty-gallon drums to fill with fuel, ready for the extensive distances I had to cover in Italy.

We were now ready to go to our next planned destination - the Old Port in Cannes. This had become my usual stop-over en-route to Malta and the Greek Islands. I found that this route was not much longer than the obvious straight line to the Strait of Bonifacio, which is the passage between Corsica and Sardinia; the reason for not choosing this latter route was because on my first voyage to Malta I was caught out in a most horrendous Mistral which is the strong to gale wind running from the Rhone valley into the Gulf of Lyons, which on some occasions can extend as far south as Majorca and as far east as Corsica and Sardinia, and I had promised myself never to do that again and to this day, I never have.

The day went well, and the newly repaired propellers were fantastic; all the vibrations had completely disappeared; in fact, I am sure the boat had become a hell of a lot faster. We arrived late afternoon in the Old Port of Cannes and found ourselves a place near the main Promenade close to the refuelling station, which fortunately was still open, so we refuelled the boat that same evening. We had already lost so much time and contrary to my widely held principles never to leave for a long passage in the evening, I decided to go for it this time.

At 19:00 we departed for Civitavecchia - *Old City* – located some 230 nautical miles away from Cannes and 50 miles north of Rome, on the main Italian coast.

Although it was only early January, this evening seemed almost too perfect; hardly any wind, a smooth sea, crystal clear visibility and a near full moon coming over the horizon. This beautiful moon lit the sea, at first with her reflections in a concentrated thin line but later becoming more wide-spread like twinkling little stars in the sky, making it a perfect evening for setting course for Civitavecchia, via the north of Corsica. I began to feel optimistic and confident once more, now that I had finally started the second half of the voyage.

We were already several hours away from the coast when we heard an almighty loud bang, but I didn't think anything of it as this could have been the drums, full of diesel, cooling and shrinking in the night's cold air.

Strangely, just after I heard this I thought that the boat was steering a little lopsided, so I trimmed her over with the hydraulic trim planes and this seemed to have done the trick. However, an hour later another even louder bang occurred and then, to my horror, I discovered that I had no steerage at all. The boat began to sail in circles; I pulled the throttle levers back and stopped the boat thinking, what in heavens name is it now?

I needed to check the linkage of the steering mechanism in the aft cabin; it could have been that by refitting the rudders in Tournus, the linkage wasn't secured enough and now, because of the vibrations, it had come adrift.

I had to move the drums of fuel away so that I could check the linkage which, to my surprise, was still intact. This puzzled me and I thought, what else can it be but then I despondently shouted out aloud, 'Oh, no! I am sure this can't be, or can it?' and momentarily I had this horrible feeling that we had lost our rudders!

But if I wanted to be sure then, unfortunately for me, I needed to get into the sea and check physically what was going on down there.

Luckily this type of boat had her stern gear fairly wide apart from the centre line making it easier to feel with my feet under the boat. I slowly lowered myself into the icy cold sea, I guess the temperature was about 10°C, until my chin reached the waterline; I then began to search for the stern gear with my feet and could clearly feel the propeller but... and I shouted '*****' this was my way of confirming that we actually **had** lost the starboard rudder, but to be sure I felt the area again as I still couldn't believe it; sadly, yes, the rudder had gone; I pulled myself across to the other side and, unbelievably, the port rudder had gone as well. What now?

Just short of hyperthermia, I slowly pulled myself up out of the sea and once more all my optimism had drained away and I asked myself the question, what on earth am I going to do now? For the first time I really didn't know what to do; now for the second time this voyage, my ability in handling extreme situations was put to the test. I knew that I needed to do something, but first a cigarette...

'We'll have to go back' I stupidly stated, but this was easier said than done. We had already covered a distance of 70 nautical miles, which had put us too far away from the South of France but alternatively, continuing to Corsica was not an option either as repairing this sort of thing on the island seemed most unlikely.

Scanning the horizon I found that my eyes became fixed into the direction of the South of France where I was able to make out the streetlights of the "Moyen Corniche", a road running half way up the mountains directly behind Beaulieu Sur Mer. Decision made, we're going back to the mainland; what a blessing in disguise!

I tried to set both engines at 1500 RPM in the hope - wishful thinking - that the boat would sail in a straight line, but soon I discovered that the boat wandered off course. I started to experiment and found that if I left the port engine running at 1500 RPM and alternated the other engine's RPM accordingly, then I was able to control the boat and could maintain a good course and, with the help of the road lights of the Moyen Corniche, this saved me staring at the compass needle.

Very relieved but exhausted, we finally arrived in the early hours of the morning in the Port of Beaulieu sur Mer. Well this was the end of the line for now and I was not in a position to keep this away from anyone and would have to tell the owner and the boatyard of my mishap with the boat.

When I finally made contact with the UK (in those days I needed to go to the post office and book the call to England and could wait up to 4 hours before they were able to make the connection with home) I was told to leave the boat where she was, and come back to England to pick up two new replacement rudders.

What happened to the old rudders? Well, I was told by the manufacturer that it was possible that the people who repaired the rudders in Mâcon had bent the blades back "cold" and by doing so had created a more serious fracture, and the continuous stress on the blades had made it easy for them to snap off!

I returned to the boat in early March with two new rudders and I am happy to say that this time I successfully completed the voyage to Athens. Sadly a year or so later, I learnt that this boat was used for smuggling from the near African continent and was impounded by the Greek authorities.

Hearing this I thought, this boat was jinxed after all!

St Jean Cap Ferrat - Porquerolles
Thursday 29th November 2001

I hadn't slept very well but awoke just as the sun was peeping over the horizon at the foot of the Italian coast hills. I had one last look over the harbour wall and gazed across the water directly onto the

Sunrise over the bay of St Hospice overlooking Monaco & Italy in the far distance

principality of Monaco and beyond. This had been my view for the past two and half years and what a view it was; I took a deep breath and with that I hoped to capture this view in my memory; I then slowly turned around and looked at the clock on the village church, which on many occasions had kept me awake every half hour - not only once, but twice just in case it hadn't been heard the first time.

I started to prepare for departure, taking in all the lines except the last one. I started my engines and, as if it had to be, the church bell chimed nine times while I simultaneously dropped the last anchor line into the water and pulled in the stern-line, symbolically detaching myself from this picturesque jewel. I slowly manoeuvred the vessel through the harbour, making sure not to create any wash; as I was passing the harbour entrance I automatically looked towards the harbour office and the Chantier Naval, and to my surprise, found that all the crew of the yard, whom I had known during my stay, were waving me off which was very moving and brought a tear to my eye; the church bell chimed nine times once more, stating that this was the end of an era.

I was just about to look back, when suddenly... I remembered the superstition in the Merchant Navy, "Never look back, or you will never see the place again." I was nearly tempted to turn around, but thought better of it. I knew that at some stage I would want to return but for now, it was enough.

The sea was calm, or at least in the St Hospice bay, where throughout the summer numerous yachts lie at anchor, some of them small but others very large with toys such as helicopters, water planes, and even another boat like a 43ft day cruiser or a 40ft sailing yacht on board - just in case the owner becomes bored with the big boat!

I pointed the boat towards Beaulieu sur Mer to pick up fuel. It was earlier this week that I had phoned around to find the cheapest fuel along the French Riviera, which happened to be right on the doorstep. I could have refuelled in St Jean by tanker lorry, but on one occasion I had ended up with more diesel on the beautiful teak deck and in the harbour than in the tanks, because the tanker lorry's pump was too fast for our boat, so Beaulieu sur Mer was the choice.

Ironically, this harbour has a long standing memory for me as I was asked to deliver an "Ocean 30" motor cruiser here many years ago; in fact, it was so long ago that the harbour had only just been completed and was still empty, except for a dozen or so boats and I wondered at the time how they were ever going to fill this place.

10:00 - I finished refuelling, 2.500 litres of diesel, and was ready to leave the marina; now with full tanks, I should easily reach the port of Alicante or even beyond, that is of course, if the weather stays favourable.

Now the vital question: what is my destination for today? Well, in the general direction of Gibraltar - I have no specific ports in mind; I find it more relaxing to let the boat and the weather take me, and then I'll never be disappointed. I wasn't planning a record breaking marathon but intended to coast-hop - *moving mostly in sight of the coast and not making extensive crossings* - most of the way.

After manoeuvring my way out of the east entrance of Beaulieu sur Mer, I headed directly towards the point at Saint Hospice's peninsular, which meant I would pass St Jean on my starboard side; therefore, without having to look back, I was able to have one last glance at this lovely port, before rounding the corner.

I fondly remembered the regular evening walk I had taken around the beautiful peninsular of St. Hospice & Cap Ferrat for the past two years; I had inevitably met many people, but one person who stood out in my mind was an elderly gentleman who slowly, but religiously, walked his dog halfway around the circuit of 3.8km. We often passed each other, exchanged a comment or two and then went our separate ways again. But one day, after I came back from leave in the UK, I noticed that something was missing and realized that the gentleman was no longer doing his walk. I saw another person who knew him too and he told me that, sadly, he had passed away the previous week whilst on his walk. I thought that was the nicest way for him to go.

The Bay of St Hospice was slowly disappearing from sight, signifying to me that the voyage had begun in earnest. It was as if the boat really wanted to go home; she moved along nicely at 8.3 knots, even with full tanks, which would normally slow her down, so I assumed that the current was in my favour.

10:30 - passing the lighthouse of Cap Ferrat at the southwest end of the peninsular, I began to see the coast and the town of Nice in the far distance. I could just make out the large war monument carved out of the rock face, and further to the right was the bay of Villefranche, which for a few years had become the anchorage for large cruise liners who used this bay for dropping off their passengers into tenders to do their shopping and sightseeing in Nice and Monaco. Sometimes there were two liners at the same time but today there were none; I suspected they had moved to warmer climates like the Caribbean; after all, it was nearly December!

The weather was perfect; the sun was shining with a visibility of more than 30 nautical miles and, with the wind blowing at 11 knots from the north, it could mean that a Mistral was in the offing.

I had set my course directly for Cap Camarat, which is not far from St Tropez, the artist town that grew in popularity because of the French actress Brigit Bardot, one of the first glamour girls who dared to wear a bikini in the late fifties/early sixties.

Passing the peninsular of Cap Camarat reminded me of the time I had to deliver a 46ft. Taiwan trawler yacht "Duck" (Page 38) and, unfortunately encountered a record series of incidents on the way.

This coastline has always amazed me with its breathtaking views of green hills filled with red roofed villas surrounded by palm trees; it almost looks like each and every one of them is trying to fight for a strategic spot overlooking the crystal clear blue Mediterranean Sea.

Just imagine that in the heat of a summer's afternoon this blue sea will be littered with numerous sailing boats leisurely cruising back and forth along the coast and, to complete the scene, there are the magnificent snow-capped mountains of the Alps set against a clear blue-turquoise sky – it's not surprising that people like to come here to chill out.

15:30 - passing Cap Camarat and an hour later it began to get dark.

Sadly the nights were going to be very long, but already the full moon was rising from behind the hills ahead of me; the sky was crystal clear and the moonlight was bright enough to see the outlines of the hilly shoreline with its street lights flickering like candle lights; a romantic and peaceful feeling swept over me - I can still appreciate a good thing when I see it.

There weren't many boats about but at one stage I tracked a boat coming towards me on radar; as she was passing me in the moonlight I noticed that she must have been doing a speed well in excess of 25 knots and I thought how foolish, one would only need to hit some semi-submerged object like a piece of wood or an oil drum or even a container, and it could do untold damage.

A flashing red light became visible in the distance, which was undoubtedly Cap Benat. This cape protrudes from the mainland directly opposite the island of Porquerolles. Checking my watch, I thought that was enough for today, even though I hadn't reached the 80 mile per day target I had set myself. It would have been foolish to continue and I was in no hurry, so I headed for the island.

I remembered that at the east end are some outlying and mysterious looking rocks, sticking up like pillars and unlit, making them difficult to spot. Luckily, the harbour east pier of Porquerolles has a light flashing with a red and white sector to guide you in, but this always seemed to bring me very near - ¼nm - to these rocks, making them look very eerie and scary in the dark. But once again I had successfully passed them and now could head directly towards the port of Porquerolles.

18:33 - safely moored, facing seawards, alongside the new visitors' quay. I stretched my legs and looked around the village but, to my surprise, it was deserted and looked like a ghost town - unlike in the summer when it is heaving and difficult to find a mooring space. It seemed that I was in for a quiet evening. I ate on board and after clearing the dishes I went ashore again to make my usual phone call home from the single phone booth on the island.

Just after I had gone to bed, a strong gusty wind started to pick up. In fact, it was so windy that the boat started to move about and it became too uncomfortable to sleep. So at 02:00 - I had to go outside, in my underpants, to secure extra ropes; luckily there wasn't anyone about to see this embarrassing sight!

The weather continued to deteriorate, and the wind changed from a northerly to a south-westerly direction, but I felt quite secure in this part of the marina.

Just after 07:00 a high speed catamaran passenger ferry arrived at the other end of the pier and a boat-load of passengers descended upon the island; it now became clear to me that most of the people had left the island for the night, returning this morning to work here during the day.

A little later I noticed the arrival of an old steel ferry which headed at full speed straight for the end of the pier and, just before hitting the pier head, made a full U turn - like a car doing a hand brake spin on ice - bellowing lots of black smoke and massive turbulence from its revolving propellers; he then shot backwards, at great speed, towards the sloping quayside and stopped the boat JUST in time to avoid crashing into the concrete wall. I wondered whether the skipper ever considered what would happen if his engine control failed.

A small number of cars disembarked and a little later two builders' trucks arrived at the port and reversed onto the little ferry. The drivers were instructed to position the trucks towards the bow of the boat; I thought this was to balance the boat, but I was wrong; from around the corner of the harbour office came a full sized refuse lorry.

The driver skilfully turned his lorry around and carefully began to back her up towards the ramp. 'STOP' shouted the crew; Thank goodness, I thought, how can this big lorry get onto this ferry, it already has two trucks squeezed on board. He then drove away from the ramp, but this was just to reposition himself and, to my amazement, he managed to squeeze this big lorry into a space on this small ferry. The ferry started her engines and left in much the same way as she had arrived, at full throttle, like the skipper had no time to lose, and as if he was in a powerboat race!

I followed the progress of this ferry with my binoculars as I was curious to see how she behaved on the high swell in the open sea between the island and the mainland.

Her progress seemed fine whilst she was running behind the island, but then, she started taking on the waves and I could clearly see how she buried her nose into the waves followed by the water spouting up high into the air and blowing across her.

After having seen this pandemonium I went to start my engine room inspection and from the depths of the engine room I heard the roaring of engines and couldn't believe it, but the ferry was back already and the skipper was repeating his daredevil manoeuvre all over again! Oddly, the ferry ran three more runs and then called it a day. I couldn't get over what I had seen and I had completely forgotten to check the weather forecast, which was displayed in the marina office.

The forecast predicted a change in wind direction, which was now to come from the north-east; this meant that I would be able to depart tomorrow morning and run along the coast-line towards Marseille, or perhaps as far as Port Camargue which is at the west side of the River Rhone. Knowing this, I told the young man behind the desk that I would like to pay for two nights and, with his cigarette

half hanging out of his mouth, he said

'OK that will be 416 francs or £42.00'

I thought this was rather steep and said,

'Are you sure?'

'Oui'

'Isn't that a little expensive?'

'No sir, in the summer it will be double!'

I told him I only had 400 francs on me, but he would not accept that.

'Up the road is a bank with a hole in the wall where you can get yourself some money' This gave me the opportunity to stretch my legs and I had a leisurely walk around the town; although the ferry had dropped off a boat load of people earlier, the place still looked like a ghost town.

Fortunately for me, the hole in the wall was out of order, so we settled on the 400 francs.

Later in the afternoon people started to gather at the harbour quay ready to board the ferry, which departed at 17:00 and now once again, an eerie silence had returned to the island for the night.

The Epic Voyage of the Trawler Yacht "Duck"
Spring 1987

This was probably one of the most daring voyages I have ever undertaken and involved no less than four boats on a single voyage from Düsseldorf via Brighton and the French canals to Viareggio (Italy), Rovinj (Yugoslavia) St Giorgio di Nogaro (Italy) and Krk (Yugoslavia). Complicated? That's an under-statement, if you like!

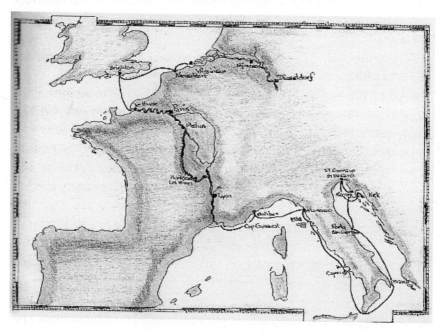

At that time, I was working for a German company who specialized in importing boats from Taiwan. I had nicknamed these boats the "Taiwan-take-aways" because they always needed a tremendous amount of "finishing off" upon their arrival in Europe.

Anyway, this 46 foot trawler yacht arrived in the Port of Rotterdam in late December 1986 on a large container vessel. After completing the formalities and mechanical checks, Pete, Martin and I set off from Rotterdam, in extreme cold and thick fog conditions, up the river Waal & Rhine to Düsseldorf and this took an unbelievably hard and exhausting two days. A sea voyage in such conditions would possibly have been more manageable, but these rivers are used as super highways to Germany, France, Luxemburg and Switzerland by a vast amount of barges, between 1200 and 5000 ton, and sometimes they would be passing each other five abreast. Upon arrival we prepared the trawler yacht so that she could be displayed at the Düsseldorf Boat Show in January 1987.

At the show, Karl, our sales executive, introduced me to the owners of the boat,

'This is Bill, our Dutch skipper, who will be able to deliver your boat. Bill does all our boat movements and I am sure he can sort out all your needs!' and with those words Karl left me with the owners.

This was very unfair as, at that time, I could hardly speak German, which made explaining the details of this complex, and nearly impossible, delivery somewhat difficult but I had many years of experience in gesticulating with hands and arms, while stringing together a number of Dutch-English words, and this seemed to work well.

'Hi Bill, we have been told that you can deliver our boat to Rovinj in Yugoslavia via the French canals. '

I took a deep breath and slowly shook my head from side to side; giving me time to collect my thoughts and find the suitable words so as not to offend them.

'I am not so sure whether your boat will fit through the canals; let me do some calculations and come back to you'. Karl, (a true salesman) had already said to them that going through the French canals would not be a problem, so their faces dropped when I had to tell them that it would be very difficult, or even impossible, because the fixed headroom of the boat was 12cm too high and must be dropped in order for her to pass under the lowest bridges in France.

After our meeting I went away to re-calculate and see how I could possibly make this happen; after tapping endlessly on my calculator, I found one possible solution - the boat needed to be filled with 200 plastic bags of sand ballast with a combined weight of at least 4000kg; this would get me through the bridges and also leave just enough depth under the boat.

It was now the end of January and with the Düsseldorf Boat Show over and done with, I had my hands full organizing and executing the logistics of getting all the eleven boats out of the hall: four of them onto lorries, seven of them back into the river Rhine, and preparing those in the water for their final hand-over to the various customers.

The only boat I didn't have to get ready for hand-over was the one I was taking to Rovinj and that would take a lot more preparation! But for now, with all the boats out of the way, I took the opportunity of taking my 10 day leave.

Upon my return from leave, armed with plastic bags and a ton of enthusiasm, I started the preparations for the delivery of the 46 foot trawler yacht; I called Karl and told him that I was ready to go; Karl answered

'Bill can you do me a favour, I need you to pick up a new Birchwood 37 from Brighton and deliver her to Viareggio' a pause, then he continued,

'I thought that as you are going through the French canals you could take her with you at the same time?'

Totally stunned and flabbergasted I innocently asked,

'You... mean... Viareggio, the town in the north of Italy?'

'Yes, that Viareggio, but don't worry, I have sorted a crew for you; Peter will join you to drive this Birchwood.'

So now, not only did I have the 46 foot trawler yacht to worry about, but also a second, brand new, untried boat to take through the canals.

Start of the Voyage

Now all I had to do was to wait for Peter and two other young lads (who were persuaded by Karl to come as a sort of a holiday) to arrive. Peter brought all the necessary paperwork and the name for the Trawler Yacht which was now officially called "Duck" and with this, the epic voyage had finally begun on the 27th February 1987.

The first day we only travelled from Düsseldorf to Emmerich, the German-Dutch border on the Rhine. Here we had to clear the boat with the German customs because the "Duck" was temporarily imported and now needed to be rubberstamped to state that she had officially left German waters - the civil servant never even came to see whether the "Duck" actually existed!

So, having stamped those papers, he left me with the new responsibility of making sure that I signed the boat, crew and myself in and out of Holland. I was told this procedure needed to be done in Rotterdam as this was the official exit point from the Netherlands.

We left Emmerich and sailed 10km down the river to the little town of Lobith on the Dutch-German border, where we filled up with duty-free fuel. The fuel barge was also the local "supermarket afloat" so we had a field-day buying all the goodies we wouldn't be able to buy elsewhere. Then, in my wisdom, I called into the Customs Office to enquire whether I was correct in clearing the boat and crew in Rotterdam but, to my great surprise, the officer told me that he could do the paperwork there, as long as I promised to leave Holland within the next 24 hours. So we departed immediately for Vlissingen (Flushing) rather than having to detour via Rotterdam.

Soon after leaving Lobith, we encountered heavy snow, which

reduced our visibility to almost zero and, with the river flowing at an alarming rate, we needed to keep a good lookout as this particular section of river was a busy crossroads and to stop the boat in an emergency would take some considerable distance. As it was getting late, I needed to find a safe mooring in the next town and after a strenuous few hours we arrived in the port of Nijmegen on the river Waal.

On the last day of February we departed Nijmegen, hoping to make the Dutch-Belgian border at Vlissingen that same day. This was a task and a half, but I remembered what the Customs Officer had said and I didn't want to break the rule.

The day went brilliantly well except for the occasional snow shower. An intense snow shower occurred just 500 metres before the one kilometre long bridge over the Hollands-Diep, and now in poor visibility and without radar, navigating in-between the bridge pylons was very scary indeed. But then all of a sudden it all cleared as if nothing had happened.

The old Moerdijk-bridges across Hollands-Diep

At around 16:00 we reached the last lock at Hansweert before entering the river Schelde. As we were so early, I told the crew that we were going to carry on for as long as possible, but because I was the only experienced person on board I needed to avoid a full night passage.

17:30 - we passed Vlissingen and slowly made our way across the main shipping lanes in order to hug the Belgian coast and although the cruising speed was only 9 knots, we still made fantastic headway; in no time we passed the sea port of Zeebrugge. Little did I know but I had set my course across the area where one of the most horrific sea disasters was to take place in a few days from now.

We finally arrived in the port of Nieuw-poort just on the border between Belgium and France. Although we arrived at midnight, I hoped to leave again at the crack of dawn.

Heading for Brighton

Today I had planned to sail to my next destination, the port of Brighton, using the edge of the inshore shipping route, south of the "West-hinder" light vessel - one of the last working light vessels in existence at the time. I then intended to cross the main busy shipping lanes towards Dover and Dungeness and along the coast, passing Newhaven and finally Brighton Marina in order to pick up my second boat on this voyage, the "un-named" Birchwood 37.

The voyage was progressing well, with the North Sea reasonably calm and not much wind, but the brilliant winter sunshine on a clear blue sky was a recipe for an extremely cold night and the likelihood of dense fog.

From Dungeness we sailed in a direct line to Beachy Head and, as I had predicted, it became misty; I just crossed my fingers and hoped that this was the most we would encounter.

22:00 - we passed the "Seven Sisters" cliffs and, as I had feared, the earlier mist became more dense in places and eventually became thick fog; not having radar, auto pilot nor GPS made it very difficult to keep a good course and, in order to avoid drifting towards the beach I had set the course well off the coast, but we would soon have to close in towards the shore at Brighton. I slowed down from 9 to 7 knots, hoping this would give ample time to take avoiding action if needed.

By the sound of Newhaven's foghorn, it seemed that we had passed the entrance, with just another 7 miles to Brighton Marina.

We needed to be very careful as we closed in towards Brighton, and I asked all of my crew to listen out for any signs of life, and in particular the fog horn of the marina. Although the engines were noisy, it still felt quite eerie; the night was pitch dark and all we could see was a dark grey mass of fog ahead of us.

Then... this grey dense mass turned into a deep orange glow and before I could think what that meant I heard a loud crunching and banging on the bottom of the boat and almost instantaneously felt the boat being lifted and shuddered about, stalling both engines at the same time. We came to an abrupt stop, all losing our footing and I realised to my detriment we were stranded firmly on the beach, presumably not very far from Brighton Marina's east harbour wall.

Looking up into the sky, I could see the street lights through the fog - which turned out to be the orange glow I had seen earlier - and, as you can imagine, this was not a good place to be in the late evening; adrenaline rushed through my veins and all I could think of was to get the boat off the beach as quickly as possible because it was the third hour after high water and the tide was dropping fast; with these thoughts a slight panic had set in. Come on now, you will have to compose yourself, get your thinking cap on and try to get out of this mess!

Having had a few moments to think, I started the engines and as the boat was facing with the bow up the beach, I needed to move her stern first. I tried reversing but the engines kept stalling; however I wasn't going to give up but the boat wouldn't budge and time was marching on; I knew that "time and tide would wait for no man"; the situation became desperate and I had to get her off the beach; if only I could give more power, but every time I reversed I could hear the propellers crunching the beach pebbles. I thought it's now or never and pressed the engines to their limit and after several attempts and heavy vibration, the boat began to show signs of movement; I just hoped we hadn't holed the boat in the process. I asked Peter to stay below in the cabin and check for any signs of water ingress.

Finally, and with a huge sigh of relief, I succeeded in getting the boat afloat; now we needed to find the harbour entrance but we couldn't hear the fog horn. The boat began to shudder and shake, but at least we were moving and luckily we didn't seem to be holed. I knew, by the way in which the boat was shuddering, that the propellers were badly damaged but I wasn't too sure what state the rudders were going to be in; now I seemed to have enough steerage, so maybe they were alright; I would need to have the boat lifted, for a thorough inspection, in the morning.

Slowly we made our way towards the harbour entrance, and after a good half hour, and well shaken-up, we finally entered Brighton Marina. Having moored the "Duck" safely alongside the visitors' pontoon, I went to the harbour master's office and explained what had just happened; the young lad in charge just shook his shoulders and said

'Sorry captain, the fog horn hasn't been working all evening, but I have reported it and they will look at it in the morning.'

Thanks... the words 'horse' and 'bolted' sprung to mind... the damage had already been done.

Voyage through France

The following morning I called the office in Germany and told Karl of the incident; all he was able to say was

'Can you fix it?' and added,

'How long before you can be on your way again Bill?'

'I don't know, but I will get moving as soon as the job is done.'

The boat was lifted the same day and as luck would have it, we only seemed to have damaged the propellers. The dock master gave me the name and address of a company situated in South London, who specialised in repairing underwater gear. I loaded the shrivelled-up propellers and made my way there in a hired car, hoping that the propellers could be refurbished quickly.

When handing them over, I was told that I could pick them up the next day; surprisingly, it had only taken us just two days.

In the meantime the new "unnamed" Birchwood 37 had arrived by lorry from the Nottingham factory and was launched preceding the "Duck". We refuelled both boats and split the crew: Peter had his crew on the Birchwood and I had the other boy with me on the "Duck".

At midday we were ready to set off on the next leg of the voyage, across the channel to Le Havre, in order to wait for the incoming tide and would then proceed up the River Seine to Paris and beyond.

The day was very pleasant, the sea was smooth once again and Peter felt it necessary to open up the throttles on the Birchwood; he started playing about for a short while, circling the "Duck" – like a little dog playing around his master; his boat was fitted with very powerful engines, therefore a lot faster and perhaps he had become bored with sailing slowly behind me all the way.

We arrived on the same day, late afternoon, in Le Havre but, as luck would have it, the tide had just turned in our favour so we were able to sail straight up the river Seine nonstop to Rouen.

It was very late, in fact 2.00 a.m., when we arrived in Rouen, all totally exhausted. Personally, I was very pleased that we had finally left the sea behind; after all, it was the end of February and so far, weather-wise, we had been very fortunate.

From Rouen we steadily moved up river and made fantastic progress, only stopping once at the lock in Conflans, where we had to wait for another barge to arrive. Whilst waiting in the lock I was told that the two young crew members had had enough and said that they didn't want to continue the voyage; when I asked them why, they said that they only had two weeks holiday and as the stop-over in Brighton had taken so long, they now needed to make their way back to Germany before the following Monday.

This setback wasn't too bad; Peter had enough experience to drive the Birchwood by himself and I felt confident enough to sail the "Duck" single handed. I didn't think anymore of it and a few hours later we stopped for the night one lock just before Paris.

Disastrous News

The following morning we started early as usual and negotiated the last lock before Paris, when on the news - *in those days I always listened to radio 4* - I heard, to my horror, that the previous evening the "Herald of Free Enterprise" had capsized outside Zeebrugge on the Belgian coast. Hearing this was a real shock and, having been at sea as a professional, I was trying to work out what could have caused this; one of my thoughts was that perhaps they had loaded the vessel top heavy. I was totally pre-occupied and listened most of the day to the latest updates, but I never did find out *that day* what really happened.

Much later, it did come to light that the ramp doors were left open and, of course, even the smallest amount of water entering in the wrong place would make her top heavy - *my thoughts were correct.*

A few hours had passed since the dreadful news and we finally arrived in the centre of Paris at Pont Alexander III at the Touring club de France.

Peter and I said our goodbyes to our German lads and moved on upstream towards our intermediate destination, Saint Mammes - the junction with Canal du Centre and Shalon sur Saône. I chose this particular route rather than the Canal la Marne a la Saône because of a certain railway bridge at Vitry-le-Françoise, as I was not sure that the "Duck" would make the height, which is generally 3.60 metres. This would have been alright, but this bridge is very deep and I have been stuck on it in the past.

Before we arrived at Saint Mammes, we needed to find a crane so that we could lower the aft-deck sunroof, and also an "Aggregate Depot" where we could buy 4 tons of sand!

After a further day's sailing from Paris, we made the town of Melun where I just happened to spot a Dutch barge carrying a hydraulic crane which was used to embark and disembark their cars. I must admit, I had been anxious to find one of these barges. I hear you ask: what would I have done if I was unable to find a crane? Well, I would have tied the boat up under a bridge and, with the help of a rope and tackle, we should have been able to do the job but it was much more complicated than it sounds - lowering the roof by crane was far easier.

Anyway, I went alongside the barge and asked the owner whether he was willing - *for a fee of course* - to lift the roof for us; being a Dutchman, he was all for it, and thought it was a challenge. Within the hour, the roof was down and stored.

Time for Loading Ballast

We moved further upriver, where we found an "Aggregate Depot"; we secured the boats alongside a concrete wall with the "Duck" nearest the quay and the Birchwood alongside her. Looking on the river navigation chart I found that we had moored at Fontaine-le-Port near the town of Vulaines sur Seine.

I went ashore, found the office in the far corner of the yard and, in my broken French, asked whether I could buy 4000 kg of sand.
The girl behind a high counter replied,
'Sure, where is your lorry?'
'Oh no, we have a boat and we need to put the sand in the bags to

act as ballast for the canals.'

I really shouldn't have tried to explain this to her, as she didn't have a clue what I was on about.

I went back to the boat and minutes later a large bulldozer with flashing lights and bleepers announced its arrival.
The driver asked

'Where do you want this sir?' and I pointed towards the edge of the quayside where he dumped a mountain of sand on the ground. I said,

'Thanks' but he replied,

'No, I have another load for you shortly.'
Peter and I looked at each other and had to laugh. All I could say was, 'Sorry, Peter.'

'Don't worry, we'll get through this, but are you sure this will do the job?'

'Well, I hope so.'

'We'd better get started then, Bill.'
Well, I have done some strange things in my life but this tops the lot!

Peter sat on a bag of sand, holding the bags at the edges whilst I scooped the sand into them. Peter, being a very strong guy, offered to carry the sand on board and painfully stowed it all over the boat, starting under the large aft sundeck. We had to stow the bags in two layers and Peter had to crawl endlessly under the sunroof.

In the beginning the boat was quite stable but the more bags we positioned on board, the more unstable she became; in fact, at the end, we could only place 8 bags on one side and then we had to balance it out carefully over the other side before the boat heeled over too much.

I was aware that I couldn't sail with the bags for too long because I wasn't sure how the boat would react to the wash created by passing boats, and bearing in mind how easily the "Herald of Free Enterprise" had sunk, our "Duck" could sink for a similar reason!

Setting-off for the Canals

After a full day's hard work we lowered the boat by the 12cm, giving us a new depth of 1.65 metres and a maximum headroom of 3.60 metres - which was still, in fact, 5cm too high. However at 16:00 - we were ready to move on again.

As usual, I led the way. Because of my restricted depth, I wasn't sure how the boat would react under bridges with tow paths, where she would need to be brought to a near stand-still so she wouldn't suck too much water away from under the bridge and leave me grounded.

The following few days we covered a lot of ground and arrived at the town of Montceau-les-Mines by Saturday evening. Montceau-les-Mines is famous for its special glazed roof tiles in many different patterns and colours.

We went to celebrate our achievements by eating out, accompanied by a pint or two - or perhaps three or four - which wouldn't matter, as on Sundays the canals are closed to navigation.

We talked about how pretty the place was with all those colourful roofs and... out of the blue, Peter asked where we were in relation to a big town. I answered

'The nearest town is Shalon sur Saône, Peter.'

'Oh good' I was now really puzzled and asked,

'Why?'

Then... Peter dropped the biggest clanger yet,

'I need to be back in Germany on Tuesday.'

It took me a few moments to register and then I asked,

'What has happened?'

'Oh it's nothing serious, but I have my coach driving exam on Tuesday.'

'Peter..., I really didn't know you needed to go back; what am I to do now?'

'Sorry Bill, but I did tell Karl before I took on this voyage and he said that's fine, you should be there (Yugoslavia) by then.' *Honestly, some people have no idea how long things take!*

I was hoping he could help me finish the last thirty locks downhill, but he said,

'Sorry Bill, but I can't afford to miss this exam. I have already paid a lot of money for the course so far and I will lose it all if I don't turn up; I am sure Karl won't reimburse me, so that means I have to leave first thing Monday morning.'

I organized a hire car for Peter then made a call to Karl and asked him whether he was aware of this situation. As always, he responded in his usual deep, calm, controlled voice,

'Yes I know'

I thought, that's typical, nothing will disturb this man! Then I asked,

'Karl what are we to do? I will need two crew for the Birchwood and crew for me also!'

Karl responded,

'OK, where do you want me send the crew, Bill?'

'Well, the nearest place is Shalon sur Saône; can you send them today?'

'That's not possible, that's too soon; can't you just continue...?'

I hastily interrupted his sentence,

'Do you mean on my own?'

'If you can' and before I knew it, I had stupidly answered,

'OK. But can you please promise to have the crew ready for me by the time I get to Lyon, on the river Saône. I am now about five days away from there!'

After Peter had left, I tried to make sense of it all and asked the question, what have I let myself into this time? Now I will have to take each boat down the canals separately and when I reach the river, I will tie the two boats together; this shouldn't be too difficult as the river Saône is wide and the locks are very large.

The run with the first boat, the "Duck", went smooth enough; the locks were close together and it only took me a day and a half to reach the last lock before the river. That is except for one bridge which was extremely low, and my heart went in my throat as this bridge happened to be on a 10km stretch which meant that it was impossible for the water level to be lowered; if I hit the bridge it would be the end of the "Duck"! All I needed to do was to wait patiently and hope the water level would stabilise, all the time panicking and thinking, what if she can't make it? At the same time I was frantically trying to find a plan "B"; I didn't need to think any longer because, for some reason, the water level started to drop again; seeing this, I made the snap decision to pull the boat by hand carefully through the bridge. I held my breath and could feel my heart thumping faster and faster, constantly checking and crossing my fingers that the water level wasn't going to rise dramatically, which could have been disastrous; thankfully, the level remained low enough and once the highest part of the boat passed the bridge girders I breathed a great sigh of relief and shouted 'Yes... I did it!'

After that, all went well and I sailed the "Duck" safely to the end of the canals.

After securing the boat at the last lock I walked up to the lock keeper's control cabin. 'Bonjour Monsieur' I told him that I was the skipper of the "Duck" moored at the lock. My French was terrible but I was able to make him understand that I was leaving the boat there whilst going back, by taxi, to Montceau-les-Mines to collect another boat. The lock keeper looked totally perplexed but organised a taxi for this mad Dutchman!

It only took half an hour to get back to the Birchwood which had been patiently waiting at the quayside in the town centre of Montceau-les-Mines.

The voyage with the second boat went well and I finally met up with the "Duck" the following day, now being Wednesday 18th March. I moored both boats together along the landing stage and secured them side by side. I felt pretty pleased with myself.

Finally Back on the River

Now the time had come to execute my skills and I carefully manoeuvred away from the landing stage, a bit clumsily at first, but made it into the river Saône. In the meantime, I still had the 4 ton of sand on board, which reduced the boat's speed. "I'll have to get rid of the sand ASAP." I know what to do; I'll dump it back into the river once I have passed the town of Shalon sur Saône. After passing through the town, I continued until I was well out of sight; I stopped the boat in the middle of nowhere and dropped anchor at the outer edge of the fairway. I started to dump the sand into the river and what happened next was a total surprise to me. During all my voyages through the French canals I have never seen a police boat moored, let alone on the move, but whilst I was ditching the sand, a small speedboat with blue flashing lights came alongside and a Policeman politely asked,

'What are you doing sir?' I tried to explain that I was dropping the sand back into the river.

'That's fine but not the plastic bags!'

I pointed at the pile of empty bags showing a sign of agreement and he said,

'Have a nice day.' Oddly, he never asked what I was doing on my own with two boats and a pile of sand-bags!

After the police had left I stayed at anchor until the next morning.

I arrived in Lyon the following day, in the late afternoon. Lyon is one of my favourite towns and has the charm of a Mediterranean city with its abundance of beautiful architecture and churches; it is also the town where the Rhone and the Saône merge into one and flow for another 330km (210miles) downstream through the medieval towns of Avignon and Arles to the Mediterranean Sea, with Marseille on one side and Aigues Mortes on the other.

It was time again to look for a barge with a crane and luckily there was one just in front of me, near the railway bridge; it was a Dutch barge again, this time run by two brothers who helped me to erect the aft-deck roof on the "Duck" and put all the other large parts back into their places.

I called Germany from the main post office in the town, where I had to wait a good hour before I was connected, unlike nowadays when we all walk around with our phones and expect an answer immediately.

Surprise, surprise! Karl told me that he had not sorted a crew but if I could get to Marseille then this would give him enough time to organise something for me. Once again, I am sure he had no idea exactly what this entailed; in fact, he said that he might be able to get Peter to come back and help.

On my way back to the boats I started to have crazy ideas: I didn't think that I would have any difficulties in getting the two boats side by side down the river to Port St Louis du Rhone and if Peter was going to join me again then we should be able to tow the Birchwood with the "Duck"

So, I went to the chandlery at the Lyon's refuelling barge and bought 150 metres of 18mm diameter nylon rope and 50 metres of chain, normally used for anchors associated with this type of boat.

Fuelled-up, rope, chain, shackles, all round towing lights and re-stocked food, I left Lyon to set-off downstream towards the Mediterranean.

After the first lock, Bolene at Lyon, I negotiated the first part of the free-flowing section of river through the valley of Vienne, where I ended up with a "little difficulty"; the wind was being funnelled through the valley and blew in the opposite direction of the current, which made the river very choppy and, as the two boats didn't move in tandem, they kept hitting each other and eventually the anodized aluminium fendering was ripped out of the side of the Birchwood.

I managed to get safely through the lock at Vienne and at Condrieu turned into a newly built marina to inspect the damage; I seemed to have been lucky; the aluminium fendering was only out of shape and after some hours of careful labour I had it all back together again. After completing the repair I stood there thinking, what can I do now? I couldn't go back to Lyon and staying here was not an option either, so I continued the voyage downstream.

The following afternoon, I reached the entrance to the River Rhone. Phew!

You've Overstepped the Mark This Time!

So far, I had travelled with two boats for eight days, re-mounted all the equipment and parts such as roof, radar, mast and was still without a crew. To be honest, you only have yourself to blame!

What was about to happen was really stupid and it is only now, all those years later, that I am able to tell this story and smile about the whole affair; I was about to be brought down to earth with an almighty bump, luckily without any pain, just a very battered ego.

In hindsight, I should have insisted on having a crew before moving on, instead of having faith in Karl's 'Jaaaa, Jaaaa, Jaaaa, they will come to you soon' – this was not to be the case!

As soon as I left Lyon I started to prepare the boats for towage; I spliced eyelets in the ropes, attached shackles in the appropriate places, then connected the anchor chain of the Birchwood with the 50 metre chain; the tow had now become 200 metres. I prepared the ropes and cables on the deck so that when I left the restricted waters I could slowly lay the chain and rope behind me into the water until its full length was laid out, and a small pull and tuck on the "Duck" would inform me that the Birchwood was following me, like a dog on a lead!

I started to tow very cautiously away from the canal entrance into the Golf de Fos, which is the bay adjoining the exit of the river Rhone. I pushed the throttle levers slowly forward and reached 4.5 to 5 knots. I thought, I can handle this, although it did seem to be a bit slow for me; oh well, never mind, I will have to take it easy around here anyway because there is an awful lot of commercial traffic activity about - BIG container vessels and oil tankers.

So far, both boats rode the waves well but as the "Duck" didn't have an autopilot I needed to steer her by hand, which meant that I had to sit behind the wheel for all of the 350 miles or so to Viareggio, which made getting drinks, food and even going to the loo very difficult. But..., I had a pleasant surprise, something I hadn't anticipated, because the tow provided me with an artificial autopilot and kept the "Duck" in a straight line; this was unbelievable and a great relief as now I didn't have to be a permanent fixture behind the wheel and would be able to lead a normal life, getting my food and drink and having those essential trips to the loo!

Having cleared the Golf de Fos - and all its traffic - I slowly increased the speed and reached an acceptable 8.5 knots. Wow, this is better than I had hoped for; I now began to enjoy myself; deep blue sea, white rocks, warm sunshine; it was all ticking over nicely – **"Heaven"** what more could I wish for!

15:00 - Passing the islands of Ribaud and Porquerolles; luckily there wasn't much traffic about today except ferries running from the mainland to the islands. Brilliant, this was just what I needed because I couldn't be sure that pleasure craft skippers would notice that I was towing.

Later in the afternoon a strong breeze developed from over the mountain range.

19:00 - I prepared my dinner for the evening, not because I was getting hungry, but I couldn't leave the wheel so easily when it became dark. It took about 20 minutes to cook, which meant that my time at the wheel was "on and off". When my dinner was in the last stages of preparation I went to have my last checks around the boat, before darkness came.

When I came to check the tow rope I had the shock of my life and shouted aloud 'Oh Shit, Shit, Shit...' I couldn't believe my eyes, but... the Birchwood was no longer behind me! I broke out in a cold sweat, with the back of my throat drying-up there wasn't enough water in the world that could quench my thirst and at the same time my knees began to tremble uncontrollably and the only thought was, what have you done you stupid man! What in heavens name was I thinking of, and what am I to do now?" still swearing repeatedly.

It would soon be dark and I desperately needed to find the boat. "Yes... I admit it! I have definitely overstepped the mark this time. How in heavens name can you lose the tow?"

I stopped the "Duck" and immediately she swung sideways into the waves making her roll about violently in the choppy seas. I needed to re-orientate myself and thought that I must sail back into the direction I had just come from, but before I could do this I had to pull all of the 200 metres of tow equipment out from the depths of the deep blue sea.

I carefully scanned the horizon and… let me see… there was St Raphael in the distance ahead of me, and further back the bay of St Tropez and there, in the far distance, was Cap Camarat, Yes… No… Yes… there, just off Cap Camarat was a small dot; I am not sure, but could that be the Birchwood? Now the next question - how am I going to get her back?

Because of this episode, I had totally forgotten my dinner; never mind, my appetite had gone and I didn't think it would return that evening!

I just kept saying to myself over and over again, how stupid can you be; you were trying to be too clever; you should have known better, but on the other hand I was thinking, in business you never say 'No' and the show must go-on. I shook my head from side to side hoping to allay all the negative thoughts. Come on, let's get a move on.

To the Rescue!

I started the engines and turned the "Duck" into the direction I had come from earlier and headed directly towards the small dot on the horizon thinking, I certainly hope that this is the Birchwood, and I motored back as fast as I could but the "Duck" didn't go as fast as her namesake - *you know, the feathered winged type* - I looked at the time and noticed that I didn't have a lot of time left before the Mediterranean night was going to set in.

The daylight began to fade and the light of Cap Camarat started to send out her characteristic light flashes through the evening sky.

Having motored for the past 30 minutes or so, I finally came within range and could make out the detailed features of the Birchwood; it only now became clear to me as to why it took so long to recognize her; it was simply because she was facing me head-on; luckily the wind was still blowing her "off-shore"; it doesn't bear thinking about what would have happened if the wind was blowing towards the shore.

Upon arrival, I slowed down to a mere crawl and circled around the Birchwood to see if I could see what had gone so wrong. I must say she looked very sad and probably thought why did you let me go, please take me away from here. I uttered a sigh of relief - at least I had the boat back.

When I looked closer at the bow of the Birchwood I spotted that the anchor hawse didn't have any chain left hanging down - I expected at least the remains of the broken chain to be hanging into the water but... nothing at all.

I stopped the "Duck" downwind of the Birchwood because the "Duck" was a much larger and heavier boat which gave the Birchwood a chance of drifting slowly towards the "Duck". I rushed around making sure I wasn't slipping and tripping over my own feet and hung all the fenders over the starboard side, preventing any damage to either boat; as predicted, both boats were moving towards each other and finally touched very gently.

But now I had come up against a much bigger problem - how was I to get a new tow-line attached to the Birchwood?

I said aloud, to myself, 'you can't jump across onto the Birchwood; what will happen if you are on the Birchwood and the "Duck" decides to move away, then you will be in real shit. So... no, this idea was out of the question I wasn't going to leave the "Duck" under any circumstances. '

No, this has to be done differently; but I couldn't think how; my mind was still too confused. I scratched my head; if only I could find a way of securing the chain over the anchor winch of the Birchwood, but how was I going to reach?

I must have looked unbelievably silly as I held my right leg onto the rail of the "Duck" and my left hooked over the rail of the Birchwood, widening my groins slowly apart in the process, but as I was so nervous I just didn't feel the pain. Performing this acrobatic act made me feel psychologically in control of the "Duck".

I leaned across with stretched arms holding the chain in my hands, but my arms were just not long enough to reach the anchor winch; my mind was still steadfast in not crossing over onto the other boat, although that was very tempting. Relax, and just be patient. I had a little re-think and made a "bowline" - *a loop* - in the chain. I am sure that has never been done before but I had no other alternative. Then I threw it, like a lasso, over the anchor winch and after several strenuous attempts... Yeeesss, I had succeeded and the loop was now over the body of the winch, where it hooked itself under the little drum at one side and the gipsy on the other. I had a quick check and made sure that the chain couldn't chafe along any edges. Being satisfied with the result, I then climbed back onto the "Duck", after pulling my groin back into shape. I now needed to organize my departure and check that the towline was running freely away into the depths of the sea behind the boat. Secondly, I needed to check that the stern and side navigation lights on the tow were still switched on.

On my Way Again

Having completed all the checks, I slowly moved until the tow was back in a straight line behind me.

What next and where was I to go for tonight? After some deliberation, I decided to sail towards Cap d'Antibes, because going to Cannes or Juan le Pins would be far too complicated, especially having to manoeuvre around the Island of St Margarite, just off the coast at the Port of Cannes.

Still badly shaken-up - *to put it mildly* - I went up to the fly bridge taking my, now cold, dinner so that I could keep a constant eye on the tow. I did **NOT** fancy losing the Birchwood for a second time in one night!

I also had decided that I wasn't going to continue this voyage on my own and must find a crew. I would not wait any longer for Karl to fix me up with someone from Germany, but where could I find crew?

I should stand a good chance of getting crew in Antibes, because in the seventies I was based there and made numerous boating friends, one of whom was Michael, a South African who skippered a Trawler Yacht. I hoped that he was still in Port Vaubon - *which is the large port at the foot of the old town of Antibes* - and I was sure that he would know someone who would like to crew for me. I knew it was a long shot, but this was all I had to go on for now.

Having found this possible solution, I settled down with a coffee and headed for Port Vaubon. Some hours had gone by since I had started to tow again when, just over the horizon, the loom of the flashing light of Antibes started to show itself; fantastic, now I don't have to concentrate on the compass needle, which is always a struggle at night particularly when you are tired and begin to see double!

My watch showed it to be 04:00 when I reached the Port of Vaubon. Thank God I had made it in one piece.

I stopped just inside the entrance, behind the long breakwater, where I was able to pull in the towline and bring the boats in side by side. Believe me, I was very glad that this episode was now behind me. In hindsight, it was unbelievably stupid to try to do this single handed; no-one would have given me a medal for it and I thank the Lord that He stood by me through this ordeal.

I moored the boats safely alongside the fuel quay and went to bed but I was still far too stressed and had a great struggle to sleep, so after a few hours of tossing and turning, I had to get up and start searching for my friend Michael.

I walked to the mooring where he kept his boat all those years ago and, as luck would have it, the boat was still there; better still, so was Michael. I stood at the back of his boat and he must have had the shock his life seeing me because we had lost contact several years ago.

After catching-up and reminiscing, I told him what had happened to me last night and asked,

'Michael, can you do me a favour, do you know of anyone who would like to crew for me; I need to take these two boats to Viareggio and from there I need to deliver one of them to Yugoslavia.'

He thought a little, then in his South African accent, said

'I have just the guy for you, he is looking for a job sailing to the Caribbean, but I can try and see whether he is willing to go with you. I'll come and see you later.'

True to his word, Michael turned up later in the day together with a tall, blond, slender, young lad with blue eyes, who introduced himself as John.

John had already travelled up from South Africa earlier in the year and hoped to gain employment on one of the mega yachts moored in Antibes, but he hadn't had much luck so far. John shook my hand.

'Hi Bill'

'Hi John, I believe you want to make the voyage to Yugoslavia with me?'

'Yes, I would like to, but how do I get back?'

'Don't worry; I will pay for your return journey, of course.'

'When will we be leaving?'

'Early tomorrow morning, is that alright with you?'

'That's fine, I look forward to it; I'll go back and start packing.'

'Great, I'll get both boats ready this afternoon.'

Having finished the preparation I took the opportunity of browsing around the old town, and stocking up with food; in fact, I can't remember when I was ashore last, let me see I think it was Lyon, 5 days ago. I leisurely walked through the old town and couldn't help but pass the local bars where the crews of the mega yachts hung out, exchanging their adventures and I wondered whether their experiences could match the one I had just been through; I hope that the remainder of this voyage will be more of a relaxed nature for me!

Final Leg for the Birchwood, and Tow!

Luckily, John was punctual. We left Port Vaubon early in the morning of the 26th March. As soon as we left the piers, I laid out the tow for the last time and was able to set course directly for Viareggio a port North of Livorno and Pisa on the Italian coast.

Viareggio is famous for the building of large motor yachts and I mean **LARGE**.

John didn't have much to do but just being here gave me the security I needed and hadn't had since Peter left me ten days earlier.

This morning the sea was smooth with just a low long swell coming from the east and, although it was sunny, it still felt rather cool; of course it was still very early in the year.

John and I talked and I discovered he had left South Africa earlier this year in order to seek his fortune in Europe; he had decided that South Africa didn't have much to offer and was in awe of all the wealth he had seen so far in the south of France.

When he asked what my occupation was, I told him that I was given the opportunity of working for this German company because of my technical knowledge in boating, experience in sea deliveries and being bilingual. John must have felt envious because he asked,

'Do you think that I could work in Germany?'

'Hang on, we haven't even arrived in Yugoslavia yet and it may well be possible that you have changed your mind!' with that thought, he left me to concentrate on the job in hand.

We had an unexpected visit from a French custom patrol boat as we passed Monaco. They approached us from the coast, then slowed down and did a few circles around us; presumably being satisfied with what they saw, they left the same way as they had come. John asked,

'Is this normal?'

'Sometimes, but this is much more common in the south of Italy.'

'What do they want from us?'

'Oh, just checking that we haven't stolen the boat, you have to admit it's a little strange to see a motor cruiser being towed on a long tow by another, which indicates that they are on a long passage; what makes it even more suspicious is that we are moving away from the French coast.'

The overnight crossing to Italy went well and we arrived - *without any mishaps* - the following day in Viareggio. I stopped outside the harbour and pulled in the tow-line, ready for stowing, as the "towing job" had now been completed.

I pulled the Birchwood alongside and brought her into the port to the nearest yacht harbour pontoon. I secured both boats and went to carry out all the usual formalities with customs, Harbour Master and Military Police.

Having completed the formalities I walked back to the marina office and made a call to the owner of the Birchwood - *little did I know but he was the brother of the person for whom I had commissioned a boat in Barbados and delivered her to Martinique almost a year earlier.*

Not another Surprise!

'Hello Mr Braun, I have just arrived with your new Birchwood, when is it possible for you come to the marina and collect her?'

'Hi Bill, I am busy at the moment but I will see you this evening after work; when will you be leaving?'

'Tomorrow if that's ok with you?'

John and I smartened up the Birchwood and sprayed the sea salt off her. The engines were virtually unused, except for the crossing from England and the passage through the French canals.

Mr. Braun turned up later in the afternoon and was chuffed to bits with his new boat and brought the name for the boat which was to be called "Nikki II" and we were given the job of sticking the names on both sides of the bow and one on the stern; just think, I have just sailed a boat for three weeks without a name and no one queried it or asked for any papers. As a matter of courtesy I said,

'That's a good name', to which he proudly replied,

'Thank you; this is also the name of my first son and my previous boat was called just "Nikki"' and almost with the same breath he said,

'Oh, that reminds me, here are the keys to the "Nikki"; she is a Birchwood 33 and is a part-exchange for my new boat; I did the deal

with Karl at the last year's Boat Show in Friedrichshafen.'

I must have looked stunned because my German was only in its infancy and I thought that I may have misheard him, but he repeated it for a second time.

'You will need to take my old boat away, as I need the mooring space for the "Nikki II".' Karl had never mentioned anything about this.

This is just not real! I was always up for a challenge but this was too much and, most of all, I couldn't believe that Karl would do this to me again.

Well, this had put a whole new aspect to the job, and now we couldn't leave the next day as planned.

'John, I will need to call Karl and asked him what this is all about!'

I had to compose myself but finally had the courage to phone Karl and tell him of Mr Braun's request; Karl than answered in his usual calm voice,

'Jaaaa... Jaaaa... that's correct Bill, I am sure that you can take her to our base at St Giorgio di Nogaro.'

'Karl... do you know how far that is?' I continued in a tone that might convince him of this fact,

'It's nearly 1300 nautical miles, on the other side of Italy.'

Guess what his answer was?

'You'll be ok; you have plenty of time.'

Birchwood 33 foot in tow along the coast at Pisa

I admit that I understood his predicament because it is extremely difficult to get oversized road transport permits organized through Italy, but I was not happy this had been sprung upon me.

I walked away from the phone very disappointed; I was really looking forward to leisurely completing the delivery of the "Duck" to Rovinj; that would have been a piece of cake and now... I had to change my mindset and get ready for a new adventure into the unknown.

Entering the Bay of Naples Procheda on the left and Vesuvius under the early morning sky

On passage passing Volcano Stromboli

Now it was time to prepare the tow for the "Nikki" a smaller and lighter boat. This time I wasn't going to use its anchor chain but made up a security bridle, just in case. I also thoroughly inspected the 18mm nylon tow-rope and noticed that although it was still intact, it had been rubbing on the deck's edge, so I went in search of plastic hoses and slid those over the rope, preventing it from chafing through. Having been made aware of this weakness, I needed to carry out more regular visual checks and I greased the tow-rope with butter; well its grease isn't it?

Fully prepared for the second half of the voyage, we departed on Saturday the 28th of March in the general direction of Messina. Unlike two days ago, the weather wasn't too clever but once I had left the port, I thought it better to continue.

After a while I became used to seeing the movement of the boats and the excessive strain on the tow rope, as the heavy seas played tug of war between the "Duck" and "Nikki" and it looked like the southerly gale force 8 was really having a go at pulling the tow apart.

There was one consolation: the southerly wind kept the tow in a straight line and made steering the "Duck" easy peasy. Mind you I did have butterflies in my stomach hoping that I hadn't taken on another bad experience!

The afternoon passed without any mishaps but it was better to stop for the night and shelter in a bay on the mainland, Porto di Baratti, which is directly opposite the island of Elba. This bay gave us shelter from the southerly gale; I searched for an anchorage spot safe enough for both boats. I finally found the place and dropped anchor on a sandy bottom in a depth of 15 feet and laid an extra length of chain so that I could keep the "Nikki" on a short tow-line; this saved having to climb on board and anchor her individually from the "Duck".

Very Stormy Conditions

We had an early dinner and went bed almost straight after, in order to get as much sleep as we could, but sleeping was short lived as the boat was beginning to roll and pitch violently, so much so that I had to give up lying in my bunk. I looked outside and found that the wind was now coming from the opposite direction, making this bay totally unprotected from the now northerly gale, and it wasn't long before the waves became higher and the pulling of the "Nikki" could break the anchor loose at any time.

John woke up too and said,

'What are we going to do Bill?'

'We'll have to leave **now** John; that's for sure.'

Whilst still talking to John, I started the engines ready to pick-up our anchor but the violent wind made it very difficult to keep the boat straight; there was too much strain on the chain, which on several occasions tripped the circuit breaker of the winch, making the lifting of the anchor an extremely dangerous task. Each time the breaker tripped, we had to wait a minute or so before it cooled; if the power failed altogether then we would have to try to take the anchor in by hand, which would take too long, and we could easily drift onto the beach behind us with not only one, but both boats; the only other alternative would be to cut the chain.

It was just past 23:00 when we finally succeeded in getting the anchor on board, now I gently pulled away from the bay having to be extremely careful as the "Nikki" was still on a short tow, making it more likely for the tow to break. Moving out of the bay was painstakingly slow because the waves were now 14 feet or more and the wind was gusting 45 knots, so I needed to be sure that we were far enough away from the coast before I could take the "Nikki" in full tow; we were in a position to do that just after midnight.

'John can you hold the boat on course and check on me just in case something goes amiss'.

I made my way onto the aft deck and laid the tow; steaming broadside to the waves made the "Nikki" ride them independently from the now violently rolling "Duck". I crossed my fingers hoping that the wind direction would remain from the north so that we could make our way to the south side of this peninsular, where I hoped to seek shelter. I knew from the past that the south side also had a bay and an industrial harbour called Porto di Piombino.

I noticed that we had been on the move for 3½ hours and, to my amazement, we had only covered a distance of six miles.

04:00 - we turned into the bay of Piombino, where the waves finally let us be!

I didn't plan entering the port because it would be too troublesome; it would be better to look for a suitable anchorage just off the piers on the east side.

We eventually dropped the anchor just before daybreak at 05:00.

Although we had left a very strenuous night behind us, after only a few hours' sleep I pulled-up the anchor and left the safety of the anchorage. Miraculously, and so typical of the Mediterranean, the weather had become totally calm and the unbelievably turbulent seas of last night had turned into no more than a smooth long swell, giving us a very comfortable ride.

We started to make fantastic headway and only stopped-over in Capri where we had to refuel before moving directly south to the Messina Straits; from there we went along the foot of Italy passing Crotone and St Maria di Luca at the heel, and two days later we made the second stop-over in Otranto, which is the first port just at the entrance of the Adriatic Sea.

We pulled in the tow about a mile from the port and entered the port with "Nikki" alongside.

The Port of Otranto has a breakwater and quayside for commercial shipping and two dozen floating moorings in the middle of the bay, which is where I spotted a vacant buoy to hook onto. I had just realised this was our first night's sleep in sheltered waters since the start of our non-stop tow of 85 hours covering some 670 miles.

Surprise, Surprise, we encountered a handful of difficulties with the Italian Harbour authorities, who insisted that we needed to show a "green insurance certificate" which Karl had forgotten to give me before my departure from Düsseldorf. However, they said that we would be able to go back on board as long as we didn't leave the port until we showed them a faxed copy from Germany. I called Karl and told him what had happened and he said he would get this certificate from his German insurers. To be honest, I was glad that we were forced to stay so that we would get our rest before moving up the Adriatic.

Our first night's sleep was abruptly broken at 4.00 a.m. as we heard a loud explosion of shattering glass. Not long after, John stood behind me to see what was going on. The first thing in our minds was that we had been broken into and when we entered the saloon we found that a window pane had shattered into thousands of pieces. I still don't know exactly why, but my theory is that one of the self-tap screws holding the mosquito screens was screwed in slightly too deep through the frame and had scratched against the bottom of the glass, acting as a glass cutter.

At 11:00 the following day we were told that a copy of the Green Card had arrived through the new invention of the fax machine.

We immediately went to the harbour office, with our certificate in hand, and finalised the formalities with the Italian Naval Police Authorities. Whilst we were here, we topped up with fuel and departed Otranto at 13:00 for our next leg of this epic voyage.

Thankfully, not much happened on the next part of the voyage and we ran non-stop to our next port on the list, Porto San Giorgio, which is just above Pescara and below Ancona. This port would be the last port of call before crossing over to my final destination, Rovinj in

Yugoslavia.

We arrived late afternoon the following day in Porto San Giorgio, and stayed in port the next day so that we could get the "Duck" "Ship Shape and Bristol Fashion" for the hand-over and, apart from the broken window, everything else was as new; of course, the engines needed a good service, and I must say they really had served me well, considering what they had been through!

All-Done, or was It!

7th April 1987. Today is going to be the start of the final leg for the "Duck" and I can say, in all honesty, that I am going to miss her; she has been a jewel and completed the 3,200 mile voyage impeccably.

At 04:00 on the dot - *as always* - we left Porto San Giorgio. At first we hugged the coast northwards until Ancona, then headed in a north-easterly direction for Rovinj. We had no complaint about the weather; the sun was out and, with a small breeze on the blue-green sea, it all seemed worthwhile, and we soon forgot all the mishaps and bad adventures from the past few weeks... or did we?!

You would think that after all I'd been through; nothing else could stand in my way. Wrong! We entered the Port of Rovinj and headed straight for the quay housing the offices of the combined authorities.

But before I could deliver the "Duck" to her new home, I needed to complete all the necessary formalities. Somehow I had a feeling that I was going to have a problem with the paperwork and the non-purchase of a vignette, which is a yearly licence for the boat.

With a smile on my face, and all the paperwork under my arm, I walked into the Customs Office, where the officer entered details of the boat and owner in various books, finalising this by stamping the forms.

Now I headed next door into the Immigration Office, where I handed over our passports. The officer who opened my passport looked at me then at my passport and proceeded to do this several times, then silently handed it back to me. Now he looked at John's passport and repeated the same thing, but then he looked at me again; I began to sense that something was wrong but didn't know what it could be, and after a short silence he spoke in German,

'I am sorry, but I can't let **him** into the country.' Nodding his head at John,

'Why' I asked.

'You can enter, but your friend is not allowed to land in Yugoslavia. He is from South Africa and he must be in possession of a valid Visa.'

How could I complete the delivery if John wasn't allowed to land? I needed a solution to this and said,

'I need to deliver this boat onto the mooring over there. If I can take the big boat there, then I will leave with the "Nikki" for St Giorgio di Nogaro in Italy.'

'I see, but he can't come into the country.'

I realised that we had a BIG problem and all I could do now was to plea and convince this man that I wasn't intending to stay any longer than necessary; and I had no intention of leaving Rovinj with the two boats again!

'Please Sir, let me take the boat over there and I promise I will leave within 2 hours.'

He looked at the clock behind him on the wall and hesitated somewhat, but then, surprisingly, said,

'Alright, you can go to put the boat away, but you MUST leave before 22:00 because my colleague will then come on watch and he will not let this happen. I will not enter you or your friend in the books; therefore you are not here. But please remember you MUST leave before 22:00.'

'Thank you. Thank you.'

'Go now!' Flicking the back of his hand away from him, he quickly disappeared back into his hut.

This incident had totally worn me out, but had made me happy at the same time because now I was able to complete my mission.

In no time at all, we moved the boats across the harbour into the marina. We quickly dismantled the towing gear from the "Duck" and transferred all the gear over to the "Nikki". Luckily, I had the hindsight to clean the "Duck" in the last port - *I often did the cleaning a day before arriving at the final destination, then normally the owners and friends would immediately trample all over the boat.*

I was a bit worried about this "illegal" action because I wasn't too sure whether the officer would be true to his word; I would just have to hope for the best.

It took a good 2 hours to get the "Duck" settled at her new home port but, by now, it was getting late and I was anxious not to miss the deadline of 22.00.

Thank goodness this sort of hand-over was not the norm. Usually, I would tie-up, do the official paperwork, then... the crew and I would find the nearest bar and have a large cool beer.

Taking the "Nikki" was a bit daring because I hadn't tried her engines out; but when I turned the keys, both engines started almost instantly, what else would you expect from a BMW.

I left the engines running for a few minutes making sure they didn't stall, and, on time, I manoeuvred the "Nikki" away from the quay and slipped away, almost silently and without ripples, out of Rovinj. On my way out I looked across the harbour to the Immigration Office, but the officer was too busy watching TV and didn't even notice our departure. Thank God we had made it without any further incidents.

With Rovinj behind me, I once more headed out into the open sea and turned into the direction of St Giorgio di Nogaro which is not too far from Udine, and where Karl rented several moorings for his company. Normally I don't turn around (as I have told you) but I couldn't help doing it this time and noticed that the town of Rovinj had become a row of flickering, yellow lights which slowly sank beyond the horizon and I was thankful that the ordeal was over.

We cruised at a leisurely 8 knots and followed the coast north, but around midnight I was no longer able to keep my eyes open and said to John,

'I am going to stop John 'I **MUST** have a lie-down.'

I felt so exhausted that entering the unlit channel at St Giorgio was too dangerous and it could wait until the morning. I guess that we were two miles north-west of the Piran. I stopped the boat and left her to drift, which was a lot safer than trying to anchor,

'John do you mind keeping an eye on our position; if there is anything you're not happy with, wake me immediately!'

'Don't worry Bill, I will.'

I lowered myself down onto the settee and closed my eyes; it didn't take long before I was fast asleep.

During the night the "Nikki" started to drift slowly towards the open sea in a stiff breeze, which made her violently rock from side to side. I must have been in a deep sleep for 4 hours as I hadn't felt the movement, but when I awoke, and saw John's face, I sensed that he hadn't had a brilliant time, but at least he had left me to sleep. When I asked him why he didn't wake me, he said,

'If it was that bad Bill, you would have woken-up by yourself!'

I splashed my face with cold water and started the engines again and moved off, across the bay, towards the entrance channel to St Giorgio di Nogaro. I kept the speed down to 8 knots so that I wouldn't arrive at the entrance until daylight.

At daybreak I could just make out the low-lying coastline ahead of me; I recognised this coastline because of a single building on the east bank and some bushes and trees on the west bank. From the entrance it was easy to navigate my way up the well-marked channel.

After six weeks of strenuous travel, we were about to arrive at our final destination of St Giorgio di Nogaro... or was it the final destination?

I went to the harbour office; I didn't really expect a big welcome, but we might just as well have come from around the corner or by car! However, I did get this fantastic and very satisfying feeling that, once again, I had succeeded in getting three boats delivered undamaged - although at times it had been sheer hell!

John and I had breakfast in the marina café and took it easy for the day.

I just needed to tell the office that we had arrived safely.

'Hi Karl'

'Hi Bill are you there yet?'

I hesitantly answered,

'Yeeeeaaaass...'

I knew from the tone in his voice - as always calm-speaking Karl - that he was about to make some sort of request that other people wouldn't have the audacity to make.

'Bill, do you remember the boat "RIO"?'

'Mmmm... wasn't that the "Cytra 43" where I replaced the head gasket on the port engine last year?'

'Yes, that's the one; can you do me a favour and see what you can do with the starboard engine; it seems to have developed the same problem.'

'Where is the boat, Karl?'

'In Yugoslavia on the island of Krk in the marina of Punat'

I know the place as I had the pleasure of visiting this island during one of my earlier travels for the company, and if my memory serves me right, the island doesn't have any facilities for repairing a Perkins V6 235hp engine; in fact, repairing the port engine in Italy took some doing and, in the end, I had to bring all the necessary parts from the UK. With these thoughts I answered,

'Karl, I would prefer to get the boat back to Italy for the repairs.'

'That's alright with me Bill but how are you going to do that?'

'Well that won't be easy because I don't have transport to get there.'

I must have left Karl speechless, for a change, and there was a total period of silence at both ends of the telephone line but then I broke the spell, and did something totally stupid; before I could stop myself, I was saying,

'I have an idea... as I don't have transport, I could take the Nikki".'

'That's ok with me; when will you be going?'

'I'll go tomorrow morning; just let me prepare the boat for this voyage.'

'How long will it take you to get there?'

'It's about 120 miles and with this boat it shouldn't take more than 6 or 7 hours.'

'That's good, but be careful.'

Am I mad? Why do I volunteer for these things?

Anyway, this arrangement was fine, but I still had the problem that John wasn't allowed to land in Yugoslavia. Oh well, I thought, I'll have to take a chance and play dumb if necessary; at this moment I couldn't think what else to do!'

I sat down outside the marina café and told John of this new venture and informed him of the possibility of being stopped in Yugoslavia for his visa and asked,

'Do you still want to come?'

'Are we towing again?'

'I will look at the engine first, but if necessary then I am planning to tow her back to here.'

'I'd like very much to come with you Bill.'

'Well done, I'll call Karl and see whether he gives me permission to execute this plan of mine.'

'You sure that you're able to do that?' said Karl, and added

'If that's what it takes, then please go ahead, but you **must** try to fix the engine over there if you can!'

'Sure I'll try!'

But in my head, I had already made my decision that I wasn't going to sit on the island and try to fix an engine "ad infinitum".

No, my mind was made up already, I am going to sail to Krk with the "Nikki" and tow the "RIO" back to St Giorgio di Nogaro.

That's exactly what I did and then ironically, the "Towed" became the "Towing"!

Porquerolles - Palamos
Saturday 1st December 2001

I hadn't slept very well as I kept tossing and turning and waking up, wondering if the weather was really going to improve by the morning, but when I looked out of the window I was pleasantly surprised to find that the wind had changed and was now coming from the north.

So I said to myself 'there is no time to squander.' I had a quick wash and shave, stowed all the loose gear, generally preparing the boat for sea, started the engines, and by the time I left the Port of Porquerolles it was 06:00 on the dot. The wind blew the 2-yard red ensign straight across to port which meant, without a doubt, that Port Camargue would be my chosen destination for today. It was a good distance of 98nm in a straight line; this was a little further than I really wanted to travel but although I had had a bad night's sleep, I felt well rested; if I should become tired, I could always change my mind and run into a port nearer than my intended destination.

It was just after 08:00 when I marked off the position of Cap Sicie on my chart; this Cape is not far from the large naval base at Toulon and whilst I was passing, I could see the aircraft carrier Charles de Gaulle leaving the bay towards the east.

A little later, the weather forecast came through on the VHF radio. Although the voice wasn't very clear, I could make out that the forecast for the area was going to be more favourable than at first thought. What a nuisance, I thought, it had taken me so long to make my last decision and now it looked like I had to change my mind again; perhaps I could change course for the Bay of Rosas in Spain - I should be there by midnight, which isn't too bad and at least this will get me across of the notorious Gulf of Lyon. 'OK Bay of Rosas, here I come!'

08:30 - Right... this is it, I had made my decision and changed course directly for the west coast of the Gulf of Lyons - at the same time crossing my fingers in the hope that the weather forecast wasn't going to let me down.

After passing dozens of small fishing boats - some of them directly on the same track - and a few cargo ships sailing in the direction of Marseille or perhaps Sète, the sea became totally empty, except for the odd seagull. Who would believe this?! Yesterday the sea was boiling, making it totally impossible to move and today it appeared that this crossing was going to be perfect.

Certainly different from the last time I crossed this bay. (Page 85)

I just hope that the weather will stay this calm. I felt so peaceful and relaxed that I did some day-dreaming, when suddenly my peace was rudely interrupted by the ringing of my satellite phone.

I must say that the "sat phone" and the GPS have given me a fantastic feeling of security. They have been a God-send since their invention, especially when sailing solo.

It was the boss,

'Hi Bill, how are you doing?'

'Well... now I am in the middle of the Gulf of Lyon and I hope to be at the other side around midnight.' and after some light conversation he said,

'Good luck and take extra care, won't you.'

'I will and thanks for your call.'

I then thought, as I am doing so well and still feel perky why not head directly for Cap San Sebastian rather than the Bay of Rosas; this will get me into port at around two in the morning; that's 2 hours longer than I had planned but if I do this tonight then it will cut the corner by another 14 miles, saving myself another 2 hours sailing tomorrow.

The conditions were perfect; the sky was blue except for some high cirrus clouds crossing over from north to south-west and the sea was calm with only a low swell running in from the south-west, this being left over from yesterday.

The sun had only 2 hours left to burn and, unfortunately for me, was following a path which would touch the horizon directly ahead of the boat. Although I love the beauty of sunsets, this time it would impair my vision.

I made a cup of tea *(the Dutch way - very light without milk)* and relaxed; then at a fair distance away from the boat I spotted water splashing into the air and soon realized that a huge pod of dolphins were making their way towards the boat at speed, coming from the opposite direction. They made an acrobatic turn in order to swim in front of the boat, almost guiding me into the right direction; I could hear them flicking their tails against the hull and making high-pitched sounds as they zigzagged across, over and under each other, taking turns to be in front, all the time throwing their bodies sideways, looking up and monitoring whether I was still watching them; when bored with the slow speed of the boat they would take turns to swim ahead at torpedo-like speed then slow down and wait till the others joined them at the bow, their streamlined bodies cutting their way through the crystal clear blue water.

Like many people, I get a great thrill every time I see them enjoying themselves performing their stunts. I marked my coordinates on the chart at 16:20 and noticed that I was exactly half way between Porquerolles and San Sebastian. The sea had become like a mirror and I took another stroll around the decks; when I came to the front I stopped and looked over the bow into a deep blue sea with only the rays of sunlight piercing through the surface, converging into the abyss.

Staring at the Mediterranean made me aware of how deep it is; I know that in some places it can be as much as 2000 metres - deep enough to house several species of whales, which I have been fortunate enough to see in a variety of locations: for instance here in the Gulf of Lyon, between the South of France and Corsica and even between Barcelona and Majorca; of course I would love to have seen them today, but sadly that was not to be. It was greatly invigorating standing there, watching the sea being pushed away by the bow,

neatly laying an even trail of white foam, showing a pathway behind the boat. Other than the occasional squeak coming from the forward hatch lever swaying about with the motion of the boat, I was overcome by this wholesome and peaceful feeling and thought, how lovely this is, totally isolated from the hectic world in which we live, just surrounded by nature. "This must be heaven!"

Just before sun-set another group of dolphins decided to have a last exercise before dark, but this time it didn't last long and they remained in the same area, which meant that the weather was fine and I had nothing worry about.

My observations and past experiences have told me that when dolphins swim at speed in a certain direction and do not want to play in front of the boat, you can be assured that they are likely to be swimming away from a storm, but if they stay to play, you can expect reasonable conditions for hours to come.

As I predicted, the sun was setting directly ahead of me, nearly on the course line of 240 degrees, and the sunset was as beautiful as ever, turning the reddish yellow glow of the horizon into a light then navy blue sky; it had become totally dark behind me where the brightest stars began to twinkle in the sky.

I sighted land at 17:40, although I could only just see the tops of the Pyrenees mountain range. Strangely, the swell had become slightly larger, but the wind - although just a breeze - came from the east and as long as it remained from this direction I could be assured of a fine night. Although the sun had set over an hour ago I thought it was still twilight, but it turned out that the waning moon was accompanying me for a second night running. The weather was so perfect that I was able to make myself a cooked dinner and I thoroughly enjoyed every bit of it.

Everything was really going well and at 20:40 I spotted the loom of the Cap San Sebastian light whizzing through the starlit sky; this was absolutely amazing as the coast was still a good 35nm away.

00:45 - After what seemed like ages, probably because I was so exhausted, I finally passed the cap San Sebastian with the rocks of Hormigas showing on the radar at a safe distance of 1½nm; normally I sail between the rocks and the shoreline but this morning I would take the outside passage because I was too tired to navigate between the rocks.

Just after I cleared the rocks I spotted the occulting light - *where the period of light is longer than that of darkness (4+1 every twenty seconds)* - at the headland of Palamos Bay.

I arrived at the south breakwater of Palamos at 01:30 and although there is a new marina just short of Palamos, I had to skip this marina because the starboard entrance light was not visible; and not being familiar with its layout made me continue to the old harbour and anchor at the north side of the main port. I slowed down and gradually drifted towards the beach making sure to stay away from the main fairway; carefully checking the depth, I waited until it was down to 3½ metres, which is deep enough for the short night stay. I stopped the boat and dropped 30 metres of anchor chain, switched on my anchor light and closed down for the night.

It had been a long, but very enjoyable and satisfying crossing.

Thank God it's All Over!
4th October 2000

It was at the beginning of October last year, when the circumstances were so different. I wanted to get home in time for my daughter's birthday. As usual, I was already late leaving Majorca and knew, from the outset, that this voyage back to St Jean wasn't going to be easy.

At 04:00 I bit the bullet and left the anchorage at Saint Feliu de Guixols, near Palamos, for the crossing of the Gulf towards Porquerolles.

05:30 - passed Cap San Sebastian; not long after leaving the sheltered coast, the wind started to blow more strongly from the north and the waves started to build up to 8 feet or so, making them short and very uncomfortable. Although they were high, I had become accustomed to them and didn't find them too bad at this stage, but I guess they had slowly increased and were now between 9 and 12 feet, with the additional rogue wave of 15 feet thrown in between which, most annoyingly, kept catapulting me off my seat.

By the middle of the morning the waves were so high that I had to slow down from 8½ to 6½ knots. I have to say that this remarkable seagoing vessel - despite the bad weather and lack of stabilizers, due to a broken down hydraulic pump - held her own.

Early in the afternoon it gradually became overcast and the sea was now high and very confused, so much so that my autopilot couldn't keep a proper course any longer and I had to steer by hand. I then realised that this was going to be a hell of a long crossing, as I had already sailed for 9 hours and was only just halfway. Around 3pm I saw a mega motor yacht passing to the south of me into the opposite direction and could see that she wasn't having a good time; she was pounding her bow into the waves and really struggling to stay dry for even a split second. I was thankful not to be on that vessel; the sight of it made me realize how high the seas were and it

wouldn't be a minute too soon for me to reach the other side.

Steering the boat manually meant that I was unable to make myself a hot drink, for which I was desperately gasping and I dared not switch on the autopilot again because this could have sent the boat directly sideways into the heavy seas with a great possibility of being swamped; by now, I was very tired and irritable with myself - just as well I didn't have anyone with whom to let rip!

Early the next morning, after fighting the seas for nearly 22 hours, I finally reached the calmer waters behind the Ile Ribaud "Thank God it's all over!"

Passing Ile Ribaud, I made the decision not to head for Porquerolles but to shelter in the bay directly opposite the island. Finally I dropped anchor but couldn't go to bed yet as I still had to mop up the water in places where it shouldn't have been. I eventually went to bed at five in the morning and lay there thinking 'if anyone thinks they can beat the sea then they are in for a shock.'

Palamos - Ginesta (near Barcelona)
Sunday 2nd December 2001

I hoped for a lie-in this morning but woke rather early for my liking; never mind now that I am awake I might as well get ready for an early departure as you never know what the day will bring!

Today, I would hug the coast and, weather permitting, should get as far as Ginesta which is 16 nautical miles west of Barcelona, between Castelldefels and Sitges; both these towns are favoured by the Dutch and the Germans for their beach holidays. However, a stop-over in Barcelona is not an option because the marina is too far away from the harbour entrance.

09:30 - I pulled up the anchor, slowly turned the boat away from the beach and headed into a westerly direction. It was becoming a beautiful sunny day and everything was running smoothly. I only had one small problem - it was Sunday, which meant I had to dodge a huge amount of sailing and fishing boats; it seemed many locals had taken the opportunity of enjoying this beautiful December day.

This part of the coast wasn't very exciting to look at, but it may well have been beautiful before the intrusion of the high rise buildings. The only lengthy beach I could see was a 2 mile stretch between Palamos and the next Cape westward.

During the course of the morning I had to make a decision either to set course directly across to Port Andraix Mallorca then another crossing to Cabo de Palos – *just off the west point at Cartagena* - or, hug the coast; after several calculations I came to the conclusion that these two passages would only save me nineteen nautical miles and as it was winter the weather could change instantly for the worse, so the choice was obvious, I went for the coast-hop all the way.

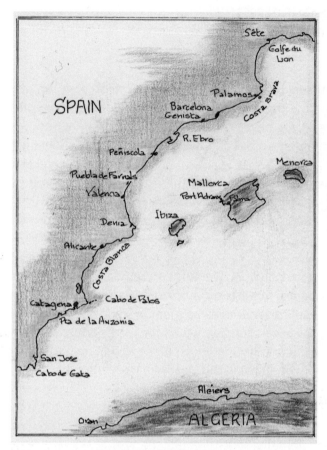

For the last 3 hours of the afternoon I was helped along by a current of 1 knot from behind, which makes a lot of difference to a craft which at best produces only 8½ knots.

17:00 - passing the anchorage of Barcelona were a few large ships anchored and rolling about gently in the long swell.

18.33 - Arrived at the port of Ginesta and, as the sea was calm, was able to moor alongside the visitors berth directly inside the entrance. In worse conditions, I would have had to get further into the port for wave protection.

I went ashore to stretch my limbs and noticed that everything was closed except for two bars which were blaring out their music against each other in the hope of attracting a few customers. But I wasn't going to be one of them!

Genista - Peñiscola
Monday 3rd December 2001

Today, I would be heading for the peninsular of Peñiscola, which is one of my favoured places in the western Mediterranean and it just happened to be strategically placed between Barcelona and Javea at the headland of Cab San Antonio. I frequently called in at this port with the smaller boats as they don't have the fuel range to cover the passage across this 180 nautical mile section of the coast, but also to avoid the occasional bad weather which can hamper this part of the Med. This was not the case today but as I had all the time in the world I thought this would be a pleasant stopover which would give me the chance to have a last glimpse of this picturesque place.

When I was preparing the boat to leave port I had a surprising visit from the port watchman, who had noticed the illumination of my navigation lights and radar scanner whizzing around in the pier lights. I stopped for a moment and exchanged a quick "Buenos Dias" – the only Spanish I knew - he then helped me with my mooring ropes and a few minutes later I moved away from the pontoon and that was the end of my visit to Porto Ginesta.

07:00 exactly - I nosed my way out into the open sea and optimistically switched on my autopilot, heading directly for Peñiscola. Unfortunately, I soon had to change course as a medium sized cargo vessel had just plonked itself directly in my pathway. Having successfully avoided a collision I switched on the autopilot again and had my breakfast in peace.

It's unbelievable but again, after the early morning low clouds the sun came out and stayed with me for the whole of the day. At lunchtime I passed the estuary of the river Ebro and spotted a large number of fishing vessels just over the horizon directly ahead of me; it was almost a full Spanish Armada coming towards me and in order to avoid them I needed to change course towards the coast which was almost too close because the depth sounder started to bleep and when I glanced at the screen I found that the depth of water under the boat had reduced itself to a mere 3 metres. However I thought, if the fishing boats are here then I should be able to make it too, and I boldly navigated through the Armada and eventually passed the last vessel 2 hours later, happily without getting caught in their fishing nets.

16:00 - 'Flipping heck' more fishing boats, but this time steaming at full speed across my bow. I could see from here that they were racing towards the nearest port in order to unload their catches before the end of the day's trading. I often wondered how these catches could pay for themselves; these fishermen go out from early morning for a full day's work and use a vast amount of diesel, just to land a few trays of sardine-sized fish.

But then to the contrary to this, it was some time ago when I was moored in Crotone - a port at the foot of Italy - when a small fishing boat steamed into the harbour at full speed heavily laden and moored just behind our boat; A few minutes later a refrigerated truck pulled up at the quayside; the driver jumped out of his cab and began a long shouting match in the usual Italian arm-swaying language with the skipper of the fishing boat. Meanwhile, a lot of people had gathered around, then two more guys came out of a shed and when the skipper saw them, he shouted something down the hatch and within a few minutes the crew started throwing an endless stream of sword fish, tuna, shark and other large fish onto the quayside. That certainly seemed to be a worthwhile catch!

Later in the afternoon I arrived in a semi lit Peñiscola. The harbour was full of fishing vessels probably some of the ones I had seen earlier. I slowly entered the port and had a good look around but I couldn't find a suitable place anywhere along the harbour wall, which was occupied by the local fishing boats. The only possibility would have been to moor alongside one of these boats, but they would probably set sail again at four in the morning and I had no intention of getting up at that hour. However, I did want to go ashore so... the best thing I could come up with was to moor alongside a fishing boat, spend the evening ashore and then lie outside the harbour at anchor.

Anchoring here is absolutely idyllic - as with most ports in the Med there are large breakwaters giving plenty of anchoring space and protection from incoming swells - the only thing to beware of, in this particular harbour, is the shallow depth, which is only suitable for craft with less than six foot draught.

Peñiscola just before nightfall

Having spent the evening ashore - and enjoying what was probably my last look at this fortress town - I walked back to the boat and

91

moved her out of the main port then carefully chose a suitable anchorage spot and finally dropped anchor in 2½ metres of water near the beach. I don't really need a lot of chain but dropped 15 metres just in case.

I sat on the aft deck thoroughly enjoying the spectacular view of the old town, which is built on a single, almost evenly sloped rocky hill. The town itself is very small and has narrow streets running up towards the fortress at the top of the rock.

Leaving the Peninsular of Peñiscola towards Valencia

This was a time for relaxing and at this moment I wished that my family could have been with me to enjoy this beautiful and picturesque port of Peñiscola.

Eventually I tore myself away to check on the engine room ready for tomorrow. I didn't find any problems; the engines seemed to have settled down and didn't require any oil or water. I could now go to bed in a very relaxed state of mind.

Peñiscola - Puebla de Farnals
Tuesday 4th December 2001

Standing on the aft deck with my morning coffee, I glanced into the direction of the town and as I suspected, the port was empty, except for a few very small boats. I must have had a fantastic deep sleep because I never heard any of the boats leaving.

I didn't have a plan for today, but just intended to coast-hop in the general direction of Valencia, but it would all depend on where I could get before night-fall.

07:00 - pulled in my anchor and left the anchorage; the weather was dull but calm which is bliss; running along the coast is fine for sight-seeing, but you do have to watch out for small sailing dinghies, fishing boats and the numerous fish farm pontoons.

Although the Almanac tells you to watch out for them, it's a different story when you are confronted with one. What do you do? Where do you go? Left or right, who knows?

Surprise, surprise, the sun showed its face just after midday and it soon became a warm and pleasurable afternoon. Later in the day I checked the chart to see where I could go for the night; Valencia was not only too far, but also a port to be avoided. In the Almanac I found a port short of Valencia called Puebla de Farnals, which was described as a port with a shallow entrance which could silt-up during the winter period.

Well, they weren't wrong because when I arrived I found an old barge with a crane mounted on her deck, still dredging. She had positioned herself smack bang in front of the entrance; the two men on the dredger waved me on and pointed towards their bow, telling me to pass as close as I could in front of them. As I was getting closer - almost on top of them - the depth sounder alarm rang frantically

93

and flashed at 0.1 metre under the keel. I knew that the sounder was accurate because I had calibrated this myself. I stopped the boat instantly, pulled the levers in reverse and slowly moved backwards away from the dredger, hoping to use the same track in order to keep some water under the keel.

Having successfully negotiated this reverse manoeuvre, I soon gained depth under the keel again and made the decision to drift around for a bit hoping that someone would come to advise me what to do next but as no-one turned up I eventually dropped anchor just off the port entrance; unfortunately, this time I did not have the protection of a harbour breakwater. Never mind, the wind was blowing off the shore and the sea was smooth so I should have a reasonable night ahead of me.

I had been at anchor for at least 20 minutes when a small inflatable boat came out from behind the dredger and moved into my direction.

'Do you want to come into the port?'

'Yes please, if possible.'

'You can come in when the dredger moves into the harbour, but the harbour will be closed until 9 o'clock tomorrow.'

I had to think for a moment; in hind-sight I should have gone into the port but I made the decision to stay at anchor and hoped that the weather wasn't going to change overnight.

What bliss, a glass of wine, an evening meal on the aft deck, watching the golden yellow-red sun setting over the Spanish hills in the background; what more could one wish for! After spending another relaxing evening, I turned in early "just in case".

Puebla de Farnals - Alicante
Wednesday 5th December 2001

The night passed without any incidents and I slept until three o'clock, but then I kept waking up as the boat had started to pitch and roll, so much so that sleeping had become impossible and in the end I had to move on. I made my coffee, prepared the boat and hauled in the anchor. I looked at my watch, 05:15 and thought, that was a quick visit, and set my course in the direction of San Antonio, which is located fifty nautical miles or so opposite the island of Ibiza's west point.

It was still pitch dark and the wind was blowing from the south-east at 16 knots giving the sea a slight chop.

My intention was to run to Alicante today, firstly to refuel and secondly just to be in a port, giving me a proper night's rest.

I had set the course directly through the main commercial anchorage at Valencia and at one stage I noticed two vessels ahead of me, directly on a collision course; they both had their navigation lights on but weren't moving. As I moved closer, I could see that the larger container vessel was drifting - most likely waiting for a pilot - and the other must have just dropped her anchor but forgotten to switch off her navigation lights.

Javea   Denia *behind mountain*   Cap St Sebastian

95

A quick temporary course change on my part solved that problem.

It was only another hour before daylight and as I was scanning the horizon I found myself being followed by a feeder ship - *a small cargo ship who takes her cargo mainly from large vessels and delivers the goods to their ultimate destinations at the smaller ports* - who seemed to have set course for Ibiza and, as I was heading in a similar direction, she kept me company for a while; eventually she overtook me and went towards the sunrise where she finally disappeared over the horizon.

Not much happened after that and, as I had moved away from the

coastline, it was a fairly easy journey with little to do. The sea had become calm once more and I was astonished at the fantastic weather I was having - who would have thought it was December!

11:00 - Passing Cabo San Antonio with Denia located just behind me and Javea just coming up on the other side of the Cape.

Javea does hold a number of memories for me but the most vivid one was the time when I skippered a motor cruiser with the most beautiful name called "Cara Mia". At first, I was just asked to deliver the boat from the

Cabo de la Nao

boatyard in Brundall in Norfolk England to Javea and that would normally be the end of the contract, but whilst en-route I was asked to skipper the boat full-time; I wasn't really interested in full-time skippering because I was doing very well with sea deliveries and really enjoyed that type of work. However, this gentleman was extremely gentle but persuasive and we made a suitable arrangement whereby I would go ahead to prepare the boat then spend the time skippering the boat for his holidays and after the cruise I would clear the boat ready for the next time. This arrangement went on for four years and once a year we would sail to the South of France for the Monaco Formula One races and whilst we were there we would throw in a mini cruise to Italy for good measure then return the boat to Javea via the Balearics.

Remembering this type of cruiser also reminds me vividly of a near-disastrous incident I encountered with a similar boat in the German Bight on the Elbe estuary (Page 99)

11:30 - passing Cabo de San Antonio and when I fully rounded the cape I was able to see the harbour and town of Javea and from here it didn't appear that much had changed since I was last here, apart from the large number of high-rise blocks of flats.

My next heading was Cabo de la Nao where the light-house was balanced on the edge of a cliff. I always liked going very close under the cliffs, and today was no exception. They were made from the most beautiful coloured rocks and the most amazing part is that the depth close to the cliffs is still a staggering 40 feet.

Having gasped at the sheer beauty of Cabo de la Nao, I changed course directly for Alicante, narrowly missing the peninsular of Calpe and the Isle of Benidorm.

The sea was a little choppy here, but still comfortable for this boat. Not long after Cabo de la Nao I passed Morayra, which in the seventies didn't have a port, but only a well protected bay tucked away from view.

I often anchored there, sheltering from the storms which can hamper this area frequently in the summer; at times I have had to alter my course from Cabo de Palos to Ibiza for the safety of this bay in order to sit out a storm, usually until the next day.

The afternoon passed fairly quickly, possibly because I had lots to look at as I recalled many of my memories.

I made good time and ran into Alicante just before nightfall. I have been here on several occasions, but the last time was sometime ago and I had forgotten what to expect. I knew that I had to sail into the far corner of the harbour complex and remembered that the basin on the portside was used by the Navy, but when I arrived I found a beautifully built "all-purpose" marina.

I moored alongside the refuelling station which, to my amazement, was still operating. That was brilliant as it would save me refuelling time in the morning. I took on 1000 litres, which was enough to get me to Gibraltar, and paid my harbour dues, which I must say were very steep, but at least I would get a good night's sleep.

After dinner I walked around the marina and at the far end they were still driving piles for the additional pontoons. Surrounding the harbour were several restaurants, bars and casinos which could occupy one well until the early hours of the morning. But all I needed was to stretch my legs, stroll around for a while and have an early night, my usual thoughts being... *you never know what tomorrow will bring!*

The Misadventure of the "Marauder 103"
1st October 1977

The Dutch agent for J.C.L. Marine had the custody of the "Marauder 103", a fast 46 foot motor cruiser by Colin Chapman the creator of the Lotus Formula One and the Lotus sports cars in the mid twentieth century.

It was the 27th September 1977 when I was asked by the boatyard to take the "Marauder 103" to Hamburg where she was to be exhibited at the Boat Show the following month.

My crew John and I made our way across to Monickendam - which is at the edge of the Marker Meer located at the lower part of the IJsselmeer (former Zuiderzee), not far north from Amsterdam.

John had crewed with me before and said he had a few days to kill; as this voyage was only 200 miles or so I thought we should be able to complete the job in two days.

I planned the route as follows: turn south across the IJsselmeer passing through the Port of Amsterdam; over the North Sea canal; through the large sea locks at IJmuiden and follow the Dutch and German coasts up the River Elbe where we would moor her in the heart of Hamburg.

The boat we had to deliver was the "cutting edge" in fast cruiser development and a real innovation for the seventies.

We arrived in Monickendam the evening before our intended departure but the weather didn't look too promising so we stayed there an extra day. Monickendam is a quaint village with the usual Dutch windmill, drawbridges through the town centre and the quayside with its Friesian flat-bottom sailing barges (these barges were especially designed to deliver their cargo across the shallow

Zuiderzee until the mid-20th century) and amongst them a few modern cargo barges.

We left on Saturday 1st October at an early hour and headed into the direction of... well to be honest, I hadn't really planned where we would end up today; I intended to basically "go with the flow". The day started off rather well and we arrived at IJmuiden much earlier than expected; even the large sea lock - which can take up a lot of time - was ready for us to enter. We skilfully negotiated this lock,

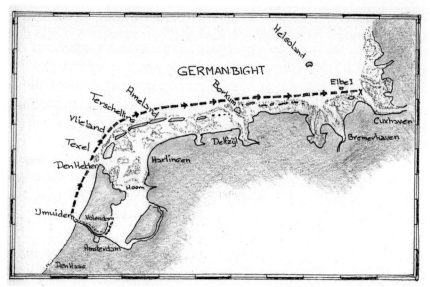

accompanied by several fishing vessels and a barge, and after the lock had transferred the water level we departed via an air bubble bath - this is to keep the sea water separated from the fresh water.

After leaving the port of IJmuiden I found that the North Sea was smooth which gave me the opportunity of opening-up and increasing the speed to a comfortable 23 knots. I looked at the time, and to my surprise it was only just after midday. Great, now I could think ahead and all being well we should arrive at Cuxhaven around 21:00.

We were really moving along and I commented on the amazing timing, but I spoke too soon because as we left the sheltered waters of Terschelling I started to see a noticeable increase in wave height which made the boat start jumping over the waves - if this continued then I would have to slow down so that the length of the waves matched the length of the boat. Shame though, this would add some extra time to the voyage.

16:00 - Passing the entrance to the River Ems. Blast! This is going to be flipping late tonight. I wondered whether I should call into Delfzijl for the night, which is the last town between the Dutch and German borders, but this would mean that I would have an additional 20 miles to do in the morning and it would also add another day to the voyage, and the staff at the show were expecting the boat to arrive tomorrow. So my decision was not to call into Delfzijl but to continue the voyage. However, an hour further along the coast the boat started to vibrate.

'Oh what now, I think we have something in the prop.' That was strange because the speed hadn't dropped, which is normally the first indication of having fouled the propeller. I pulled back the throttles and brought the boat to a standstill; I then put her into reverse gear in the hope of shaking off the debris.

But there didn't seem to be any improvement, and after some thought I decided to check the engine room, I don't know why I did this because I seriously thought that the vibration came from the outside. Everything seemed to be fine down there, but when I turned around ready to crawl out of the engine room I noticed that one of the six bolts holding the rubber flexible coupling had sheared off and therefore the shaft had become slightly out of balance. I told John what I had found, and said that we would have to keep an eye on this and we hoped this would be the only bolt.

I increased the boat's speed slowly to an acceptable level of minimum vibration and after playing with the throttles she seemed to settle for a reasonable 17 knots. Oh well... this means that we will be arriving a lot later than I previously thought. But little did I know I had worse to come...

The weather slowly started to deteriorate and unfortunately, the wind was still coming from the east and had increased to a good force 4-5 on the Beaufort scale; the tide was running in the opposite direction which made the boat slam badly onto the water; having passed my last "escape port", I was left with no other alternative than to continue towards Hamburg - the ports on the German Friesian islands are inaccessible at low tides and local charts are needed for these areas, which of course I didn't have with me on this voyage. So, I am afraid we had to grin and bear it.

I had a feeling that the speed had dropped but of course this could have been an optical illusion. I checked the log and found that it showed an average of 15 knots but the engines still showed 2300 rpm, the same as it had been earlier this afternoon. I thought that was strange but didn't understand why. Could it have been because of the strong easterly wind? Or had the tide changed? But checking on the latter - no it had not! Anyway, we still seemed to be doing relatively well; we had passed the "large-ships anchorage" on the river Weser at 19:18. Brilliant, just another 3 hours to go then we would be in Cuxhaven.

Just after 20:00 we passed the "Elbe One" - a light vessel marking the entrance to the river Elbe.

I don't know whether it was my imagination but had the boat slowed down even more since the last time I looked? Now I began to get a little nervous.

It was very strange; the engines were still running at 2300 rpm; this really puzzled me and I wondered what the hell was happening. I had never experienced anything like this. I think maybe my sixth sense was telling me something and I said to John,

'Can you please go down and have a look in the forward cabin to check whether we have pushed in one of the windows?' This was my foremost thought, because the boat was fitted with acrylic windows set in rubber frames, which was not the norm for fast sea-going cruisers.

After a short while John came up from below and very calmly stated,

'Bill, we have a lot of water on the floor but all the windows are still intact; what do you want me to do?'

I glanced at the switch of the electric bilge pump and I hadn't previously noticed that it was frantically trying to pump the water out of the forward section of the boat but it wasn't keeping up with the volume coming in.

John was still calm, but I detected a slight panic in his voice

'Bill, the water is still rising and its ankle deep now!'

I also tried to stay calm,

'Can you possibly start pumping with the hand bilge-pump?'

'I'll try Bill.'

In the mean time, I had to make some decisions; different thoughts were wildly running through my head; if I slow down or stop, what will happen to the boat? On the other hand, what if I don't do anything for now and see if I can make the port of Cuxhaven which isn't too far away? The latter seemed to be the better option.

So   far, so good! The boat was still making reasonable headway, probably because the flood tide was going in the same direction, "up river",   but   unfortunately this favourable tide was only going to last for another 2 hours and then "God help us" - we would have to push a strong ebb (outgoing) tide which would drop our speed to 11 knots or even less; I really hoped we would have reached the port before that happened. But all of a sudden…, I was woken up from my deep thoughts when I heard a shout 'Bill, Bill, I'm sorry but I can't keep it up, the water level is still rising and it's now a good foot above the floor boards; soon I won't be able to reach the handle of the pump!'

I pleaded with John to keep trying,

'I am going to try to get as near to Cuxhaven as possible and every minute counts; **PLEASE keep pumping!**'

But 10 minutes later he said,

'It's no good, it is now coming in at an alarming rate and I can't cope with it!'

Right... **PANIC STATIONS!**

'John, leave the pumping and put on your life jacket; after you have done that can you throw me a life jacket and get my briefcase from the aft cabin and take that with you, then go onto to the aft deck and prepare the life-raft, which you can find under the aft bathing ladder steps; let me know when you are ready and stay on deck, only then will I stop the boat and when I do then I suspect that she will most likely sink instantly. I don't know how much time we'll have to get off the boat!"

Whilst John was carrying out all my instructions I called the Cuxhaven Harbour Master on the VHF radio and I told him about our situation. He replied,

'What is your position?'

'We are in the vicinity of the starboard hand buoy K.'

'OK sir, the police boat is already on its way.'

After I had put the phone down, I started to get my mind set in preparing to leave the boat in case she was going to sink. I had a careful look around, staring into the dark and noticed a set of navigation lights belonging to a large vessel creeping up behind us; I picked up the VHF radio again and called,

'Attention the ship just passing buoy "J" inward bound, this is the motor yacht Marauder do you receive?'

A reply came almost immediately,

'This is the North Sea ferry bound for Hamburg calling the Motor yacht Marauder.' 'Yes good evening sir, I have a problem; we are filling up with water fast; please be aware I am going to stop her but don't know what will happen to her when I do.'

'Do you want us to call the coast guard?'

'That's kind of you, but I have just called Cuxhaven and the police boat is on her way to me as we speak; many thanks anyway. Please standby on channel 16.'

All very calm and civilized – outwardly!

I was closing in towards the next starboard hand buoy which was quietly flashing green. I was getting cold and very nervous because I didn't know what would happen when I stopped the boat.

John came back from preparing the life-raft and said,

'I am ready Bill, I have your briefcase and the life-raft is ready.'

Now it was time to make my final decision,

'Just leave the saloon door open for me John, so that I can get out of the boat quickly.'

I took a deep breath and slowly pulled the throttles back into a neutral position and... as I expected, the boat came to an abrupt halt; not only that, but the bow nosedived and in a flash, just like a submarine, the seawater rushed into the forward part of the boat at an alarming rate; I didn't wait for the final result but ran out of the saloon virtually missing all the 5 steps which led to the aft deck. John pulled me up from the stairs and when I had found my footing, I noticed that the limping yacht had already swung around (now facing outward bound) and, to my amazement, the boat had stayed partly afloat with the foredeck and cabins totally submerged, but strangely the saloon, engine room and aft cabin areas had stayed buoyant; even more amazingly, we ended up within arm's length of the green flashing "K" buoy.

Quick as a flash, I said 'John, lets get a rope onto the buoy,' and after three attempts we succeeded in getting a loop around a hook welded to the buoy; however, in my haste and not wishing to miss the opportunity, I forgot to pass the rope through the appropriate rail and now the tide was turning which made the boat swing on the rope and it tore away all the handrail stanchions along the port passageway in one go. But we had managed to secure her to the buoy.

We lowered the life-raft into the water, but needed to stay for as long as we possibly could on the limping yacht and wait for the rescue boat to arrive. After a short while the boat had stabilised and was lying there like a lame duck, helplessly held on by the buoy in virtual silence, except for the sound of rushing water passing the buoy indicating that the ebb tide had begun to run seawards. What a stroke of luck we were able to secure the boat onto that buoy, which under normal circumstances was totally illegal - if we hadn't been able to do that, goodness knows what could have happened! It doesn't bear thinking about; we could have been swept out to sea, run aground on the exposed sand banks or even worse - hit by a ship.

It wasn't long before we noticed a blue flashing light coming towards us out of the dark, and finally the Police launch was alongside our stricken Marauder.

The officers helped us to get across onto their launch.

'Thank God John, we're saved, what a relief.'

It was now just short of 02:00; we were totally exhausted, cold and not far short of hyperthermia but very relieved to have been rescued so soon.

The officer in charge asked me,

'What do you want to do with the yacht?'

'Honestly I don't know sir.'

'Well, we can't leave her here because she's a hazard to shipping; she will have to be brought into the port!' and before I could respond, he called the tugboat station and instructed them to collect the boat.

The police officers kindly asked whether they could arrange a hotel room for us and when we arrived in the port they gave us a lift to a small hotel in the town centre of Cuxhaven.

We walked back to the Police Station at the port later in the morning and were told that we had been extremely lucky to have survived the incident. We certainly agreed with that, and soon realised exactly how lucky when we saw the tugboat sweeping round the pier-head into the port with our forlorn-looking Marauder at her side; the crew had laid a VERY LARGE rope through the saloon windows and all the way around the hull, holding the yacht up like a babe in arms. It was so sad to see her like this and we still didn't know why this had happened.

The tugboat slowly zigzagged its way through the inner harbours and waited for the town bridge to be lifted; after passing through the bridge she stopped in front of a slipway and within the hour our poor

Marauder was hauled up onto the high and dry.

We could see, from a distance, that the yacht had lost her outer skin from the rear of the forward cabin to the rear of the saloon. This meant that we had been sailing on a boat held together by a thin layer of inner skin and foam; we then realised that this was no ordinary incident. I called the "Big Boss" who was shocked and sympathetic and simply asked me to cover her with a tarpaulin and wait until the transporter arrived to collect her. Our misadventure had come to an end and, sadly, this boat was not going to be exhibited at that year's Hamburg Boat show.

Alicante - Pta de la Azonia
Thursday 6th December 2001

I opened my eyes to a dark grey, overcast Alicante and it felt quite fresh; in fact that was an understatement - it was **freezing**, which made me wonder if my luck was about to run out!

Well, I should be grateful for all the good days I have had so far. I was uncertain how far I would get today but first things first; I always check the engine room everyday, prior to departure and at least once every 2 hours when I am at sea, in order to inspect for oil or water leaks, smoke and fumes - yes, fumes which can fill the engine room without one even noticing that something has gone amiss. This regular checking has saved me from disaster on numerous occasions and it also disciplines me to complete the logbook on a regular basis, which is a very good and useful practice.

07:00 - pulled the last rope on board and departed the mooring; I was surprised that even at this time in the morning the fuelling station was already open and little day-boats were waiting like ducks for food; It was mid-week and I thought, that's strange, doesn't anyone work around here?

After having left Alicante harbour I plotted my course directly for Cabo de Santa Pola. I had to be careful to set the course quite close to the shore in order to pass between Cabo de Santa Pola and the Ile de Tabarca.

By midday the sun started to pierce through the clouds, and the sea was again littered with fishing boats, particular near Cabo de Palos; it intrigued me so much that I had to find out what it was all about, so I opened my Nautical Almanac and discovered that today was a Spanish National Holiday. Well, that answered my question.

14:00 - rounded Cabo de Palos hugging the coast and must now choose a port to arrive around 18:00, as it was far too early in the day to stop at Cartagena for the night. Cartagena is the major Mediterranean Spanish naval port, and the run-up to the marina is a long way from the entrance, that's why I wanted to continue westward for the time being. I don't know what made me do this next, perhaps to stretch my legs, but I thought I would have a stroll around the decks when..., faintly from a distance I could hear a human voice screaming out! *Well, that's it! Now you are hearing voices at sea too*; then, I heard it again! I concentrated into the direction from where I had heard the voice and it seemed to come from the sea surface. I looked around and to my horror... yes, I could just about make out a human head, with diving goggles reflecting in the sun, bobbing on the wavelets and next to this head was a small red ball which was supposed to signal to others that there was a diver around.

Imagine this, I could have easily killed him and no-one, including myself, would ever have known. This guy was about 1½ miles from the beach and he didn't seem to be asking to be rescued but just wanted to let me know that he was there. In all my years of sailing I have never been confronted with this kind of situation and I had to compose myself after the shock; I went back into the wheelhouse and wrote the incident in my logbook, just in case of any repercussions. All sorts of horrific thoughts ran through my head, but I eventually had to pull myself together, so I could get on with the job in hand!

I reached the coast at Cabo Tinoso, about 7 miles west of Cartagena later in the afternoon and from here I ran fairly close under the shore and noticed that at the other end of this headland was an extensive fish farm, and guess what? Yes, once again it was just on my course!

I didn't know whether to pass this floating pen on the inside or outside but then I spotted a large fishing boat which was heading in the same direction as me. I followed him to the far end, where all of a sudden I found myself in a bay with a small fishermen's village with numerous dinghies and fishing boats pulled up on a long white sandy beach, and some larger fishing boats moored on colourful small buoys. It looked well-sheltered and when studying the chart I could see that I was in the bay of Pta de la Azonia. I slowly moved towards the beach and found a perfect anchoring spot just a little away from the moored boats.

18:10 - finished anchoring, and I must say this was a pleasant surprise and so peaceful after a full day's sailing; I was able to relax with a glass of wine and enjoy the scenery while listening to the wavelets gently dispersing onto the light coloured sandy beach.

Pta de la Azonia - San Jose
Friday 7th December 2001

This was the fourth night on this voyage that I had been at anchor, once more I had a peaceful night and I couldn't get over the fantastic weather I was experiencing.

Well... I shouldn't talk about the weather as it is one of those superstitions of Seamen, including myself: "Never talk about the weather or whistle, for in doing so, you are asking for the wind" In fact I had never found this to be true, but I wasn't going to tempt fate.

I prepared for departure and intended to sail in the general direction of Almarimar which is a good thirty miles east from Cabo de Gata at the SE corner of Spain and is a busy shipping route for all vessels moving in and out of the Mediterranean.

06:00 - pulled up anchor; departed from the anchorage avoiding the unlit fish-farm and slowly left the peaceful bay of Punta de la Azonia behind.

I was presented with a mixed bag regarding the weather, (oops I wasn't going to talk about that); after the early morning fog it turned into overcast with a reasonably smooth sea, but when the sun came out just after midday it also became a lot more windy (I should have kept my mouth shut!), but not as bad as I have experienced when passing through this area, where at times the waves have been as high as 15 feet.

11:00 - I could just make out the coastline at Garrucha. I often used to visit Garrucha for its strategic position, which functioned as a halfway-stop between Gibraltar and Alicante, mainly to refuel the smaller motor cruisers which didn't have the long-range fuel tanks.

111

12:20 - passing Messa de Roldán at the safe distance of 2 miles. Whilst plotting the position on the chart, I let my finger glide over the paper and noticed that the distance between my position and Almarimar was still another 53nm; this meant it would take another 7 hours or so, which was well within my daily run, but, what if...?

14:00 - started to close-in towards the coast and it had become a fine afternoon; the seas had becalmed and the temperature was a pleasant 18°C - *not bad.*

I was just about passing the bay of San Jose near Gabo de Gata when I thought, why not anchor here - I do have all the time in the world; so I slowly edged forward into a small inlet, but when I anchored I found that the sea wasn't **that** smooth after all and half an hour later I changed anchorage. I moved slowly towards the next bay which wasn't far from the small port of San Jose; unfortunately, this port was far too small for me, but I was able to tuck the boat comfortably behind the extended outer wall.

16:00 - finished for the day, completed all the checks and prepared my engine room ready, as always, for the unexpected getaway.

The weather was warm and pleasant so I was able to sit on deck in my T-shirt sipping tea and alternating my listening between the World Services of the BBC and Radio Netherlands which is broadcast in both Dutch and English languages; this always gave me the opportunity of listening to the topics of the day on both sides of the water.

While I was enjoying my tea I began to reminisce about the time when I had to vacate this anchorage in a hurry; it was on one of my "solo" voyages from Rungsted - *6 miles north of Copenhagen, in Denmark*, via the German and French canals into the Gulf of Lyon at Sète and onto Jose Banus near Marbella. (Next page)

She was about to Break Loose
November 1978

I left Garrucha earlier that afternoon and ran fairly close to the shore.

I plodded on for a while but gradually much larger waves started to come from around the headland at Cabo de Gata; finally I had to give in because the boat was almost standing on end and the slamming was becoming so severe that I could hear the dishes and other bits and pieces rolling around in the boat, so I turned around and headed back along the coast and I ended up here at "San Jose".

I anchored the boat as close as I dared to the beach, where she settled in nicely.

It was around 2:00 in the morning when the boat started to pitch up and down and violently roll from side to side and I could hear the anchor chain grinding over the ground - this indicated that she was about to break loose.   This was not good and I had to get up; in order to orientate myself I looked out of the cockpit windows in search of the shore lights but to my surprise the lights weren't where I thought they should be; no wonder, the wind had changed direction and was now coming straight off the sea; this meant that the boat was now slowly drifting towards the beach.   Until then she had seemed quite happy; but, for how much longer? I had no intention of waiting to find out. I started my engines and struggled to the bow, holding on for dear life; but now I was faced with a more dangerous task of having to pull in the anchor chain.   This was difficult and strenuous on this boat because she was fitted with a manual winch, and therefore it took some considerable time to pull in the chain, leaving the boat at the mercy of the wind which blew her towards the beach at an unprecedented speed; I pulled in as much chain as possible onto the deck and waited for the anchor to break ground;

113

when it finally did I quickly secured the chain and ran as fast as I possibly could - without slipping and tripping - back into the wheelhouse and moved the boat slowly away from danger and into the open sea, and only then was I able to bring the anchor safely on board.

If I had not been able to pull that chain in so quickly, I could have run aground and the waves could have pounded the boat and smashed her to pieces.

San Jose - Almarimar
Saturday 8th December 2001

Last night the boat started to rock about quite a bit but not enough for me to move away from the anchorage; although I didn't get up until eight o'clock, I still felt rather tired and decided to have my breakfast before moving off this morning.

The sun was shining across the sea against a deep blue sky and the visibility was endless; my experience tells me this normally means a northerly wind, and it was true once again. Some three miles off the coast was a large motor yacht travelling in a northerly direction and even from this distance I could see the vessel moving rather rapidly into the oncoming waves; a northerly wind in this area usually means that along the bottom part of Spain there will be a strong easterly wind.

Oh well, as I am heading in a westerly direction the waves should run in from the stern which should give me a comfortable ride today.

10:25 - passing Gabo de Gata and as I suspected, the strong wind from the north had become more easterly and eventually settled down from a north-easterly direction; but now that I had moved away from the protection of the coast, the sea had built up to 2 metres or so, which made steering a straight line a bit of a problem - this boat wasn't one of the better boats for steerage - even the autopilot was having difficulties staying on track; I tried steering by

115

hand for a while but that was not easy and after 10 minutes I handed back to the autopilot again.

After a strenuous passage across the bay of Almeria I finally reached the port of Almarimar at 13:30, but when I rounded the pier head into the opposite direction I really felt the boat being shaken about and noticed that the wind indicator was registering between 35 and 43 knots (Force 8/9). I had a good look around for a place to moor and found a small space along the visitors' quay but this was not going to be easy as the wind was going to blow me away from my position instantly. I could really have done with some help but with a bit of a struggle I finally managed to moor her safely alongside. 'I can't believe it!' I momentarily lost my footing as I stepped ashore and found myself staggering and swaying from side to side - as if in a drunken stupor - into the harbour office where I had to complete the usual paperwork. I took the opportunity of asking the Marinario what the weather was going to be like for the next few days; he rummaged around amongst a disorganised pile of documents and after a few minutes handed me a shrivelled up piece of paper which did, in fact, look like the weather map. I must say it didn't look too healthy; there were at least three storms in the offing and I thought it better to stay put for a while.

I couldn't grumble, because I had been very fortunate and... I needed a break anyway. I was given a berth opposite the harbourmaster's office and the minute I'd secured the boat, my mobile rang; it was my wife to see whether I was ok. It's funny, but she always seemed to know when something wasn't as it should be, almost as if she was watching me from just around the corner. It was very comforting.

Later that afternoon the weather really began to close in on me "big time" but what can you expect at this time of the year. I was certainly glad to be tucked away safely in port!

Almarimar is situated on the Costa del Sol in the Alboran Sea. This port was an invention from the seventies and it looked as if they were trying to copy Ampuria Brava, a rather glamorous marina in the northeast corner of Spain, but they hadn't quite succeeded. It is a vast complex, based on a "Complete City" idea, which had been started some 30 years ago and they were still building blocks of flats and shops in places.

The buildings along the route to the harbour office were 3 stories high and seemed to stand on breezeblock pillars which looked rather flimsy. This whole city complex can only be reached from a road on top of the hill via a slip road of at least a mile long. Behind the hill is the Mountain range of the Sierra Nevada. The hill has almost flat slopes which are littered with white washed greenhouses making them appear as if they are covered in snow. Other than that, the place is featureless, almost like a desert.

The harbour quaysides are already crumbling away from underfoot; the concrete reinforced construction wire has started to rust and the expansion of the rust has broken away the concrete in large chunks. I have the feeling that when this city is finished they will have to start it all over again.

So it wasn't the most attractive place but I was safe and secure.

Now safely in port, I was going to chill out and take it a day at a time; I still had plenty of time to reach Gibraltar before Christmas, but if that proved to be a problem I could always leave the boat here for the Christmas period.

I started to get into a daily routine by stretching my legs and walking all the way around the harbour to the harbourmaster's office, which took 20 minutes, even though the office was literally only a stone's throw away from the boat; that was my exercise for the day. I soon realised that the weather forecast on the notice board was not frequently updated, so found it better to watch the forecast on the TV. This I did regularly, waiting for the storms to abate so that I could continue my voyage.

Almarimar - Caleta de Valez
Thursday 13th December 2001

It took a few days for the weather to improve but seeing the forecast on the TV last night, I established that I could leave this morning because I would be running along the coast in a westerly direction which shouldn't give me any problems; mind you, the easterly wind was still here but down to a comfortable force 4.

I wasn't going to walk all the way around the harbour again this morning - I still needed to pay the harbour dues and collect my passport, which the marina kept in lieu of any outstanding harbour dues, which was a clever way of making sure one paid the bill.

Therefore I untied the boat and manoeuvred her across to the office where I came to my first hurdle as I had to wait for the club secretary to arrive because I was told that she was the only person who had the keys to the safe; never mind, chill out and see how it goes.

08:50 - departed the marina, with a little help from the marina staff, and once outside the piers I found that the swell from the previous days had completely abated and the sea was smooth once more.

With these impressive sea conditions I was able to coast hop close to the shore, something I had never done along this particular section of the coast-line; you see, I normally don't have time to sight-see; my main route is always in a direct line from Gibraltar to Almarimar or Puerto de Garrucha.

I headed in the general direction of Motril, a large commercial port but just after an hour into the voyage, I sighted a vessel in the distance which seemed to be heading straight towards me; at first I saw her as a little dot on the horizon but shortly after I could make out that she was a grey warship with the marking P14 which meant that she was a Patrol Vessel and she was still heading towards me; in fact she came so close that I had my doubts about her intentions; then, almost at the same time, a helicopter emerged from over the hills and headed directly towards the Patrol Boat and me; I quickly looked at my chart and the Almanac and couldn't find any reference to this area being an exercise area nor being for any other activities.

The Patrol Vessel, still going at speed, switched on her blue flashing light ordering me to stop; I wasn't going to dispute this, and shortly after the ship had slowed down, some crew hung out several almighty fenders ready for the captain to manoeuvre the vessel along my port side; a uniformed officer stood at the bow of the Patrol Boat and, through a megaphone asked me,

'Where do you come from?'

'Almarimar' I replied,

'Where are you going to?' I couldn't think quick enough and said,

'Malaga.'

'How many persons do you have on board?

'One'

'Are you sure?'

'Yes'

'OK sir, sorry to have troubled you, have a safe voyage.'

I couldn't think what they wanted - maybe it was an exercise or were they looking for someone specifically? I hadn't drawn their attention to the fact that I was on my own and although I had said to them that I was going to Malaga, I actually hadn't planned to do so.

The day went well and I was enjoying myself so much that the time had flown and it was already 16:00. It was time for me to start looking for a stop-over and it seemed that, strategically, it would have to be Caleta de Velez or Torre del Mar for land-lovers.

Looking at the speed log, I had covered 54nm since Almarimar and an early arrival wouldn't be such a bad idea. This part of the coastline started to look flat and was littered with a horrendous amount of high-rise blocks of flats, so distinguishing a port amidst them was nearly impossible. Then luckily for me fishing boats started to appear from all directions, all heading for the same block of flats so the best thing for me to do was to keep an eye on them so that I could see where the harbour entrance was.

There is a reason for my apprehension because written in the Almanac was a warning of a semi-submerged part which had broken away from the espigón (breakwater).

As I approached the blocks of flats I began to make out the harbour entrance and, as luck would have it, I noticed a fishing boat leaving the port on the left of the espigón and I gave a sigh of relief – phew, I needn't have worried after all.

When I turned the boat into the harbour I noticed that the port was, in fact, a large commercial fishing port rather than a yacht marina.

The port was chocker-block with fishing boats unloading their catch from the day's fishing accompanied by hundreds of seagulls screeching and fighting for the left-over scraps thrown overboard into the harbour.

Totally mesmerized I slowly passed through the hive of activity and called the marina office on the VHF but after several attempts I still didn't get any reply. I couldn't find an available mooring and desperately needed the help of a Marinario in getting me a berth. I waited and waited for at least 15 minutes and then finally, a Marinario came from behind some boats standing tall on the quayside and told me to lie at the end of a pier alongside another boat.

I couldn't believe my eyes but this boat was called "Midnight Sun", a sixty foot boat built in Taiwan, and I happened to know it very well (*how very spooky)*; in fact, I had delivered this boat in April 1992 from Düsseldorf to Arenal near Palma de Mallorca. Well, here was a bit of nostalgia and who would have thought it? Slowly and carefully I manoeuvred the boat alongside the "Midnight Sun" facing seaward, ready for an easy departure in the morning; I turned off my engines at 19:00 and as I had never been here before I had a good look around to get my bearings, from the comfort of my wheelhouse seat.

It didn't take long for the security guard to arrive, who told me to report to the office in about 10 minutes. He pointed in the general direction and said,

'It's just along the quay in the high building.'

Ten minutes later I walked along the pontoon, where there were numerous small boats moored, full of seagull excrement - the whole place looked as if it was covered in snow. It appeared that the seagulls occupied this area every night, together with the fishing fleet.

I had difficulty finding the right building, but eventually found it; the little security guard was sitting behind the high counter and I could barely see him but he'd seen me first and told me to fill out the usual forms.

'That will be 1500 pesetas.'

'Will you take a card?'

'Sorry I can't, I don't have the key for the drawer with the machine.'

'How can I pay you, I don't have the cash?'

'Well, of course you can pay in the morning; we open at nine.'

But I didn't want another late start so I walked into the town where I found myself a hole in the wall and withdrew just enough money to pay the harbour fee, because next year Spain would no longer deal in Pesetas but would be changing over to the new currency of Euros.

While I was ashore I had a quick look around but I couldn't really see the attraction of this place, which was supposed to be a "holiday resort". A fishing port... yes, but a marina and holiday resort? - I don't think so!

I paid the security guard the 1500 pesetas and asked him for the weather forecast for tomorrow. This proved to be very difficult for him and when he eventually tapped into the computer, the whole system crashed. I apologised profusely for the trouble I had caused and said I would check the weather on the TV later.

I went back on board, checked the engine room, and made dinner with my glass of wine.

Caleta de Valez – Gibraltar
Friday 14th December 2001

The first thing I did this morning - *and this had become second nature to me* - was to look out of the porthole in my cabin to check the weather. It was rather breezy in the harbour and the wind seemed to be coming off the mountains which meant that I couldn't see any danger in crossing the bay because the furthest I would be away from the coast would be 8 miles; this in turn meant that the sea would only be slightly choppy. Alright, I didn't get the TV weather forecast last night but it must be ok out there because all the fishing boats and the hungry seagulls had already left.

07:00 - I nosed my way out of the piers; this time I knew exactly where low-lying boulders of the outer breakwater were and I carefully manoeuvred my way around them.

I stopped the boat outside the piers in order to bring in the fenders because the wind was too strong inside the harbour and could have seriously endangered me by causing the boat to drift towards the quay.

Using the radar at short range gave me a perfect distance from the coast and I was able to navigate close inshore as far as Tore del Mar lighthouse, from where I could set the cruising speed at 8 knots and head directly for Punta de la Calibres, a distance of 41nm - *about 5 hours*. This gave me some time to settle and have breakfast in peace.

It gradually became daylight and the sight of numerous fishing boats silhouetted against a black/dark blue sky, gradually becoming yellow/red, made me believe that today was going to be a fantastic day.

The sun rose this morning at 08:22 - *this was 20 minutes later than a few days earlier at Toulon* – and I was already 10 miles from the fishing port of Caleta de Velez.

It began to dawn on me that this was going to be the end of the first half of my homeward bound voyage and if I succeed in reaching Gibraltar today I will have covered a distance of 849 nautical miles since St Jean Cap Ferrat and completed this part of the voyage in 11 sailing days.

10:50 - passing Punta de la Calaburras which is near the holiday resort of Fuengirola where I changed course for the last time and pointed the boat into her final direction towards Gibraltar; the wind had remained the same for the past 2 hours but had only produced a slight chop on the sea; as I was nearing the coast the sea had calmed once more and from my unique position - *close under the shore* - I was able to see the road traffic busily going back and forth, thinking how fortunate I was. Two dolphins showed their dorsal fins as they lazily pottered about, making no attempt to move towards the boat; this once more gave me the impression that fine weather was ahead of me.

The next heading I had chosen would steer the boat slowly away from the coast and, just ahead of me, I observed the first tidal-rips since my arrival into the Mediterranean 3 years ago. These tidal-rips can also create choppy seas, but that's the Med for you - one minute calm and the next... everything comes from all directions! All of a sudden the wind gusted to 35 knots, directly from the west and straight on the bow, making it very choppy and uncomfortable for me.

Not long after passing through the first tidal-rip zone I began to see the hazy outlines of the "Great Rock." YES... finally, Gibraltar was in sight; from here the Rock looked half submerged; seeing Gibraltar, I changed the radar setting up to 24 miles and found that "The Rock" was still 23 miles away and I was sure that the African coast would soon be visible too, but as the sun was over the African continent I was left partly blinded as I looked across a silvery glittering sea and this blocked the view of the mountains in Morocco. I would have to wait a little longer; then far over on my starboard side I could just make out the mountain range behind Marbella and Puerto Jose Banus.

Puerto Jose Banus holds several memories for me, but this one has to have a place of priority because here in Jose Banus had lived a couple who, unbeknown to them, would change the course of my life... (Page 135)

Dark grey clouds started to gather overhead and I thought it wouldn't be long before I would experience the first cloud burst of the voyage. I rather hoped that it would rain now, because the last thing I wanted was to stand in the pouring rain whilst having to moor the boat later.

I was now close enough to the Rock to be able to change the frequency on my VHF to channel 12, which is used by Gibraltar's Port Authorities and would enable me to build up a picture as to what was going on in the bay and the port alike; to be fair, I had really forgotten how busy it was within the Gibraltar Straights, the bay and the various ports.

The Mediterranean gives a false impression as to what real navigation is all about and I must admit that I prefer tidal navigation, which gives a sense of achievement when calculating tides, dealing with adverse weather and general challenges encountered on the high seas; there is also a real buzz in "almost" mastering the sea. I say "almost" because the sea can play havoc with us and we must remember that nature will always win in the end.

It is interesting listening to the pilots as they guide the large vessels in and out of the bay; most of them have come to refuel before their long crossings either to or from the Americas.

Gibraltar Europa Point

My attention was particularly drawn to listening to one of the vessels which wanted to come into the bay and it sounded like this vessel had a Chinese crew and didn't quite understand the message they were given; I couldn't hear the name of the vessel but the pilot said,

'Just stop there where you are, now!!'

'Ok, ok!'

I could see, in the distance, a large vessel was trying to stop. I was so involved with the ship that I hadn't noticed I was surrounded by dozens of dolphins; there were large and small ones flanking either side of the boat, swimming with me as if they were guiding me out of the Mediterranean - "Cheeky". A few more miles, then this leg of the voyage will have come to an end; I am sorry to say, this end has come a little too soon, but if this is my last voyage in the Mediterranean then "I am a happy man!"

16:12 - I rounded the famous Europa point at the entrance of the "Gateway" or exit to the Mediterranean - *Don't look back remember!!! NO, I won't look back!*

I had to pass Gibraltar's main harbour entrance very closely in order to dodge the various anchored vessels and from there I continued to the north end just short of the airport runway where I needed to turn sharp to starboard; there, in front of me, I found the Sheppard's Yard and Marina Bay Marinas opposite the Custom & Immigration and Port Authority offices.

The rain had stopped almost as quickly as it had started; brilliant! I slowly glided the boat towards the Custom pontoon, but had to stop abruptly and wait for a small sailing boat that had strategically plonked itself smack bang in the middle of the pontoon. The Skipper, a man of my age with a white beard and a skipper's cap, appeared from the Customs cabin and slowly boarded his boat, started his engine and, with an unsure smile on his face, vacated the pontoon.

I assumed that, like myself, he was a "solo sailor" and I wondered where he would have come from; perhaps a few miles, or even from across the ocean. Anyway, I started my manoeuvre alongside and with the wind from behind, this didn't present me with too many difficulties.

Now with the Custom and Immigration formalities completed, I called "Marina Bay" and asked for a berth; they replied that the marina was full for the winter, but I could see several free places and more than ample space for this boat. However, it was explained to me that during any storms from the west these places would be vulnerable and damage to the boat could not be ruled out.

I tried to call "Sheppard's Marina" but they didn't reply and after 10 minutes I gave up.

Now where am I to go?

I went in search of another place and had heard of the Marina inside the main docks called "Queensway Quay Marina" which was an inner harbour and, until a few years ago, was occupied by the Royal Navy.

Queensway Quay Marina is at the Ragged Staff Wharf in the old dock. Originated by the Spanish in 1736, it was subsequently developed by the British under the supervision of the First Lord of the Admiralty, Sir Charles Wager, with the purpose of providing "better victualling of men-at-war"; who knows, I might be at the place where Nelson and Wellington had landed.

I called Queensway Quay Marina on the VHF radio.

'Queensway Quay Marina this is Calypso II.'

'Go ahead Calypso II.'

'Do you have a berth for my boat?'

'What is your length?'

'60 foot'

Then there was a silence and I waited and waited and thought *what if they don't have a space then I will have to turn back into the Med.*

In hindsight, I should have done just that, but I really wanted to leave the Mediterranean behind, and then...

'Calypso II, this is Queensway Quay Marina come in please.'

'Calypso II listening, go-ahead.'

'How long are you planning to stay?'

I thought for a second or so and hesitantly answered,

'Oh, I expect at least until the end of January!'

'You can come into the marina and go to pontoon 'A'. We'll send someone to help you moor.'

I entered the marina, which I must say was a bit tricky, but after 2 attempts I finally succeeded in reversing her onto the allocated berth and surprisingly the harbour assistant told me that I could use as many anchor lines as I liked; I didn't know what he was on about at the time but was to find out later.

17:30 - I switched off the engines for the last time and in doing so I had symbolically brought this voyage to an end. The Mediterranean was behind me now and nostalgia swept over me.

The mooring they had chosen for me was just inside the floating breakwater which I assume was to stop the small wavelets entering the marina. However, this breakwater hadn't stopped the oil spill which they had encountered a few weeks earlier, because when I hauled one of the anchoring lines out of the water I found it to be coated in thick black oil which subsequently covered the lovely teak deck; Oh great! In addition to this, I also happened to notice that the pontoon was littered with plastic bags and other debris covered in oil. This was a real welcome to the place I must say!

Now with the boat moored securely I found myself wandering along the pontoon, my legs still wobbly from being at sea, but it was so good to be ashore again.

Although this voyage had come to an end, little did I know but a new adventure had only just begun.

I checked the Nautical Almanac regarding the shelter in Gibraltar; the remarks were: "Reasonable shelter although strong gusts'off the land can be bothersome." This remark turned out to be a complete understatement and until they build a second concrete breakwater this harbour is, in certain circumstances, extremely dangerous.

After a peaceful weekend relaxing, and enthusiastically preparing to go home, disaster struck. In all my years at sea I have never been confronted with such a dangerous situation, and in the apparent safety of a marina! I hope it will never happen again. Even on the notorious Atlantic coastal Ports I have never known such a horrendous and frightening episode as the one which follows.

Rough Weather in Gibraltar Harbour

During the night of Monday 17th December 2001 I felt the boat moving about quite a bit – I had been used to living with swell movement in the Port of St Jean Cap Ferrat when the wind came from a certain direction - and around breakfast time the boat began to pull really hard on all the lines. I went outside to extend all the

ropes by another metre, which meant that if I needed to go ashore then I would have to leap from the gangway onto the pontoon. The pulling on the ropes became even worse as the day progressed, so much so that it really began to make me feel seasick. Unfortunately, leaving the boat was now impossible and so I had to grin and bear it.

The movement started to stabilise for a while and I felt confident enough to leave the boat and venture ashore in order to stretch my legs. My first port of call was the harbour office where I enquired as to whether this situation was at its full potential or could we expect more. The lady in the office said,

'I think this is about it; we normally only get this sort of thing when the wind is blowing from the east.'

I couldn't really understand this as the harbour was well protected from the sea by the larger outer breakwater which protected the whole of Gibraltar port.

After my visit to the office I had a general look around the town which was only a stone's throw away from the marina.

Upon my return I found that one of the 3 inch thick long lines had chafed through and was now floating like a snake in the oily water of the harbour. I replaced the rope and began to get the feeling that the swell in the harbour had risen; I estimated that it was a good 4 feet; now all the boats on my pontoon began to sway in unison from side to side constantly jerking on their ropes. I could see that this situation was becoming increasingly dangerous and I called the marina on the VHF asking for permission to move further inside, but they answered that the harbour was full and I should stay where I was.

I just couldn't keep the boat secured and one by one the ropes began to chafe through; it wasn't only the stern lines I had to replace but the same happened to the bow lines too. Luckily there weren't any boats moored either side of me which enabled me to borrow the mooring lines from these intended occupants; at least having those extra lines gave me the added security for the night or so I thought!

The situation became even worse in the evening, when an occasional rogue wave of well over 6 foot would run into the corner of the harbour and set the quayside awash; it was so bad at times that making my dinner was now well out of the question; ironically though, I had never had a problem preparing and eating dinner at sea.

The weather deteriorated as night fell, becoming unbelievably windy and pouring with rain, certainly not a pleasant evening. I tried to focus on relaxing and watching TV, and surprisingly I nearly succeeded. Then, at around 10:00, I heard an almighty loud bang, like an explosion, and noticed that this was in tandem with the violent swaying of the boat to the starboard side, but then within seconds another loud bang occurred. I leapt into the wheelhouse but I couldn't see anything because of the rain lashing against the windows so, reluctantly, I threw a coat around my shoulders and slipped into my boots to investigate what had happened. I staggered and swayed to the rear and found that the crossover lines had broken and a third line had caught under the bathing platform; luckily the boat's bathing platform was sturdily built and it was the rope that had to give way.

Whilst I was busy repairing and replacing the stern ropes, another loud bang occurred, but this time it came from the bow. I ran as fast as I could to the front of the boat and, to my horror, I found one of the four anchor lines was dangling into the water and a second anchor line on the same side had nearly chafed through and it wouldn't be much longer before this one was going to part company.

Right now I couldn't do much about the broken line, but secured the partly chafed line with a special knot. So far, so good! Totally drenched and extremely cold I despondently went back inside, changed into dry clothing and made myself a hot drink thinking, I don't want to be a pessimist but sleeping in these conditions will be almost impossible. I finished my drink and checked on all the mooring lines to see whether the protection sleeves - *plastic hoses I had put over the ropes* - had stayed in place, before going to bed.

Seven of the protection hoses were in place but one needed to be adjusted; in order to do this I had to lift the rope up and slide the hose back into its position protecting the rope from the sharp edge of the fairlead *(a hole through the side of the deck)*.

I decided to wait until the boat moved and slackened off the rope so that I could slide the sleeve back. Stupid me! Suddenly, the boat moved violently over the other side leaving my left index finger between the rope and fairlead, and in a panic, I tried pulling my finger away from under the rope and I cried out; my screaming was so loud that the sound of my own voice echoed back from the building surrounding the port and for a split second I thought someone else was in trouble too.

The pain in my finger was excruciating and I couldn't bear looking at it otherwise I might have fainted; I ran into the wheelhouse and quickly picked up the wet towel I had used earlier to dry myself; I tightly wrapped it around my finger and staggered into the saloon; I sat down and it took a few minutes to calm down and compose myself, then I finally had the courage to unwrap the cloth and replace it with a bandage. Now I needed to think what to do next: I can't get off the boat and jump onto the moving pontoon, but what if I need to go to the hospital, who would look after the boat in the meantime, and how do I get back on board again now the boat is too far away from the pontoon for me to jump. Exhausted and with my injured finger up in the air, which reduced the throbbing, I fell asleep on the settee.

Thank goodness, the night passed without further incidents, but the following morning I felt like death; I had hoped that the pain would have eased and the throbbing would have stopped, but it hadn't. I thought I'd better get to the hospital to check on the severity of my injury and see whether it had been infected by the dirty towel and oily residue.

I tried to have a wash and shave but this was a joke and I thought I'd better stop before I cut my throat!

I was finally ready to leap ashore, but had wait for the right moment and eventually managed to jump onto the shaky pontoon.

After finding my footing I waddled like a duck onto the shore towards the marina office where I was optimistically greeted by a young lady,

'Good morning sir, can I help you?'

'Yes please, I hope you can – I *pointed my finger at her, although it wasn't meant to be rude* - I had an accident last night and I think that I should see a doctor.'

She suggested if I didn't know the town then it would be better to get a taxi and ask for the General Hospital.

I thanked her and walked onto the main road and hailed a taxi; we zigzagged through the town "formula one" style and stopped in a very narrow street in front of the hospital main entrance, halfway up the mountainside "Rock". I walked into the entrance hall where a large number of people were already waiting to be seen, but surprisingly I was attended to within the hour.

The doctor took off the bandage and said,

'Mmmm that's not good, it looks like the top of your finger is broken; we can't do anything about that; you'll have to wait until it heals by itself.' With this diagnosis I despondently walked down the mountain back to the boat.

The day had finally come for me to fly home for my Christmas break. I hoped the weather would stay kind to the boat whilst I was in England.

My return ticket to Gibraltar was for Thursday the 3rd of January which is earlier than normal, but I was not happy about the position of the boat and the incident before Christmas, so I thought it better to return to the boat as soon as the festive season had passed.

In the Right Place at the Right Time
March 1971.

At that time I was freelance skippering on behalf of Moonraker and part of my job was to demonstrate their "Moonraker Soft Rider 36" along the coast of Great Yarmouth.

One day, upon my return from a demo, I walked towards the office door when John, the Moonraker salesman, who was with some customers at the Marina café, called me over and introduced me to Michael Sullivan and his wife Dany. Michael had just purchased a Moonraker called "La Princess" for Dany's birthday.

Mike and Dany were accompanied by their friend Jack. Jack did most of the talking and, unbeknown to me, had sized me up and I must have ticked all the boxes because at the end of our conversation Mike and Dany decided to take me on as their skipper; this was the beginning of a long and delightful friendship.

A few days after the launching of "La Princess" - *with champagne and headlines in the newspapers* - we started to plan our voyage for the warmer climate of the Mediterranean. Dany asked whether we could take the boat through the French canals, but I was led to believe that this boat would not pass under some of the bridges and so had to tell her that we would need to sail her across the Bay of Biscay and Gibraltar to Marbella.

This posed a bit of a problem as we needed to plan the voyage to arrive in Marbella in time for the birthday of Dany's son Robin. We managed to do this and when we arrived in Puerto Banus, just outside Marbella, Mike and Dany left the boat and stayed with some family friends in the mountains. A few days later they returned to the boat and we departed for our next destination, Palma de Mallorca, where we left the boat securely moored in Club Real

Nautico until the next time.

In early July I flew out to the boat, prior to Mike and Dany, in order to get her up and running again. Mike and Dany arrived two days later full of enthusiasm.

We made our plans for the next voyage and agreed to sail from here to Minorca, Sardinia, Palermo, Messina and Crotone, to arrive in Corfu two weeks later.

With all preparations and plans in place we went out for dinner, just across the road, to a little square tucked away from the main drag just below the Cathedral of Palma.

We had a most enjoyable evening; Mike, being himself, recited endless jokes, with a cigarette in one hand and holding a stiff glass of Irish whiskey in the other, and in between... a little bit food.

After dinner we leisurely walked back to the front of the marina office where we had moored our dinghy, and just as we stepped into the dinghy we heard a voice asking if we were from "La Princess".

It was the night watchman who was trying to say something; Dany was able to grasp a few words and thought she heard him mention the word "fire" but we didn't think it had anything to do with us, so we proceeded to untie the boat and just as we were about to move off the watchman frantically shouted,

'No, No, No you must stay here and wait; England will call you soon!'

We looked at one another in total confusion and Dany suggested that Mike and I went back to the boat whilst she waited for this "mysterious" call from England.

After sometime, Dany returned on board crying her eyes out.

Mike asked,

'What's the matter ma petite?'

Dany, who was normally very composed and kept her emotions to herself, couldn't stop crying and could barely get her words out but was finally able to utter,

'Môn amour, our lovely home has burned down!'

It was their friend Jack who had the task of informing them of this awful news. We sat down totally speechless and after they had come to terms with this dreadful news, it was obvious to me that I couldn't take them away on this voyage, and suggested,

'I think you should both go back to the UK and sort things out.'

Mike said,

'Jack can do that for us Bill.'

'No, môn petit, I think Bill is right; we should go and see for ourselves.'

With this it was decided that I should stay and await their return.

Not long after, we experienced a fire on "La Princess"; this was due to a turbo-oil pressure gauge tube which had split and sprayed hot oil all over the un-cooled turbo exhaust and had instantaneously set fire to the sound-proof insulation under the wheelhouse floor but luckily I dealt with this without too much damage.

But in 1995 in their Paris apartment, they tragically met their death and no-one knows exactly what caused that fire.

I spent many happy years skippering for Mike and Dany and had become part of their family because during this period I was asked to skipper the boat for Mike's sister and family; it was then that I met my future wife who was to become the mother of our three lovely girls.

So you see, I had been in the right place at the right time!

Gibraltar
January 2002

I had booked an early morning call - **really early** - and took a taxi to the airport. I was most surprised to see that there were so many people out and about and when I arrived at the airport I found the place in full swing.

At the check-in desk I asked,

'Is it always so busy early in the morning?'

'Yes sir, it's the early morning rush hour. It's busy from now until eight then it tails off. This is your ticket and boarding card sir, the flight is slightly delayed but I wish you a pleasant flight.'

'Thank you.'

I had been allocated a seat on the right-hand side of the aircraft. I always choose an aisle seat as I suffer from claustrophobia in a plane, and I like the extra arm and legroom despite getting bumped into occasionally by the cabin crew dealing with the passengers.

After take-off, the pilot welcomed us on board and gave us the "pleasant" news that they were currently experiencing a storm and heavy rain in Gibraltar and that we might have to divert to Malaga.

Here we go again; before Christmas I had left Gib with atrocious weather and it seemed that this hadn't changed. The aircraft cruised for a while at low altitude and then, as we climbed through the lower cloud layer, I looked out of a partly-frosted window and noticed that we were accompanied by at least four other aircraft running virtually in a parallel direction at similar speed; I now understood the ground staff's reference to the so called "rush hour". I suppose this must be it.

The flight was fairly smooth, except when we crossed over the mountain range of Granada, but once past the mountains I could see the blue Mediterranean Sea ahead, near the port of Malaga.

The pilot then gave us the good news that the rain and wind had moved away from the "Rock" and we would now be landing at Gibraltar after all.

Sitting on the right side of the plane gave me the opportunity of seeing the "Rock" and I must say it is a magnificent sight. The sea looked calm and the sun shone brightly onto the Rock face depicting the grandiose and magnificent stature it represents.

Flaps out, loud whistle, clonk, wheels down, engines revving up, more flap and rudder adjustments constantly trying to line up for the final approach, but hang-on a minute, the sea was getting closer and closer; it began to look as if the plane was just about to land on the water but after having fought-off the crosswinds, which violently shook it about like a rag-doll, it finally plonked itself down hard on the runway; the pilot immediately reversed the engines at full blast and, with screeching brakes, we finally came to an abrupt halt at the very end of the runway; here the pilot turned and steered back over the live runway, across the main road into Gibraltar and eventually stopped at a building with a large sign "Welcome to Gibraltar". We walked across the tarmac to the building, where I cleared Immigration & Customs, picked up my luggage and walked through the green sign and out of the airport.

I didn't have anything to declare because you can buy all your needs here on the Island. Well it's not really an "Island" but the Spanish had closed the border for such a long time that people began to think they were on an island.

I recollect that on one of my previous visits I had met a Gibraltarian who told me of the awful situation the Gibraltarians had to endure and he thought that the plight of the people was quite similar to that of the people in Berlin who were also denied access to the other side.

'Look' he had said, pointing across the runway from where we were standing,

'Over there are the relatives of the people living and working on the Rock and the only communication they have is a pair of binoculars and a two-way radio set.'

'Can't they visit each other at all' I had asked,

'Yes they can, but they would have to travel to Ceuta, the Spanish colony in Morocco then turn around to the Gibraltar Bay on the Spanish side at Algeciras.'

'That's a crazy situation, isn't it'?

'I think so; the sooner they get this sorted the better.'

Little did he or I know that a few years after our conversation this particular problem would be resolved.

I came out of the airport and grabbed a waiting taxi. The driver steered in the direction of Gibraltar which meant that we had to cross the runway which I had crossed earlier in a different direction.

Thinking I was being funny I said,

'I hope there isn't another plane coming!' to which the taxi driver replied,

'Well, last year we had a man driving a car passing the wrong side of the barrier just before an incoming plane; this crazy person was trying to avoid the customs at the border with Spain; luckily for him he got away with it, but the Spanish Customs did catch him in the end.'

After a ten minute ride we arrived at the Queensway Quay Marina and I was back to reality. The boat looked fine but they hadn't cleaned the pontoons from the oil spill last year. I went to the office and asked whether I could move the boat further into the harbour and, to my surprise, I was given a much better berth, one which wasn't so exposed to the swell.

Although I had returned to the boat, we weren't planning to leave for the time being as the owner, who was going to join me for this section of the voyage, didn't have the time and it wouldn't be advisable for me to tackle this part of the voyage on my own. At least this laying-up time gave me the opportunity of getting the boat ready for the second half of the voyage and getting to know the "Rock" and her people.

I needed to have some sort of exercise because being on the boat all day does stiffen the joints, so I took a daily walk around the town with a regular "pit stop" at the Safeway Supermarket located in the new development over in the old commercial docks.

Doing the daily walks made me realise that this place was in a different world altogether. Gibraltar has a population of 40,000 or so and each and every one of them seemed to have a car; I had this funny feeling that the M.O.T didn't exist or, if it did, they weren't worried about it because most cars were bellowing blue smoke into the atmosphere and if you were not being choked to death by the smoke you certainly may have experienced an early heart failure from the young drivers sounding off their audio capability - they only seemed to know **VERY LOUD** music; I would have liked to have said to them 'you may want to drown out the traffic noise but soon you won't be able to hear any noises at all!'

Nevertheless, Gibraltar has something other places don't have and I couldn't help feeling that I was walking in history.

I have visited many places in my time, which in their own right have a lot to offer, but here there is a special magic and a diverse culture oozing out of it. You can definitely see that the British - who have been here for over 300 years - have left a distinct mark on the place, as part of the town could be set in Cornwall a century or two ago; other parts are straight out of the 1960's with their two story buildings mostly made out of concrete pillars and covered by glass, and the commercial area looks more like the new high-rise buildings set in the London Docklands.

Whilst I was walking through the upper town level I came across what looked like a setting in French Morocco with typically French designed houses, small alleyways, steep stairways and wrought iron balcony railings, finished off with the distinct archways seen in Morocco.

One day I took the cable-car to the top of the Rock and from there I enjoyed a breathtaking panoramic view over the Gibraltar Bay, across the Gibraltar straits and, in the far distance, the African continent with its Atlas Mountains; I could visualise the numerous sailing ships weighing their anchors and pursuing the enemy passing through the Straits. Gibraltar is so strategically placed that it is not surprising that no-one has ever been able to capture it, and if they were about to succeed then there was always the 100-ton canon at "Nelson's Anchorage" with which the enemy had to contend; I am sure that this gun must have caused a lot of damage to the unwelcome visitors at that time.

The month of January had gone by rather quickly and I still hadn't heard anything about a possible departure date from Gibraltar.

It was not until the first week of February that I received the call saying that we were going to be on our way soon but, of course, February is the most difficult time of the year for sailing around these waters; any sailor with common sense wouldn't, and shouldn't, attempt to leave the safety of a port; in fact, whilst I was in Gibraltar very little pleasure craft traffic was seen to be moving and the new crafts coming from the UK had all arrived on specially designed cargo vessels. Having said this, I did usually seem to be lucky, weather-wise, but perhaps this time I might be overstepping the mark.

With this information under my hat, I began my routine checks and made a horrible discovery in the engine room: the port engine's exhaust manifold had corroded through the external part and had started to pour seawater into the boat; I panicked a bit and quickly phoned the owner, explaining that we needed a replacement part; the owner replied that the part we needed was not on the shelf and I would have to make-do with a temporary repair; this meant that I would have to improvise a way of blocking off the hole.

I found some high temperature chemical metal which could be spread onto the hole and hoped it would work. I left the repair to settle for 24 hours and thank goodness it worked - at least for the time being!

A few days later the owner arrived in his corporate jet, two days before our departure. Having familiarised himself with the situation, we took the boat for an extensive sea trial; unfortunately we had to limit our trial to the Gibraltar side of the Bay, because should we go further afield then we would have to re-enter Gibraltarian territory and go through all the necessary Customs and Immigration formalities again – we did not think that was an option.

Gibraltar - Marina Cherry
Tuesday 12th February 2002

Oh my goodness! I hadn't realised that we had been in Gibraltar for over a month already and sadly we now needed to leave, although I wished that we could have postponed the departure at least until March, when the weather improves. - Oh dear, I am beginning to sound like some skippers who prefer an easy life and will give their owners any excuse to avoid going to sea; well, this owner just happened to love the sea and adverse weather or did he?

This morning the weather was not looking too promising with thick fog first thing which later changed into a very low cloud base and a howling wind from around the north side of the Rock. This really had put a dampener on our departure but the owner insisted that we needed to move-on anyway because he didn't have a lot of time at his disposal.

After some deliberation we departed the marina at 10:00 and moved westwards across the Gibraltar Bay towards Tarifa point, which is at the most southern tip of Spain and the most southern point of mainland Europe. Traversing the bay needed my full concentration as I had to cross paths and collision courses used by many vessels, i.e. the fast and slow moving ferries departing and arriving from Algeciras to Ceuta, refuelling barges and numerous fishing boats trawling in the bay. In addition to this I needed to make numerous course changes in order to avoid the ocean-going vessels lying at anchor waiting for fuel or new sailing orders.

After safely crossing the bay I started to hug the coast in order to avoid the current which enters the Mediterranean, but somehow I still caught a bit of this easterly going current until just before the point of Tarifa.

Slowly, a long swell started to develop from a westerly direction, although the wind was blowing from the east at 24 knots; this became much more noticeable as we were nearing the point.

Sunset, East of Tarifa, most Southern Point of Spain.

We passed the point of Tarifa just after midday which gave me this unbelievably weird feeling that somehow the door had closed behind me for the very last time. - Ironically this month forty years ago I passed this point for the very first time on the Cargo vessel "Schelde Lloyd" on our way back to Rotterdam from a round-the-world voyage.

All of a sudden the sky started to clear from the west which meant that better weather was in the offing and yes, within the hour we were in bright sunlight, but I noticed that the swell had become much higher and measured between 9 and 12 feet. Seeing this, I thought it better to stay under the coast for a little while longer, but having made this decision I realised that it would increase the length of the voyage for today. Luckily the current had changed and was now coming from behind and we actually made good timing and arrived at the Trafalgar lighthouse a lot earlier than I would have done if I had chosen to travel the direct track.

The voyage was uneventful, that is until mid-afternoon when we noticed that at Pointa Camarinal a full scale rescue was taking place on the beach with the assistance of a helicopter. I don't know what had happened, because we were too far away from the scene, but through my binoculars I was able to make out that a stretcher was being lowered from the helicopter onto the beach.

I changed my VHF radio setting to channel 16 but unfortunately I don't speak any Spanish and therefore couldn't understand what the problem was; I suppose with the big breaking waves rolling onto the beach it could well have been a surfer in trouble.

Cape Trafalgar is a lighthouse which holds a few memories for me; on several occasions I have had to give up attempting to reach Gibraltar because of adverse weather conditions, mainly due to the cross-over currents and short waves over the sand banks. My diversion usually ended up in Cádiz or, weather permitting, I would run into the Port of Barbate de Franco. The latter was not as interesting as Cádiz, which has a fantastic wealth of history, especially with the British. The lighthouse can be easily recognized; it is a tall and single-standing structure on an island surrounded by flat land. I had set my track 2½ miles off Cape Trafalgar so that I could pass the island on one side and a shallow patch on the other. I aimed to stay in the 23 metre depth zone; this was to avoid the short breaking waves as they ran over the shallows.

Fortunately, the wind was still from the east at 20 knots, which made the voyage running along this coastline very comfortable.

Then…. something began to puzzle me; why were we suddenly accompanied by a large pod of dolphins? They don't normally swim in the shallows; they only do this when the weather is rough in the open sea!

I followed the coast towards Cádiz and since I had passed Trafalgar the sea had become totally smooth, that is except for the low Atlantic swell rolling onto the beaches.

17:30 - I rounded the west cardinal buoy at Castello San Sebastian - a fortress on the corner of the Bay of Cádiz just off the main coast - and as I was turning onto the final heading to Cádiz the owner suddenly

asked,

'What's that over there?'

He pointed his finger in a different direction to that of the Port of Cádiz.

'Oh, that's the new yacht marina called Cherry.'

'Let's go there, shall we?'

As I have said, you never know the destination, but that's what keeps the job exciting!

I took the south channel, which is not well-marked but with these sea conditions and superb visibility I was able to spot the off-lying rocks just off the main channel.

Puerto America (Cádiz) was now at my starboard side and from here I had a clear run to Puerto Cherry but we were intercepted by a Spanish Customs cutter just before we arrived at the port. As always, the Calypso II attracted a lot of attention from many seamen who appreciated a beautiful ship when they saw one, and this Custom cutter crew was no exception.

We entered Puerto Cherry at 18:30 and the Marinario, who was just about to go home, provided us with a mooring. The place resembled a modern concrete jungle and it felt uncomfortably dark and mysteriously spooky. We asked the Marinario where we could find the restaurants and he said,

'Sorry they are all closed for the winter, but if you travel a few miles down the road you will find a place called Puerto de Santa Maria.'

Having taken note of what the Marinario had said the owner thought better of it and stayed on board. This wasn't bad actually; it just meant that I had to cook dinner for us, which was quite easy for me, with the assistance of a few glasses of red wine!

Marina Cherry - St Maria - Cadiz
Wednesday 13th February 2002

We were ready to go but the marina office was still closed and would remain so until nine o'clock.

I thought that if we were making our way towards the UK then we needed to start a lot earlier in the mornings than this.

After paying the overnight mooring we finally left the marina at 09:30 and - wait for it - the owner asked to move to Puerto Santa Maria, a mere 3 miles away and up a small river called the Rio Guadalete, just adjacent to this port; I had this funny feeling that this so called "returning to the UK" wasn't going to happen for now and that my owners had decided to have a short winter break instead. Oh well, I couldn't blame them and I really didn't mind because not knowing where we were going made it a mystery tour and skippering this vessel gave me the opportunity of exploring many new places.

I slowly sailed up the short river to Puerto Santa Maria, where my owners suggested heading further into the town centre, rather than the marina, which was fine with me because the marina moorings looked too flimsy for this vessel. I found a space alongside a restaurant barge and told the owner that if I was chased away, then they would have to call me on the mobile when they had finished so that I could come and collect them, and so they went ashore to explore the place.

Soon after they had left, the restaurant owner came to see me and I thought he was going to tell me to leave but actually he invited me to stay, as he thought that the presence of the Calypso II would attract customers for the lunchtime service.

We didn't stay long in Santa Maria and headed a mere 2 miles across the bay straight for the port of Cádiz. Here we had the choice of two marinas: the first was Puerto America and a little further along a smaller marina which seemed to be for the local boats only. I opted for the first one which looked newly built. I nosed my way into the marina and had a look around but the only place suitable for us was just ahead of the Spanish lifeboat which was, as you would expect, a very large craft; I had been here in the past, when I had to shelter from mountainous waves and I recalled that the concoction of shallow grounds and partly submerged rocks made this a hazardous area, to say the least.

As soon as we finished mooring the boat I insisted that they should pay a visit to the town as it was buzzing with history.

Me... well, I spent my time, as usual, hooking up the electricity and checking the technical matters and whilst carrying out the checks in the engine room I received a phone call from my owner saying,

'Did you know that they are having a carnival in the town today? there is a great atmosphere and we are really enjoying ourselves, so we won't be eating on board and could you possibly find out whether we can sail to the city of Sevilla?'

Wow, another surprise destination!

After finishing my checks, I walked around the harbour to the office to pay for the night's stay but when I arrived there I found the place closed. I scanned around for a while but couldn't see anyone. I suppose they must all have been at the carnival. But then I spotted a small harbour bar tucked away - the only one around for miles; I went inside and found a few customers staring at the TV. I enquired at the bar as to what time the office would be open; a middle aged man with a weather-beaten face, sitting at the bar, carefully guarding his glass of schnapps, slowly turned his head into my direction and grumbled,

'Who wants to know?'

'Me, I am the skipper of the motor yacht over there.'

'Oh, that's a very beautiful boat!' he said in a more pleasant tone and continued

'But the office won't be open today, haven't you heard its Carnival?'

'Yes I have, but we would like to leave very early tomorrow morning.'

'For you, Sir, I will open now as long as you can pay by credit card' That was fine by me because I didn't have any Euros on me anyway. We walked over to the office and I apologised profusely for disrupting his afternoon off.

'Oh, I nearly forgot, where can I get information regarding navigation up the river to Sevilla?'

'Everywhere is shut for Carnival Day, but you could try asking the captain of the lifeboat; he will definitely have that information.' I thanked the Marinario and wished him a good afternoon.

The lifeboat shed was a 42ft container which didn't only hold lifeboat equipment but was also a mess room for the crew, who were having their tea.

'Buenos Dias. Could I speak to the coxswain, please?' A small Spaniard answered in perfect English,

'Good afternoon, what can I do for you?'

'I am from the motor yacht and we're looking to go to Sevilla tomorrow but we don't have any charts for that area; is the river difficult to navigate?'

'No, not really, big ships travel regularly to and from Sevilla, but I have a chart and by all means you can have a look at it.'

Although I have a photographic memory I wasn't able to absorb all the information I needed, and as there was no facility to photocopy the chart the only alternative was to sketch a river map outlining the most important features.

The coxswain allowed me to borrow the chart, as long as I returned it before closing time, which gave me only 15 minutes in which to copy all this information onto a scrap of paper. Exactly 15 minutes later I returned the chart and thanked him for his help.

I made my dinner and settled down for a peaceful evening; that was... until the owners returned and found that they couldn't get on board because the water level had dropped and had left the boat down in the depths of the harbour. I am afraid I hadn't noticed but I soon moved the boat towards the rusty steps built into the wall and succeeded in getting my owners safely back on board.

Cadiz - Sevilla
Thursday 14th February 2002

Last night we planned that today we would leave early, but this morning I woke to a thick blanket of fog – what am I to do now? Well, I would have to wait until the fog lifted a little; I thought it would be wiser not to venture out and get swallowed up in this thick soup. The owner wasn't up yet and I didn't see the need for waking him. Ironically, I could have gone to the shop this morning and bought that chart for Rio Guadalquivir after all.

The morning was marching on and the fog still wasn't lifting. Although I had a fantastic radar at my disposal I did not want to take any risk because the previous day I had observed how the little ferries, coming from Santa Maria, approached the pier head at full speed then swung around and reversed at an alarming rate for 300 metres, which made me think that leaving now would be suicide.

The fog slowly started to lift, and at around 10 o'clock the visibility was about 100 metres, which was safe enough for me to navigate; I hoped that the sun would burn off the rest later; at least there wasn't really any wind, which is always helpful for motorboat lovers.

I reached for my sunglasses because they give a better vision in fog and switched on the navigation equipment then manoeuvred the boat gently away from the quayside, using 3 short blasts on our powerful air horn warning mariners that I was going astern. I then turned around and pointed the bow at the marina entrance and headed for the main breakwaters out into the bay. I must admit that I felt a lot easier seeing the pier head disappear into the fog behind me.

I had set my track just outside the shipping fairway but at one stage I had to cross over to the other side of the fairway making sure at the same time to stay close to the markers so as not to run onto the rocks which I had seen a few days earlier.

I slowly moved along the outer edge of the port-hand marker buoys ticking them off the chart one by one. Then on my radar I noticed a big bleep coming towards me in the channel and shortly after that I saw a large red painted LPG (Liquid Petrol Gas) tanker which came steaming towards me like a bullet out of the fog and passed me just 200 metres on my port side – phew that was hairy!

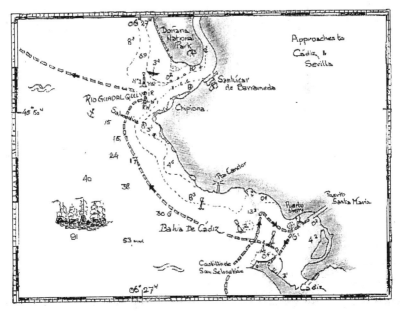

A little later, I passed the last port-hand buoy at Punta Rota just off the coast, and a short distance behind the buoy I could just about make out the low-lying coast-line with its buildings along the sea front; I always think that buildings seems so much larger on low lying land.

Seeing the coast also meant that the visibility was now ¾nm; at last the fog was beginning to lift. I was so relieved that the weather was clearing, because I was still very apprehensive about entering the Rio Guadalquivir without the proper chart. I had studied the Reeds

Nautical Almanac carefully, but nevertheless!

After passing the last buoy I was able to change course to a north-westerly direction, running parallel to the coast of Casa Breva and just clearing the Bajo Sal Medina rock by a mile on the west side. Just after passing Pointa Candor the visibility started to diminish again and then I noticed another small blip on the radar travelling at an alarming rate towards me, with no obvious intention of diverting its course; I chose to make a positive course change to my starboard, hoping to avoid a collision.

Then... just in front of my bows appeared a dark grey inflatable boat occupied by two uniformed officers; when they were beam-on, I noticed that they had a radar dome so they would have known exactly where I was and were quite happy to aim for me head-on at full speed. But, they should have complied with the "rules for avoiding collisions at sea", which is to pass port to port; they obviously thought they knew better! They didn't even wave or slow down; maybe they were just observing but I thought they were behaving recklessly, absolute madness!

It wasn't very long after the "loonies" had passed me, when the weather closed in again. The visibility dropped back to 50 metres or even less - this was just what I needed! My time was now divided between looking at the radar, feeling my way in the fog and studying the river approaches. I have always studied the pilot books before entering a strange port and thank God, so far, it has always had a positive outcome.

12:25 - I measured the distance, and by the angle of Sal Medina island on the radar it appeared that I was ready to turn towards the number 1 marker buoy at the mouth of Rio Guadalquivir. Thank goodness this marker was fitted with a Racor signal transmitter - *this is to identify the difference between the buoy and the numerous ships on the radar screen.*

I wasn't feeling at ease with this situation because not only did I have to cope with the fog but also the numerous blips on the screen, which unfortunately were all lying in a direct line towards the marker-buoy; it looked like all these vessels were waiting for the incoming tide. I thought I had successfully dodged all the blips on the radar until I was unexpectedly confronted with a dark grey mass of steel coming out of the fog, just off my course-line and for a brief moment my heart went into my throat, but I passed him without incident, thankfully.

As usual, I had set the VHF radio to Channel 12, the pilot station, which gave me a fair indication as to what was happening in the area.

The fairway was marked on either side every ¼ mile with the appropriate coloured buoys which echoed in a perfect line on the radar. Now my biggest problem was that I didn't know how much depth there was outside the fairway and I had noticed on the chart that there were some rocks on the starboard side and an almighty large sandbank on the port side but my small-scale chart didn't give me the accurate distance away from the navigation channel, so I stayed very close to the inside of the fairway, along the starboard-hand buoys.

I let off a sigh of relief as I finally passed the last ship and now had a clear run up the fairway; mind you, this was still rather a tricky affair in this fog because the fairway was relatively narrow and there wasn't very much space for vessels passing either from behind or coming down stream.

13:30 - it was nearly low water; the pilot station had started to instruct the vessels to prepare for running up river with the coming flood, which made it perfect for me to run up river also, with a 3 mile current pushing me from behind; this would shorten the voyage by at least 1½ hours.

Listening to the pilot station's broadcast I couldn't help hearing the conversation between the Spanish pilot and the captain of a Russian vessel, who was instructed to prepare for departure up river and their conversation, in Spanish/English went as follows:

'Sir, will you please prepare to lift your anchor'

'Yes sir'

'When you have lifted your anchor sail to the fairway marker, be sure to be at the marker at 13:45'

'Ok sir'

In the meantime, I was still fighting my way up the fairway in the fog and... I couldn't believe it but suddenly it was as if I had left the fog out to sea behind a "curtain" and now in front of me I could clearly see an armada of small fishing boats making their way to the open sea and into the fog, making use of the falling tide.

Fantastic, now I had a clear view all the way up river with the town of Bonanza on my right and the Doñana National Park on my left. The river at this point is at least a ¼ mile across but I still did not know if the whole width of the river was navigable A replica river steamer crossed my path and started to hug the river bank a ½ mile in front of me so I was able to follow him knowing that there was enough water in which for me to navigate.

It seemed that the pilots had rounded-up all the vessels ready for the convoy up river, but then I could hear the voice of the pilot station radio operator who began to get irritated with our Russian friends:

'Whereabouts are you captain?!'

'I am at the buoy where you told me to go and wait.'

'Well captain, I am at the buoy but I can't see your ship! You will have to get a move-on otherwise you will miss the tide until tomorrow.'

Then the Russian captain said,

'Please sir, can you blow your horn so that we can find you?'

The pilot, who was obviously puzzled, replied,

'Do you not have radar, captain?'

'Yes we do, sir' was the answer,
Then even more irritated but still in a polite tone the pilot said,
'Do you know how to use it, sir?' he didn't wait for the reply but added,
'You'll need to sail to the blip on the screen with the Racor marker that is shown as a thick line with a specific set of dark sections under-breaking that line!'
To which the captain replied,
'We don't have this on the screen, sir.'
The pilot, now getting impatient, gave him the ultimatum and said,
'If you are not at this buoy in 10 minutes I suggest you remain at anchor until tomorrow. OUT!' The subject was now closed!

Running up the Rio Guadalquivir seemed to be relatively easy; the landscape was nothing to write home about; I could not say "wish you were here"; it was almost featureless with only a few trees scattered about and not a sign of life other than the fishermen on their numerous craft bound together like rafts and anchored just off the main shipping fairway. But at marker 43, and not far from the fishermen, I did get it wrong somehow, I thought that going for the middle of the river was a safe bet and hoped to pass a batch of rafts on my right side, but as I moved closer to the rafts I noticed that the river had become shallower and the water level under the boat had dropped down to 1 metre. I pulled the gearlevers back and stopped the boat instantly because it was written in the pilot book that there was at least 5 metres of water in the river; this puzzled me and I couldn't understand why those rafts, anchored in the middle of the river, didn't have markers stating on which side to pass them; the fishermen waved me on, but I was still a bit wary and made a move towards the right-hand side of the river. Great! Now I had lots of water under the keel again.

With this tricky event out of the way I needed to take this river a little more seriously and to make good use of the shore-markers, which were really meant for the commercial shipping.

. Towards the outskirts of Sevilla the river became more attractive, being lined with trees which still had all their green foliage; from this distance I could just about depict small orange and bright yellow specs in-between the leaves - I had come to the English marmalade country. A little further up-stream I had the pleasure of seeing a whole colony of storks nesting high in the treetops at either side of the river; that was something really spectacular; I was told as a child that we had storks in Holland, but I had never actually seen one in real life, but here they were in abundance, gliding so gracefully to and from their nests, feeding their young - what a magnificent site to see!

The afternoon passed by quickly and we covered a distance of 42 miles in 3½ hours, because I had taken advantage of the strong current from behind, and now I only had 9 miles to the lock at Seville; I looked back down the river and noticed a full sized container vessel steaming up from behind but still a fair distance away.

Camariñas
Finisterre
Sangenjo
Vigo
Bayone
Póvoa de Varzim
O'Porto
Figueira de Foz
Peniche
C.Raso
Lisbon
Sines
Portimão
Cabo de São Vicente
Villamoura
Sevilla
Cadiz
Trafalgar

I kept an eye on her as she was on the same track as me, but having experienced the earlier difficulties with the depth of water I thought it better to continue for as long as possible in the main channel.

It wasn't very long before I noticed that the vessel had caught up with me - she was really steaming on - and I had to move out of her way, to the right, to let her pass; I felt our boat going down a dip as the passing vessel sucked the water down by at least 2 feet from the embankment; it was as if there was a huge tidal surge, or a resemblance to the river Severn bore.

The vessel was steaming well ahead and although I was doing a good 12 knots, I wasn't able to keep up with her and it didn't take long before she rounded the river bend and I lost sight of her.

So... why get worked up about it?

Simply, because it was written in the Almanac that a pleasure craft needed to pass through the lock in conjunction with a commercial vessel; the Almanac also stated that there was a bridge in the town which needed to be raised and this had to happen before 18:30; being 17:00 already didn't give me much lee-way. If I missed the lock with this vessel, then it might be too late and no doubt I would miss the lifting of the bridge. I had already had a very trying day so I was looking forward to finishing the job and having a relaxing evening with a glass of wine.

Although the vessel was a lot faster than me, I began to see her stern through the trees and this made me feel very optimistic in getting to Seville on time for the bridge lift.

It turned out that this vessel had to wait for another one to come through the lock in the opposite direction. That was a bit of luck; now I needed to find out whether I was able to pass through the lock in conjunction with my friend ahead of me. I called on the VHF,

'Sevilla Pilots, Sevilla Pilots, this is Calypso II come in please.'

I was waiting for a reply but when I didn't get one I called again. This time they responded:

'This is Sevilla Pilots go ahead Calypso II,'

'Good afternoon sir, is it possible for me to enter the lock behind the container vessel?'

'I don't know sir; I will get in contact with the pilot on the container vessel and come back to you.'

'Thank you sir, standing by.'

It took a little while, but then:

'Calypso II, Calypso II, this is Sevilla Pilots?'

'Yes Sevilla pilots this is Calypso II.

'Sir, the pilot on the container vessel is now aware of your intentions and when the time comes he will let you know whether you can enter the lock behind him.'

Now all we could do was to wait. The lock gates started to open and a large vessel gently glided out of the lock, passing us, and slowly disappeared around the bend. The vessel ahead of me was already edging her way into the lock; I noticed that she had only inches to spare, which made me less confident in sharing the lock with her.

I waited and waited just outside the lock gates then... on the vessel's bridge I saw a small uniformed man waving his arms about gesturing that he wanted me to proceed into the lock.

Now it was time to show my skills - which only the canals can teach you - and I slowly proceeded into the lock; I momentarily stopped just inside the lock gates to see what influence his propeller's turbulence was going to have on our boat; having made my calculations I slowly edged my way forward close to the stern of the other vessel.

The owner stood at the front and kept looking into my direction as if to say, 'are you sure that you can do this?' Little did he know, I was inwardly praying that all would go well and that I wouldn't make any mistakes. The vessel's large propeller turbulence was pushing me well over to the side of the lock chamber - for which I had calculated -

but now it was up to me to make sure that the Calypso II stayed parallel to the lock-side wall so that when the boat touched the wall it would be with the full protection of the balloon type fenders, which were evenly spaced out along her side.

With some fine throttle adjustments I was just about able to get her alongside but then found there was nowhere to tie the boat onto, which left me with no alternative than to keep her in this position with the help of her two Perkins engines.

After 20 minutes or so the water level in the lock was even with the upper river and the large vessel started to use forward propulsion to edge her way out of the lock. I waited until she had completely left the lock and then it was my turn. But what was that? The vessel had stopped just outside the lock where she was preparing to dock immediately to the left. I slowly overtook her and continued the few miles upstream passing through the commercial docks towards the south town bridges, but the railway bridge, which needed to be opened for me, was already in an open position. All that worrying for nothing! All I needed to do now was to pass through the two bridges and moor the vessel immediately beyond the second bridge at the left of the river at the Yacht club of Sevilla.

I dropped the anchor well into the middle of the river and reversed the boat towards the quayside edge of the Yacht Club.
I finished mooring the boat and tried to get the electricity going, but I found that the shore power wasn't enough for our requirements, so I ended up having to use the on-board generator.

The "Yacht club" was charming and a well-designed place; it also had facilities for: a few canoe clubs, an indoor/outdoor swimming pool, a 'kiddies' ground, tennis court and football areas. The people were very pleasant and extremely helpful. Little did I know but my stay in Sevilla was going to be the most pleasant stay since the start of this homeward bound voyage.

The next few days I spent clearing and preparing for the next leg of the voyage, whilst the owners explored the sights in Sevilla. Two days after our arrival they needed to go back to the UK and suggested that I should go with them so that I could have my first break since Christmas.

I was invited to fly home in the company's jet. At first, I tried to make any excuse for not flying in the small plane; although I had flown since 1962 I was still apprehensive about flying in a commercial aircraft let alone a small jet.

In hindsight, I am glad he persuaded me to go with them as it was an opportunity I should not have missed.

River Guadalquivir left the Yacht Club ahead the town of Sevilla

The plane was a new twin-engine Cessna jet with the latest navigation equipment and seating for five passengers in luxurious comfort - much better than an ordinary airliner.

We flew at 40,000 feet, which I believe is higher than most commercial aircraft fly, and it was extremely smooth and comfortable. Now I think it is the only way to travel - I should be so lucky!

Two weeks later I returned to the boat after a well-earned break - this time slumming it on a commercial airliner! I wasn't too happy leaving home on this occasion, as I would miss out on the birthdays of my Mum and my own; in addition I would also miss the Easter season which was in early April this year and who knows where I will be then. However, on the plus side, I had left a very cold England behind and there was the possibility of enjoying an early spring here in Spain.

There isn't much to do on the boat at this time of the year other than carrying out general maintenance and, out of boredom I overhauled the generator, a task which was well overdue. Whilst I was waiting for the owner to arrive to help me to sail the boat back to England, I took the opportunity of exploring the many historical sites in Sevilla.

It is a most fascinating and interesting old city and I can wholeheartedly recommend this place to anyone who is hungry for beauty, art and culture. However I have heard that the middle of the summer is not the time to come here because of the immense heat in the city; unfortunately for me we were now experiencing many low pressure systems coming across the Atlantic, which was depositing a huge amount of rain on the place, but between the showers there were some great spells of warm spring sunshine.

What I didn't know at the time was that I would end up spending almost the whole of March in Sevilla, the reason being that the owner had found a potential purchaser for the boat; you see, the boat had been up for sale for some time in the south of France and now that we had left there, the owners had found this potential buyer. Ironically, if the boat is sold she will have to return to the south of France, which would suit me fine as this would mean returning to the Mediterranean instead of waiting for a crew to run along the horrendous Atlantic coast.

It had now been a full month since our initial arrival in Sevilla and, so far, no further progress had been made regarding the sale of the boat and I began to get the feeling that the departure to England was now imminent. Yes, the day had finally arrived when the owner phoned and asked,

'How long will it take you to get the boat to Villamoura?'

I innocently answered,

'A good two days.'

Without any hesitation he added

'Then you can leave when you are ready and I will join you there!'

Funnily enough, this time I didn't suggest taking the boat solo but the owner seemed to have taken it for granted that I would and, as you can imagine, I was totally perplexed and extremely disappointed but found myself uttering,

'Ok, I'll see you there!'

I slowly put the phone down and after the initial shock thought, I hope someone will be looking after me, but then more positively, I suppose it won't be so bad now that the winter has passed and at least I will be on the move again.

The owner's call came somewhat inconveniently as it was just before the weekend, which made stocking the boat with food and fuel a bit difficult and now that he wasn't going to join me I needed "running expenses". Luckily I had my credit card on me and would be able to extract the cash through the hole in the wall.

You would think that would be easy enough – WRONG! The bank only allowed me to withdraw a set amount per day which didn't suffice my needs but when I tried to get an additional amount the bank blocked the card. There I stood in front of this machine in the middle of Sevilla thinking what now?!

After several calls to the credit card fraud squad in the UK they reinstated the card for me and I was able to get the remainder of the money required. I was pleased that they were checking on the protection of my credit card, but it was most inconvenient and for a time had made me very nervous.

During my stay in the past month I had made many friends, all of whom happened to be sailing boat people who had fallen in love with the place and had chosen to stay here over the winter period. These friends were of mixed nationalities: English, American, German and a

Dutch family too.

But the most outstanding friends in my mind were Roger and Ann, a young couple who had two dogs and lived on a small motor sailing boat. Roger had had an unfortunate motorbike accident a year earlier back in England and had lost the total use of his arm and with the insurance payout they decided to buy a boat to leisurely tour the Mediterranean. He told me that he had started out as a total novice in boating but now, two years later, he seemed to have mastered most of the tasks which needed to be carried out on board, despite his disability.

Ann had thrown in a good job back in England so that she and her dog could join Roger and his dog on this adventurous trip around Europe. So that Ann didn't get bored she invested in a special sewing machine which could produce complex embroideries; she used this mainly to embroider boat names on clothing and she also produced dinghy covers and so was able to pay for the running expenses of their boat.

The dogs were called "Indy", a German shepherd, and "Solomon", a terrier, and it never seemed to amaze me how these two dogs kept themselves occupied together on this small boat.

Roger had trained the dogs to play hide and seek which they seemed to enjoy immensely, and the way in which he did this was by sending both dogs into the aft cabin down some very steep angled steps, which we could easily have fallen down if not careful, but the dogs didn't seem to have any problem with those steps whatsoever; once they were down in the aft cabin Roger told them not to look and he would hide their toys; then, Roger would count down from ten to zero and would tease them by stopping short at number one, the dogs knew not to start looking until Roger had said zero, then they would try to climb out of the cabin at the same time looking for their fluffy toy; sometimes they found it, other times they didn't but always ended up getting a reward!

Sevilla - Pta de la Malander
Monday 18th March 2002

Having done some tidal calculations this morning I came to the conclusion that I would need to leave at 10:00 which would give me enough time to reach the lock for 10:30 because I was told that was the time they were allowing vessels to lock-out into the river.

On the dot of ten I cleared the last mooring line from the stern and hauled in the eighty metres of anchor chain; I had laid extra because I knew that the river was a poor holding ground and this extra length gave me added security in case of a storm causing the anchor to drag over the bottom, which could move the boat from her secured position; unfortunately, I had already experienced this one night earlier this month.

With the anchor fully home I was ready to move off but I nearly forgot to lower the 18 feet RT (Radio Telephone) whip aerials in order for me to get under the road bridge. I left the fenders out as I needed them for the lock walls. Slowly I moved away from the marina and blew my horn three long blasts to say good bye to my friends who were at the quayside waving me off; and then... I don't know what came over me, but all of a sudden I felt very lonely; I would have to get used to that feeling again because I had a long, long way to go.

The boat just cleared the road bridge, and shortly after I passed through the railway bridge - which always seemed to be in the open position - and slowly sailed through the main commercial harbour which only had a few ships this morning.

A few hundred yards away from the lock I noticed that the lock gates were in my favour but then..., hang-on! Am I seeing this correctly? The lock gates slowly started to close in front of my eyes. Oh well, I thought, that's the end of a well-planned departure and "that's Spain for you". I was very annoyed; if I didn't get this lock, I would miss the full ebb tide and this would make it impossible for me to reach the mouth of the river before the bottom of the tide and as I only have small engines it would be a struggle fighting the flood. I called Sevilla Pilots and after several attempts they answered,

'Yes, Calypso II what can I do for you'

Although I was still annoyed, I politely answered,

'Can you please tell me when I can pass through the lock?'

'Which side of the lock are you on?'

'The town side, sir; I would like to go to sea please.'

'I will get back to you.'

'Thank you, standing by.'

I stayed in the middle of the harbour making sure that they were able to see me and this must have worked because within a few minutes the lock keeper slowly opened the lock gates again; I looked around to see whether there was another vessel in sight, but the re-opening of the lock seemed to be just for me. *Thank you pilots.*

I had the lock all to myself so it was easy to pick and choose a place along the wall and I knew that the water level wasn't going to drop too much (high water being at 11:00) which gave me the chance to tidy away all the mooring lines and stow the fenders at the aft end of the boat.

The lock gates opened exactly at 11:10 and looking through the opening gates, I noticed that the water level had only dropped one metre which meant that I would be well in time for the falling tide; Yes! Just as I planned it.

I cleared the lock gates and sailed around the first bend and immediately saw an approaching cargo vessel. They had obviously closed the gates on me in order to prepare the lock for this vessel; was I glad I didn't have to wait for her; that really would have thrown a spanner in the works for today.

The voyage downstream was a pleasurable experience apart from the gusty winds and the occasional showers and I had time to observe the storks once more.

The river journey took 5 hours and I arrived just as the tide was turning to become the floodtide once more.

Now I had to make a decision whether to anchor at the mouth of the river, or to sail through the fairway to the Marina of Chipiona. My friends in Sevilla had told me about this marina. I thought it was an attractive proposition, but as I was nearing the river mouth I noticed the Atlantic swell rolling-in. The decision was made for me; I would go to the anchorage on the river just outside the fairway, opposite the town of Bonanza and within reaching distance of the Doñana National Park.

I dropped anchor in 4.7 metre depth and laid out 30 metres of chain and just after this, a catamaran sailing yacht arrived from seaward and dropped his anchor just down-stream of me for the night.

I started my engine room inspection so I was ready for any emergency "get-away" and also in preparation for tomorrow morning's departure.

I did my usual checks on the starboard engine's cooling water, engine and gearbox oil, loose wiring and for any possible leaks; so far, as I expected, everything was in order, but when it came to the port engine, I found that the oil level was well above the maximum mark! This was most alarming and mysterious; I am sure that the engine was fine this morning and I definitely did not over-fill it on my last inspection.

Totally dumbstruck, I went upstairs and made myself a cup of tea and staring into space was wondering what could have caused this high oil level.

I thought aloud: 'If the oil cooler was leaking, then this would escape from the cooler into the sea rather than into the oil; then there is the possibility that the head gasket has blown, but then again, the internal fresh water cooling would diminish in the reservoir and the engine temperature would be high, and that has not happened either.'

After finishing my cup of tea I lowered myself slowly down into the engine room and started to pump the excess oil out through the attached pump and found that I had actually pumped 1½ litres of water out of the engine sump before it became clear engine oil again.

The problem was most likely staring me in the face, but I couldn't get my head around the fact that it was clear water; so the water must have entered the engine after the engine had stopped otherwise the water would have been mixed with the oil, making it milky. I sat in front of the engine and stared despondently at the exhaust manifold which had been temporarily repaired earlier in Gibraltar and now... I started to suspect that this repair had something to do with it, but how?

I went back upstairs and found the magnifying glass so that I could inspect the edge of the exhaust repair. It looked like the metal had come away from the outer jacket, but I couldn't find a leak into the engine. I cleaned the surfaces and added some additional metal putty and then I just had to "wait and see".

Just before dusk I went to have another look at the repair, and checked the oil level in the engine to see whether it had risen again, but luckily it seemed to have stopped.

Although I hadn't been able to find the problem, I thought it better not to let it play on my mind, but instead to enjoy this beautiful prime spot amongst nature; I am so glad that I stopped in such a very tranquil place and, as an added bonus, I was presented with a most spectacular sunset with a red/yellow reflection on the water and from behind the trees on the shore.

Later in the evening, whilst having dinner, I heard a very mysterious humming noise which is normally associated with revolving propeller(s) of a passing vessel. I went outside but there wasn't a ship in sight but the noise was still evident. I then followed the noise which took me to the engine room where I found both propeller shafts turning quite rapidly.

Not quite believing what I saw, I went outside and looked overboard and saw the water flowing rapidly past the boat; I switched on the instruments and the log was indicating a flood tide of 5.3 miles per hour! All I can say is that I am so glad this boat possessed a substantial anchor and that I had laid enough chain to keep the boat firmly in her place.

With this peace of mind I was then able to enjoy the remainder of the evening in this beautiful anchorage.

Pta de le Malander - Villamoura
Tuesday 19th March 2002

Looking out of the window this morning I found that I was enshrouded in a thick blanket of fog; it did worry me a bit but I just thought, oh no, not again! Still, this wasn't going to dampen my spirit because I was really looking forward to going to sea today and sail to my next port of call, Villamoura in Portugal.

At first, I thought that the fog had set-in for the morning, but the sky began to clear overhead and the sailing boat who had anchored overnight had already left the anchorage; seeing this I was in two

minds about my own departure and, somewhat hesitantly, I lifted the anchor so as not to miss the last of the ebb tide. Whilst navigating down the final stretch of the fairway, I noticed the Atlantic swell rolling onto the sandbanks and thought, you definitely cannot afford to make a navigational mistake here; however it seemed that some skippers had done just that as there were already two vessels lying high and dry on the sands.

Finally I cleared the fairway, passed the main entrance buoy and headed out into the open sea; as soon as I had cleared the restricted waters I checked the oil level in the port engine and found, to my great surprise, that it hadn't taken on any water. That's strange, but... at least I didn't have to change course and return to Chipiona;

171

now I felt confident in continuing the planned voyage for today.

The dense fog finally lifted although it stayed fairly misty and grey until after lunch when, surprisingly, the sun came out and with a calm sea and in between dodging a few fishing vessels, I had a truly pleasurable and relaxing afternoon.

When I had planned this part of the voyage I had worked out that my ETA (Estimated Time of Arrival) would be around 19:00 and unbelievably, having sailed the distance of 90nm in 11 hours, I entered the harbour of Villamoura bang on time.

My phone rang whilst I was busy manoeuvring the boat alongside the visitors' pontoon almost as if the caller could see me. Well, it was the owner.

'Hi Bill, how did you get on today?'

I was chuffed to bits with my achievement and cheerfully answered,

'I have just this minute arrived in Villamoura', to which he replied,

'Well done. How far is the Airport from where you are Bill? Innocently I replied,

'Oh, not more than 20 minutes; as a matter of fact I passed Faro Airport about 2 hours ago by boat.'

'Oh that's good.'

But I wasn't prepared for what he was about to tell me, although I should have expected it.

'How long will it take to get to Lisbon?'

I answered cleverly,

'Well, it will take *us* 3 days, all being well, but if *we* travel day and night then it would take *us* half that time.'

After a short silence he said.

'Mmmm I am sorry Bill, but I can't make it right now; do you think you could continue to Lisbon by yourself... of course you can take your time?'

Before waiting for a reply he added,

'I'll meet you there on Friday.'

'Well, if it's all the same to you, I would prefer to wait for you in

Casçais; there is a newly built marina at the edge of the Tejo estuary; this would save me sailing up the river Tejo.'

'By all means go ahead and I'll see you there.'

I was taken aback and astonished with this conversation and had to pause for a minute to take in its implications. I don't believe it! I had just agreed to something I had never attempted before and to tell you the truth, I wasn't comfortable with the idea of roaming around the Atlantic coast on my own, but having had a thorough look at the long-range forecast and sized up the distances between the various ports, I thought it was worth trying.

I sincerely began to believe that I wasn't taking a risk, although there is **always** an element of risk in going to sea anyway. But what would I do if the weather turned really bad? Well, I worked out that I would be able to reach the safety of a port within a maximum of 3 hours which, hypothetically speaking is manageable. However, having said this, I remembered that the Portuguese seem to close some of their harbours when the large Atlantic waves roll in over the entrance bar making navigating a real hazard.

"Entrance Bar" is an area just before a harbour entrance that is the dividing line between the relatively deep sea and the shallows of the river or harbour, and the water running down the river creates a large but short wave.

Although my owner told me to take my time, I made the decision not to linger-on but to continue the voyage as planned. But for now, I had to check on the engine and sort out the problem of the leaking exhaust manifold.

This time, I found water in the engine again and the amount was similar as that of yesterday except that the water was salty, which made me think: funny, not a drop whilst sailing but almost an accurate measured amount when the engine stopped!

It didn't take long for me to realize that the exhaust manifold had not only leaked to the outside - which incidentally had stopped - but into the exhaust port. I think what had happened was that when the engine stopped, the remaining cooling water in the exhaust jacket had poured into the engine through the leaking part; this accounted for the engine oil not being emulsified.

The boat didn't really need refuelling but I like to keep the tanks fully topped-up in order to avoid the sludge in the bottom of the tanks fouling the filters; changing filters at sea is not easy, but refuelling in the morning would mean that my departure time would be late again but then... it is better to be safe than sorry.

I stretched myself out over the charts on the table and worked out a series of possible ports and anchorages to run into "just in case"; I let my finger run over the chart passing over Portimao, Lagos, the bay at Sagres and after that well up the Atlantic coast line where the Port of Sines was only 58nm from Cabo Vicente; these were all possibilities.

I had stopped several times in the first two ports, but never in Sines; but let's see what tomorrow brings; I could always change my mind if needed. I knew that it was a daring attempt to sail a 60 foot motor yacht, on my own, along the Atlantic coast – it gave me butterflies in my stomach!

After dinner I had a walk around the harbour and quickly scanned the place and came to the conclusion that not much had changed since the last time I had the pleasure of visiting this port.

Now... let me see, that was in September 1982 with a Dutch Aluminium built 52 ft motor cruiser called "Jimali" which I had delivered from the port of Oss in the Southern Netherlands to here. (Next Page)

One in a Million
September 1982

It was late summer and the voyage had gone well since our departure from Oss. I don't know why, but I decided to run for the port of le Palais on Belle Ile before crossing the Bay. I ordered the fuel, as usual, which arrives by truck to the quayside edge and filled the boat to the brim so that I didn't have to refuel until Vigo. After refuelling I went into town to get food supplies and to leave that same afternoon; this was an unusual thing to do as I normally leave in the mornings but the weather was so superb that I couldn't resist leaving now.

At around 16:00 we departed from the island over the east side and headed into the direction of Gijon and I must say that it was a real pleasure and dangerously relaxing to be out on the ocean; it was amazing to see the Atlantic so flat, no wind and hardly a swell to speak of, which gave me the opportunity of maintaining a good cruising speed of 16 knots; I calculated that the crossing to Gijon would be 16 hours and I should arrive at around 11:00 in the morning. Later in the afternoon, the crew and I had the pleasure of seeing a most spectacular sunset, with the sun showing itself as a bright red-yellow ball set against a clear blue sky and slowly sinking beyond the horizon into the sea; this gave me peace of mind knowing that the night ahead would be fairly calm and without any nasty surprises.

Shortly after the spectacular sunset I slowed down to a comfortable 9 knots just in case we hit a submerged object; travelling at this speed meant I only had to check the engine room every 2 hours for oil and water leaks etc.

23:00 - it was time to do one of my engine room checks; I crawled my way through the aft section and stopped at the rear of the engines thinking I might as well change over fuel tanks, because I had calculated that this needed to be done at around midnight anyway.

I started to pull some levers and finally changed the valves so that I was using the tank in the rear of the boat; having completed this task I sat down and had a last look before crawling backwards out of the engine room, when... were my eyes deceiving me? Whilst crawling back I caught sight of the fuel water separators which have a clear plastic bowl *and* they were literally full of water.

'STOP THE ENGINES!' I shouted but I wasn't heard and I couldn't climb out of the engine room fast enough; Oh no, it's too late... both engines had come to an abrupt stop and seconds later the boat became eerily silent.

I tried to work out why and what had happened.

This must be one a million; the first thing on my mind was to get the boat going again. I emptied the filters of water and luckily, the engines started with no bother at all but... a few minutes later the bowls started to fill again.

Now I was in a real panic and immediately started to swear and blame the fuel delivery guy who had given me contaminated fuel from his truck!

Blaming him didn't help solve the problem and I couldn't fathom out why there was so much water in the fuel. I sat down and paused for a minute, then thought the only sensible and logical thing to do was to switch the tanks back and to use the third tank instead – I was reluctant to do this because this was my emergency supply. But thank God it worked, although I knew I would have to run the remainder of the crossing on a single engine so as not to contaminate the whole system again and also to save precious fuel.

02:30 - good gracious me, this whole affair had taken me 3½ hours but at least I was on the move again. Now I had to rethink my destination and changed direction straight for La Coruña. I know it's a bit further but the port has a large fishing basin and I am sure that they have the facility to remove the water out of the diesel tank.
After a further 15 hours sailing we arrived early evening in La Coruña; totally exhausted we rested-up for the night and would look at the problem with fresh eyes in the morning.

The following morning I went ashore and found some 50 gallon drums and a pump. I opened the inspection lid of the aft tank so that I had easier access to the fuel. But strangely, every time I extracted fuel, which was clear and not contaminated, the tank level slowly rose again and finally... the penny dropped. That's it! As the tank was part of the hull, maybe the hull had split, allowing seawater to penetrate the tank.
Now all I had to do was to close the inspection hatch, seal off the valves and place two 50 gallon drums on the aft deck filled with diesel to replace the split tank; in this way I was able to continue our voyage to Villamoura.

Villamoura - Sines
Wednesday 20th March 2002

I slept rather well considering the circumstances I had created for myself. After breakfast I went across to the office to clear Portuguese Customs and Immigration as there wasn't anyone on duty last night. This took up some of my valuable sailing time and on top of that I still had to refuel the boat which meant leaving Villamoura a lot later than I had hoped and I couldn't see me getting to the port of Sines much before 22:00.

Never mind, the weather looked fine, but this was no guarantee that I would encounter similar conditions around the corner at Cabo de São Vicente.

09:30 – that's not bad after all! I slowly manoeuvred away from the visitors' pontoon and was soon through the piers. Outside I found the sea almost flat which was a bonus as this coast was unbelievably littered with many small fishing boats trying their luck at catching the local "Fruit de Mer". There were also numerous fishing buoys mainly constructed of a stick bound together with a polystyrene block and a bit of coloured plastic at the top representing a flag
.

12:12 - passing the large breakwaters of Portimão, which is at the mouth of the Rio Arade and about half way between Cabo de São Vicente and Villamoura.

This place has a fantastic sheltered anchorage just inside the breakwaters and I was fortunate to visit it in 1973 for the first time when skippering a 78ft Motor Yacht "Colleen Bawn", *which was built at Dagless of Wisbech, England*. Since that time Portimão had become a favoured stopover of mine and would often have been my first break from the high seas since leaving England.

I continued towards the headland at Pta de Sagres and Cabo São

Vicente which has a sheltered bay but this can only be used with the northerly winds, not that I have ever needed to anchor there; I had marked this off as one of my security stopovers for this passage, but today the weather and the boat were doing well so I could safely tick this place off the list once more.

As I was nearing Cabo de São Vicente I found that the wind started to pick up from over the land and from a north westerly direction; this normally signifies stormy conditions but distant skies were contradictory and didn't give any indication of a weather change.

Gradually the large swell came rolling in from around the headland but it didn't look too high from here, but then... ten foot is enough to get your sea legs going!

Near the Cape I was joined by a lonely sailing boat - under power - which had come from a southerly direction and seemed to have taken on a race with me towards the Cape; I needed to keep

Cabo São Vicente

an eye on her; although she was on my port side, I would still have to correct my course, if necessary, in order give her a wide berth.

I rounded Cabo São Vicente at 15:15 closely hugging the coast. According to the old sailors' tale, the lighthouse at Cabo São Vicente, at the SW west corner of Portugal, is manned by monks, and the sailors believed that a prayer was being said, wishing the passing ship

179

and its crew a safe passage across to the Americas.

Rounding the headland I was pleasantly surprised to see the Atlantic so smooth and the wind had dropped, which is most unusual, so I continued the voyage towards Sines, which was just another 58nm up the coast. This place is strategically positioned between Cabo São Vicente and Lisbon, making it a perfect stopover.

The boat was performing well; that was until I spotted a fishing buoy between the large swells, seriously close to the boat's port-side; that in itself is nothing because this coast-line had been littered with them, but this one was slightly unique as it had a long loose line trailing along the surface, just like a snake swimming in the direction of the current and it just happened to cross my bows; for a split second my heart stopped pumping and I feared the worse. I tried stopping the boat in time but was too late to prevent the trailing line from drifting under the boat. I held my breath momentarily but luckily the line was only caught in front of the starboard stabilizer. It was a thin line and had just jammed between the hull and the front end of the fin-blade, which left the fin in an off-centre position.

I was able to grab the loose end of the line and the fishing buoy with the boat hook; I forcefully jerked and pulled on the line, hoping to free the other end, but after numerous attempts I had to give up and decided to cut the excessive length so that the line wouldn't get caught in the propeller. Thank goodness the sea was calm, because now I had to continue the voyage without the use of the stabilizers.

Despondently I re-started the engines and continued once more. This affair had cost me a good hour but that was nothing compared to what could have been a real disaster if the rope had fouled one or, worse still, both propellers.

I promised myself to watch out more carefully and suspected every fishing buoy near the vicinity of the boat of having a long line attached to it, and now a further thought went through my mind:

what happens when it gets dark? I would have to find a way of avoiding these damn buoys. The only solution was to use my radar to its full potential so I adjusted the range to the lowest scale possible, which on this radar was down to ¼nm - equivalent to about 465 metres.

I began to experiment with the fishing buoys coming towards me by fiddling with the knobs. I should explain that the visibility was very much restricted because the fishing buoys needed to be on the same wave as the boat itself or on top of a wave, which is usually short lived and I hoped that the radar would pick up the weak signal.

Not only did I succeed in picking up the fishing buoys but also the seagulls resting on the sea surface! This was a whole new challenge and I had never experienced anything like it before. I am happy to say that the radar was a hundred percent successful in spotting the fishing buoys and avoiding them had become a very effective way of staying safe.

However now the radar was focused on the fishing buoys I was left with the additional task of keeping a look-out, which put an intense strain on my eyes. This will make me unduly tired, and that's all I need!

The ocean had become like a mirror, so much so that the sea and sky had become the same shade of dirty dark grey so I didn't have a proper horizon on which to focus but thankfully, except for the odd vessel in the far distance, I had the sea all to myself.

It had now become pitch dark and I had a real struggle keeping a good look out; in fact the compass and instrument lights had become a nuisance and I needed to switch them off for most of the time.

19:30 - I plotted my position on the chart as six miles off Cabo Sardao. Yes! No! Yes, I am sure that I spotted the light of Cabo de Sines. The boat was bobbing up and down and the large swell made the sequence of flashes appear irregular so it was difficult to know whether it really was Cabo de Sines. Ten minutes went by and I counted the flashes again and yes, they were the flashes of Cabo de Sines lighthouse, still 20 miles away.

This gave me my horizon back and I was able to navigate by sight rather than constantly having to check the compass.

Now that I had visual contact I could afford to have a coffee and something to eat; although the boat was moving slowly, I still needed to be vigilant and couldn't leave the radar screen for too long. All was going well and finally I had lost the butterflies in my stomach, caused by my earlier experience and the responsibility of sailing solo.

Anyway, I made my hot drink and with a complicated balancing act I managed to bring it up and place it on the anti-slip mat without any spillage and felt well-chuffed with myself. I went back down and switched off the cabin lights then continued my lookout.

What the hell is happening now? The light flashes over my port bow had totally disappeared. At first, I tried to be optimistic and didn't take it too seriously as this can often happen when the sequence of lights are out of synch with your eye co-ordination, usually through tiredness, or having looked into bright lights for a while.

Not having been able to spot the light again made me panic slightly and I quickly looked at the compass which, thank goodness, was still showing 010°; so at least I knew I was still heading in the right direction; I leant forward, pressing my nose against the glass, staring into the darkness, scanning the horizon and counting the seconds in the hope of seeing a light, but to no avail, then I went outside onto the foredeck so that I could shut out all the light pollution from the wheelhouse; I even dared to switch off the navigation lights; sadly, the flashing light had definitely gone, but the shore lights over my starboard were still shining in full glory.

Where the hell is the light? Then... for a few seconds I thought I saw it again but this time it looked rather dull and reddish; that's it! It had become obvious to me that a bank of fog had rolled in from the

Atlantic; I just hoped that it would clear when I needed to enter the port. However if these conditions persisted then I would have to re-think the setting of the radar and either leave it on the short-range for the fishing buoys or change it to the six-mile range, which I preferred at night and certainly in foggy conditions.

I kept changing the range on the radar, making sure not to touch the tuner and sensitivity settings; it seemed to be working; I could see the coast clearly on the screen and I spotted a fishing boat two miles away, which was also marked on the radar, so I carried on sailing towards my destination still hoping that the fog would lift by the time I got to Sines.

But as time went by, I became more sceptical about the fog lifting because I was only 4½ miles away from the coast and now I seemed to have lost the sight of land altogether. I was so busy that I hadn't noticed that the time was creeping up on me and I was now fast approaching the port.

I had to reset the range on my radar again to give more accuracy on the close-range targets; as an extra precaution, I started to study the port layout and port procedures in the Pilot Book.

The Port had a VHF working channel for pilots and as this had served me well in the past I tuned in and listened.

I lifted my wristwatch near to my face and saw that it was now 22:10 with only 1 mile to go to the harbour entrance and there was still no sign of the fog lifting. Now I can't even see the front of the Calypso II; it's time to slowdown Billy. I dropped the speed to 3 knots making the boat glide slowly towards the harbour and all I could hear was small wavelets breaking at the bow, the humming of engines in the distance and the occasional clanging of the bell fitted on a buoy giving away its location; other than that the Calypso II silently made her way through the water.

The radar showed two large blips on my starboard side at a distance of ¾ mile; slowly the blips became larger which made me believe they were vessels lying at anchor. I kept concentrating in that direction and although I couldn't see anything, I could clearly hear the generators humming; then the radar showed that I was passing one of the two blips at a distance of 0.10nm or 185 metres.

Brilliant! I had successfully passed the two mystery vessels. Now I could slowly edge my way forward to the inner port, but then... I became rather apprehensive because I had never been here before and, not knowing the layout, wondered whether I should wait outside until the fog lifted - but that would be very uncomfortable wallowing about in the large heavy swell - or continue towards the inner port which was now only a stone's throw away?

Again I reduced the range on the radar to a ¼ mile and I could see a wall-like shape appearing at the top of the screen just like the one drawn on the chart, but what puzzled me was that I couldn't see an entrance; I hoped it would become visible on the screen when I was a little closer.

I called the Pilots on my VHF but didn't get any response and although I continued calling, the radio stayed silent. I started to get cold and began to shiver a bit, probably because I was so tired.

The whole situation had become rather intense and now I had my hands full: I had to steer by hand, keeping a sharp eye on the compass and a good look-out, but I couldn't see a thing; I switched on my automatic foghorn and hoped to get a response from someone, but everything stayed eerily silent; it then became clear to me that I was the only idiot on the water; this did have its advantage because I had whole the port all to myself.

Slowly the boat edged its way towards the wall and after a good 10 minutes the radar started to show a small gap in the line but the opening looked far too small to be an entrance.

The screen indicated that I had no more than 231 metres to go, but I still couldn't see anything in front of me; I now slowed down to a mere 1½ knots, the minimum speed to which this boat's rudders would respond.

Then suddenly…! Not far on the starboard side was a large black mass appearing out of the fog and this was such a shock to me that I instantly reacted by pulling the control levers full reverse to stop the boat. Now that I had stopped I took the opportunity of familiarizing myself with the new surroundings; my eyes searched along the black mass from one end to the other and from the waterline upwards; then, high up, through the fog, I spotted streetlights which were neatly spaced out as far as the eye could see. I had reached the harbour wall after all.

I went back into the wheelhouse, turned the boat and followed the wall to the end where a faint green light was flashing trying to pierce a hole through the fog. Brilliant… I am safe but what on earth is that in front of me?

Suddenly, I was upon a large fishing vessel that had plonked itself smack bang in the middle of the harbour entrance. I slowly passed her very close-by, still concentrating on not losing the lights on top of the wall, because then I would have to drop anchor too and I didn't think lying in the harbour opening was a safe option for me.

Although the inner harbour was well tucked away from the main entrance it didn't stop the moored vessels lurching violently back and forth with the movement of the Atlantic swell.

I found myself a mooring alongside a pontoon and it wasn't long before an official came knocking on the boat. He was a pleasant guy who took the basic details from me, saying that I could do the remainder of the paperwork in the morning and he wished me a good night.

Totally exhausted I laid my head on the pillow and once again thanked the Lord for bringing me safely into port after this eventful day.

Sines - Peniche de Cima
Thursday 21st March 2002

In contrast to last night, I woke up to a bright sunny morning which gave me a real "feel good factor". This did surprise me because last night's fog was so dense that I thought that it would hang around at least until the middle of the morning.

The tide was on its way down and I found myself looking against this high wall again; of course, the fishing boat blocking the entrance last night had already left; over on the other side of the port I was able to see part of the old town with its ancient city wall and I must admit that it looked rather interesting, but sadly, I wouldn't have any time to explore; instead... I went to check the machinery and again found that the repair I made at Rio Guadalquivir had held so I felt secure enough to continue the voyage.

Oh dear, I nearly forgot all about it, but I had to check whether the engine had filled up with water again and not surprisingly, yes... it had.

After my engine room checks I wondered what I could do regarding the stabilizer, which was still in the locked position from yesterday.

I had moored the vessel last night - *most conveniently for me* - on her starboard side, which ironically also happened to be the side of the jammed stabilizer.

I jumped ashore and started to play about with the frayed line; as luck would have it, the line was just long enough to pull on but unfortunately I wasn't strong enough and it wasn't budging an inch for me.

I sat down, sipped my coffee and stared into the crystal clear Atlantic water from where I could see the stabilizer with the jammed line; I noticed that the boat was surging quite strongly back and forth in the swell, momentarily putting a heavy tension on the mooring lines.

Eureka! I came up with an idea, it was a strange idea and I didn't know whether it was going to be successful, but I thought, I'll have a go at it all the same; what do I have to lose!

Firstly, I tied a mooring line onto the bit of string, then took the other end of the line and walked it well past the boat and secured it to a cleat on the pontoon.

Now for the test; I slackened-off all the mooring lines - still keeping the boat attached of course - so that the boat could freely move back and forth, hoping to pull on the string and free the stabilizer.

I waited a while but nothing happened and it looked like this wasn't going to work; I think there was too much stretch in the line. It was obvious that I had to take the slack out of the line; now all I had to do was to sit and wait again and... after a short time, with a muffled bang; the rope catapulted into the air and freed the stabilizer. Well done; you must admit this was a genius idea!

This had taken a good hour but I felt very relieved with the result; at least I didn't have to take the boat out of the water or, worse still, to sail the remainder of the voyage without stabilizers.

09:30 - the boat was now ready for sea and all I had left to do was to complete the usual Customs and Harbour formalities. I climbed the steeply angled walkway, towards the Customs hut, with my ship's papers, passport and Immigration documents from Villamoura under my arm.

After the few minutes walk I reached the wooden hut and was just about to knock on the door when, from around the corner, a uniformed officer arrived on his moped; he greeted me with a nod, un-locked the door, threw his coat nonchalantly over one of the two chairs facing his paper-littered desk, but keeping his official hat firmly on his head, ushered me in.

'Good morning, are you from that lovely yacht over there?'

187

'Yes I am, and I would like to clear Customs.'

I handed him my passport and a photocopy of the ship's papers. He looked at the papers, shook his head slowly from side to side and said,

'I am sorry sir, but I can't accept these photocopies; I will need the original ship's papers.' I thought, Mmmm, here we go again.

'That's all I have sir. I have been travelling all around the Mediterranean with these papers and I have never been stopped before.'

He had another look but again shook his head and said,

'No, sorry, I can't accept them.'

Humbly I replied

'But sir, I have just come from Villamoura and they cleared the boat without any problems.'

'Well, let me see the papers you have from them.'

I handed them over to him, then, perhaps saved by the bell, my mobile phone rang, and guess what? It was my owner.

'Hi Bill, how are you keeping?'

I wasn't going to tell him what was happening here, as I didn't believe in making him unduly worried, so I said,

'Thanks for asking I am doing fine.'

'Where are you at the moment?'

'I am in a place called Sines; it's about halfway up the coast between Cabo Sao de Vicente and Lisbon.'

'What's the weather like?'

'It's really pleasant, sunny but fresh and the sea is good too, so I hope to leave as soon as I have cleared Customs.'

I was very proud to tell him that the sea conditions were **so** good and I hoped to arrive in Cascais that evening.

'Well Bill, I was coming to that!' and after a short pause he said,

'Sorry, but something has come up at the office and I won't be able make it to Cascais; it looks like it will take me at least until early next week before I can join you!'

I could hear the hesitancy in his voice

'Are you alright to continue the voyage by yourself?'

I had to think for a minute - if I wait in Cascais then this will prolong my journey home; on the other hand I don't really like sailing on my own but what choice do I have? *So* I answered politely,

'Sorry to hear this, but I would like to continue whilst the weather is good, if that's ok with you.'

'That's fine with me but don't take any chances with the weather, will you! Good luck and bon voyage'

'Thanks.'

I slowly put the phone back in my pocket, feeling a little disappointed again.

Whilst I was on the phone, I noticed that my officer friend was studying the papers from Villamoura intensely and made several calls. He finally put his phone down, looked at me with a distinct disappointed look on his face, shook his head and said,

'No... I can't let you go.'

Well, my heart went up into my throat and I gave him a huge "please feel sorry for me" look, but to no avail.

I was stunned and couldn't say much for a while but could see that he wasn't too happy with his own decision in taking the matter further and, excusing himself, said,

'I am waiting for the return call from my superiors.'

I patiently waited.

Another hour went by but his antique Bakelite phone on the corner of his desk didn't ring once. Then I broke the silence,

'I am losing valuable sailing time,'

He looked at me for a second and then, totally out of the blue, said

'You'd better go!'

As you can imagine I had no intention of questioning his decision; I moved off my chair, shook his hand, thanked him and left. I momentarily stood still on the step, taking a deep breath and was about to turn towards the boat but thought better of it and instead turned left to the harbour master's office to pay for my overnight stay; mind you, I was tempted to skip the payment and leave the port as soon as I could before the officer changed his mind again.

The harbour office personnel were extremely pleasant and co-operative; they handed me the receipt and asked whether I had a pleasant stay. What could I say!

'Yes thank you and do you have the latest weather forecast please?'

The harbour master produced a long scroll of paper consisting of a full bulletin and weather map. I had to dismiss the bulletin as I couldn't read Portuguese and while I was studying the map he asked,

'Where are you going today?'

'I am planning to run up the coast towards Oporto.'

'Then you should do well, the weather looks settled for the next two days with only variable winds and perhaps this will last until Saturday.'

This valuable information made me feel better already. So far, I had been blessed with good weather, which is really unbelievable for this time of year and it seemed this might continue at least until the end of the week.

I left the marina office from where I could see the Calypso II; she looked rather grand lying there in the depths of the marina. This business had made me rather tired but I still had a long day ahead of me. At least, now I could get on with the voyage.

Walking across the car park I noticed a large grey vessel turning into the harbour; it was a Customs boat and... Yes, I knew it! She steamed straight for the pontoon where the Calypso II was berthed.

From this safe distance I watched her moor up, then two officers disembarked and walked past her towards the walkway but then doubled back and knocked on the Calypso II. Oh well, I thought, they will have to wait until I get there and I slowed my walking pace hoping they would move on, but they seemed to be nailed to the spot. My feet were getting heavier and heavier as if blocks of lead were attached to them. I finally made it to the boat and the two officers greeted me,

'Is this your boat?'

'Yes' - this time I didn't feel in the mood to be **that** polite.

'Where did you come from?'

'Villamoura'

'Where are you bound for?'

'Oporto'

'How many people are there on board?'

'Me, just myself' I emphasised it so they heard me correctly.

'Can we see your papers?'

That was easy; I still had them in my hand so once more this morning I handed them over and hesitantly waited for the dreadful reply, but then to my amazement he said,

'That's ok sir, have a pleasant voyage.'

Now I politely replied,

'And the same to you thank you.'

Now that was easy - don't get so neurotic!

The two officers turned around and walked back to their vessel and minutes later they went out to sea again; it looked like they had come into port especially to see me.

I looked at my watch and said aloud, Oh No! It's eleven already! My departures seem to start later and later each day. I opened the chart hoping to find a reasonable distance for today's trip. A run to Cascais seemed to be the most obvious choice with a distance of only 52nm; that's alright; I should be there at around 17:30.

So... decision time: either I run for Cascais the port near Cabo Raso and not far from the river Tejo's Estuary which leads to Lisbon; or continue to Peniche de Cima another 30 or so miles further up the coast. Oh well, let's wait and see. I'll just head into a northerly direction for now.

I untied the boat at 11:10 and made a graceful turn towards the entrance of the marina while being watched by a few locals who, as always, were admiring the splendour of this boat.

Slowly and majestically I departed from the inner harbour and came into the large outer harbour. Now in clear daylight I was able to see the whole of the port, including the two vessels from last night; it all looked as I had imagined it to be; the only thing I hadn't been able to envisage was the immense length of the outer breakwater which, due to the continuing pounding of the Atlantic

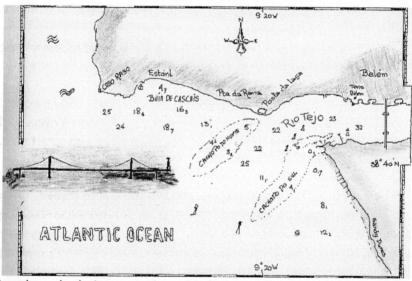

breakers, had given way in several places; the far end had become partly submerged, but that section was clearly marked with a tall, rusty cardinal marker buoy. The two triangular cones pointing down - meaning it was the south end marker - were half hanging off; this buoy was being swayed about by each of the large deep blue waves which were pushing it sideways, then angrily hitting and swamping the submerged pier with a great thunder, leaving a high sea spray in the air.

I finally cleared the large breakwater and headed straight into the huge waves where I switched on the autopilot; after clearing the last marker buoy I turned the boat into a north-westerly direction and now the waves started to come from the rear, which gave me a most comfortable ride.

An hour or so had passed when in the distance I spotted a sailing boat fine on the starboard bow. I slowly began to gain on her and when I was about to overtake her I noticed that this was the same sailing boat I had passed yesterday afternoon at Cabo de Vicente; I suppose they must have been sailing through the night in order to get this far.

16:00 - I was able to make out the shore line in the distance near the entrance to the River Tejo leading to the Port of Lisbon.

Seeing this place reminded me of the time when I was involved in a "non-self inflicted" incident with the Maritime Police, and since that time I have been very reluctant to return there. (Page 196)

But I had my sight set for the newly built marina at Cascais. This marina didn't exist in the early 1970's but I clearly remember that we were able to shelter from the strong northerly wind in the bay; refuelling with diesel was rather primitive; it consisted of a hose and hose-gun which resided at the bottom of the bay and, when needed, you would pick up a plastic bottle and carefully pull in from the sea a tatty, flimsy string, followed by the hose, shake out the gun and fill the tanks; once you finished refuelling you just dropped the hose back into the sea and had to somehow get yourself ashore to pay.

As Cascais was getting nearer I noticed that the time was only 16:30 and I thought it was far too early to pack it in for the day and that I might as well make the most of it with this gorgeous weather; I still had a few hours of daylight left and since I did not now have to meet the owner in Casçais, I was free to do as I wished.

Decision time – where shall I stop tonight? I grabbed the chart and found that it was feasible to make the next destination Peniche de Cima which was now an additional 42nm up the coast. I'll have a cup of tea and something to eat and then I must make up my mind. This took some doing as I had to go back and forth to the wheelhouse in order to keep an eye out for small fishing boats and the numerous fishing buoys; the latter were still my biggest enemy as getting a line caught in the propellers would put an abrupt stop to the smooth voyage which I was enjoying right now.

Finally I brought my tea up to the wheelhouse and made my decision which was to continue to Peniche de Cima after all; I only had to alter my heading slightly and now headed for Cabo Paso.

16:40 - finally passed the headland at Cabo Paso and turned the boat onto the new heading for the Port of Peniche de Cima. I had to lay the course well off this coast as the Atlantic rollers were hitting the coast with such a force that they were bouncing back for at least two miles, making the sea confused and sailing very uncomfortable; even with the stabilizers switched on I would have a roller coaster ride, that's ok for a few minutes, but for an extensive period it would be rather painful on the joints, and the vast amount of fishing buoys bouncing up and down between the waves would keep me on my toes.

I let my dividers walk over the chart and measured the distance to be another 40nm and at this speed my arrival time would be 23:00. This boat was a little gem and I normally could rely on her speed but, having said this, I still crossed my fingers hoping that she wasn't going to let me down today.

194

Tonight there didn't seem to be too many fishing boats around and I was able to avoid them all by using my radar at the close-range setting but, unlike last night, I had clear visibility and didn't need the radar for spotting the coast or other vessels.

It began to get busy five miles before the harbour with the movement of fishing boats and I had to start dodging some of them but they did help me to find the entrance to the port, as the town lights in the background made it difficult for me to see the green (starboard) entrance light.

23:05 - I moved slowly into the large harbour behind a small fishing boat but I could only see his stern light which was occasionally being shrouded in the mist of his own exhaust fumes. Ten minutes later and a bit clumsily for my liking, I moored alongside a yacht pontoon which was mainly occupied by the local community fishermen.

The marina office was shut and I could see with my binoculars that the pontoon was secured by a "code protected" gate, but it was late anyway, so this gave me a good excuse to have my well-earned drink and go to bed early as I did want to have an early start - weather permitting of course!

Lights or No Lights
August 1984

This bizarre event happened to me when I was delivering a 60 foot Italian built motor cruiser accompanied by the owner and his daughter from the Hamble in the UK to Palma de Majorca in Spain, calling in at Lisbon's yacht harbour of Belém where I needed to refuel for the next leg of the voyage to Gibraltar.

I suggested that we stay for the night which seemed to be a good idea because we had already spent five days at sea and it would be good to have some solid ground under our feet and spend an evening ashore.

We had to move the boat from Doca de Bom Sucesso to the next marina Doca de Belèm - luckily much nearer the town - and moor the boat on the allocated mooring buoys, but this meant we needed to be ferried ashore, which was a bit of a pain. However, it did have the advantage that we would be able to depart the marina without the assistance of the Marinario.

Finally we were ready to paint the town red (I wish!) and we had a most enjoyable summer evening sitting at a café terrace watching the world go by and finishing off with a superb meal at a local restaurant recommended by the harbourmaster.

We agreed last night that we were going to leave at a reasonable time so that we could round the Cabo di Vicente at approximately midday, expecting to arrive in Gibraltar at about midnight.

05:30 - dawn was just breaking in the east. I started the engines and as we were untying the boat I found that one of the lines had caught under the boat near the stern-gear - *the propellers and rudders* - and in order to free this line I had to walk along the deck from the bow towards the stern, while leaning over the railing at the same time; in doing so I had to pass a section that can be opened; unfortunately, this section of rail gave way under my weight and I fell head first overboard. Not a good start to the day - I can still hear myself warning the owner a few days earlier about this railing!

Well, obviously, this had put a halt to our early departure. I pulled myself back on board, with the help of the owner, and stopped the engines; then, totally drenched and smelling awful from the oily water, I walked into the shower. It didn't take me long to get changed and now we were ready to depart once more. "Take Two." I re-started the engines and at 06:20 successfully departed our mooring.

Still a bit shaken, I gently edged the boat through the numerous moored vessels to the harbour entrance and, as my vision was restricted by the high harbour wall, I made the boat drift towards the river.   I didn't really expect any traffic at this hour of the morning, but there just happened to be a small boat passing the entrance seaward. Because I was coming out of the harbour I had to give way and just to be sure, I looked up-river to see whether there was anyone else on their way down, but I couldn't see properly because the sun, which had just risen, shone from under the expansion bridge linking Lisbon with Mon Almada on the Southside of the river Tejo.

Feeling assured that the river was clear; I turned our boat seaward and followed the little boat which was now ahead of us. What now?! She made a sharp U turn in front of me and was almost on a head-on collision course with us and, as per the rules of the sea; I made a sharp manoeuvre towards the starboard in order to let her pass on our port side but then... 'What the hell are they playing at!!?' She had now made another unexpected U turn and was heading directly towards us.

When the little vessel had caught up with us I noticed that the wheelhouse door was opened and a stocky person in uniform was frantically waving his arms about and trying to tell us to go back into

197

the port; I handed the boat over to the owner, while I tried to persuade this little man to let us go but he insisted that we had to go back, which in the end we reluctantly did, and we were soon back where we had started half an hour earlier.

In the mean time, I had established that this was a police boat and noticed that they had moored their boat a little away from us. This time I had chosen to go alongside the small visitors' quay, because all I could think of was that they wanted to see our paperwork which shouldn't take more than a few minutes, but it was damned inconvenient to us.

The two officers waited for us to finish mooring and then the stocky policeman, who had insisted I returned to port, now waddled towards me and told me in Portuguese to go with him onto his boat. I assumed he would want to see the ship's papers, which I took with me, but he sternly told me he wasn't interested in them and said I must come **NOW!** The tone of his voice was like a military command to a subordinate!

I climbed on board the police boat and he impatiently gave the helmsman the order to move off, violently gesticulating and shouting, 'alee, alee;' the helmsman headed for the harbour entrance but then turned up the river Tejo towards a small commercial harbour called Doca de Santo Amaro, just under the expansion bridge.

I couldn't get to grips with this situation, but this little fellow must have been very upset about something because his behaviour on the boat was far less than friendly! He kept shouting to me in Portuguese and he became more and more agitated as I was unable to answer him in his own language. He then stood behind me so I couldn't see his face and kept pushing me with his full hand on the back of my shoulder, which almost made me fall over, but it was too early in the morning to even contemplate having a discussion with this guy, let alone having a fight with him.

After about 20 minutes we turned into the small harbour of Santo

Amaro and moored alongside, opposite some office buildings.

The stocky, impolite policeman now decided not to have anything to do with me, climbed off the boat and walked across the quay into a building, leaving the helmsman to escort me there.

We passed through a small door and entered a dark, almost black passageway, where it took some time for my eyes to get accustomed to the dismal light.

The helmsman quietly asked me to sit on the bench outside one of the office doors and I was left there without any further comment from anyone.

Time was marching on; it was now 10 o'clock and the prospects of leaving today were becoming more remote and leaving late in the day meant two nights and one day sailing to Gibraltar; needless to say I would have preferred the reverse.

Then... just before noon I was summoned into the room directly opposite the bench and the person behind the desk handed me an old fashioned Bakelite black telephone and in broken English said...

'Here, for you! I looked astonished at him as I couldn't think of anyone who would want to speak to me; I spoke hesitantly,

'Hello.'

'Hello, I am a representative of the British Embassy and would like to translate that we have been informed that you are in serious trouble.'

I took a deep breath and asked

'Can you please tell me what my problem is?'

'Don't you know?' he stuttered a bit saying, 'well... all I am allowed to say... is that you are in deep trouble and I advise you to get yourself a lawyer!'

I now began to get a little nervous and asked him,

'How did you get to know about this apparent problem?' to which he replied,

'The police officer at the station called us and said they were holding an Englishman in connection with a very serious crime, and it is our duty to help British citizens as much as we can.'

Now totally confused and very upset, I stupidly replied,

'But I am not British, I am Dutch.'

'Well in that case, we can't help you any further and it would be better for you to contact the Dutch Embassy.'

Feeling shocked by this conversation, I slowly handed the phone back to the man behind the desk and ignored the advice the clerk had given me, thinking to myself, if it's such a serious crime why don't they handcuff me or even lock me up!

This affair had become very frustrating; I was now back on the hard wooden bench in a very dark and draughty hall-way with people walking in and out of different rooms, some of them smoking the most awful cigarettes which left thick blue smoke lingering behind them as they were passing me. I thought, maybe they were trying to kill me with the smoke rather than wait until after I was "tried and found guilty!"

The whole afternoon was spent sitting and waiting; thank goodness I am blessed with a tremendous amount of patience. Then, out of the blue at five minutes to five an officer walked towards me and said in perfect English (*Surprise, surprise someone did speak English after all),*

'You can go back to the boat for the night, but you MUST return to this office in the morning promptly at eight o'clock.'

I thought maybe I could take this opportunity of leaving the port but the officer must have read my mind and said

'The harbour master is aware of this situation and it would be unwise for you to leave the port.'

'I have no intentions of doing so sir'. I fibbed.

I made my way out of this grubby building as quickly as possible and once outside I took a deep breath and enjoyed my freedom; then a sudden chill came over me as I thought what if I had ended up in jail today? I shook my head to eliminate that dreadful thought and started my long walk back along the tree-lined avenue to the harbour of Bom Sucesso.

Back on board the owner poured me a cold beer and we sat on the aft deck reminiscing about what had happened, both knowing full-well that we were unable to leave today.

Later that evening the harbour master came on board and introduced his son to us; Carlos was a young man of sixteen and was learning English at school. Of course the topic of the evening was my encounter with the Portuguese Police, and Carlos said,

'I have the day off tomorrow, would you like me to come with you to the police station?' and without any hesitation I replied,

'That's very kind of you; I really could do with some help, thank you very much.'

The following morning we set off well in time to be at the Police station for 8 o'clock. No-one seemed to mind the presence of my companion. We sat down on the same bench to which I was attached for the whole of yesterday, but fortunately only for a short time on this occasion before my nasty officer came towards us; he pointed in the direction of the main entrance, spoke something in Portuguese and with that, Carlos stood up and I followed him outside to where an old Volkswagen bus was waiting for us. Four officers and the two of us squeezed ourselves into this sardine tin, which started to splutter and cough and finally moved away; the driver drove us through many winding roads passing Lisbon town centre, where we had spent such an enjoyable evening two nights ago, sitting at the cafés watching the world go by.

After a while the bus came to a halt at the bottom of a very long and wide staircase - Like a "stairway to Heaven!" Looking up, I could see that we had arrived at the Palais of Justice. We all walked up the steps into the main entrance hall, and were told to wait in the middle of a massive lobby which had several numbered wooden veneered doors most likely leading into separate court rooms; after a few minutes waiting we were told to go to one of the doors where a guard said, '**wait there**!'

I passed the time by looking around and noticed that at the far end of the hall stood a person in handcuffs surrounded by several policemen; this gave me shivers up my spine as I realized the terrible reality of the situation I was in.

'You can go in now.' I heard the guard say in broken English.

We entered the courtroom which was empty except for two people: the policeman who had driven the boat and our nasty friend who was responsible for me being here. The guard told Carlos and I to sit down then left the room and silently closed the door behind him. Five minutes went by, then a side door opened and a smartly dressed woman came through the doorway; all of us stood up then the lady Judge told us to sit down.

She began to speak in Portuguese and then spoke to me in perfect English saying

'Good morning, you know the crime for which you have been accused, Sir?'

I replied,

'No Madam.'

'I will have to speak in Portuguese first, and then I will ask you some questions in English.'

After having conversed with our policeman the judge turned to me and said,

'You have been accused by the Maritime Police Officer of trying to leave the Port of Lisbon yesterday morning in the dark without your navigation lights?'

Is that all? I thought. Stay calm and only reply to what you are being asked - this whole affair was beginning to look like some TV detective drama!

The Judge went over all the questions relating to the crime and finally asked,

'Is this the officer who remanded you yesterday?'

'No Madam, this is the helmsman; the officer who remanded me is the other person in this room, and I would like to add that he man-handled me and tried to provoke a situation in which I could have committed a crime.'

The Judge then spoke to our friend and, following his reply, asked for a newspaper, which arrived within a few minutes.

The Judge now turned once more to our friend, who was questioned for at least another 20 minutes then... she stood up, looked into my direction and said,

'Sir, you're free to go, good morning.'

Then with her newspaper and books under her arm, she walked out of the courtroom.

I was flabbergasted. Why this positive conclusion? Carlos and I walked out of the building straight into a taxi and as we drove off Carlos explained

'Well, your policeman friend had said that you drove the boat away yesterday morning in the dark without navigation lights but the helmsman confirmed your story giving the time of the event and the daylight time, so the Judge ordered a newspaper in order to confirm the official time of sunrise, which proved that you drove away in daylight!

The other discrepancy the Judge had to consider was your story regarding the man-handling by the officer; the helmsman said that he couldn't confirm any physical manhandling as he was looking ahead but he said that the language the officer used was certainly provoking.

We returned to the harbour and I thanked Carlos profusely for all his help. After paying the harbour dues and feeling rather relieved, I went back onboard and said to the owner,

'Lets get out of here and I will tell you the story later.'

Totally against my principles, I left the harbour almost straight away, which meant sailing two nights and a day, but I didn't care this time. Let's move... shall we!

Peniche de Cima - Poroa de Varzim
Friday 22nd March 2002

I must admit, I didn't get much sleep because there was so much traffic throughout the night with the arrival and departure of numerous large and small fishing vessels; not to mention the motion of the Atlantic swell running in from around the outer breakwater.

Because of this constant disturbance I woke early and was ready to go and at 05:30 I departed Peniche de Cima – Wow, for once today I was setting off early.

It was still dark but around these areas daybreak is almost instant  and should be with me soon. I turned the boat around and followed the little boat ahead of me out of the port and, not long after having left the breakwater, I turned the boat straight into the heavy swell which was

Cabo Carvoeiro

running-in from the SW. I slowly made my way towards the lighthouse of Cabo Carvoeiro at the headland, accompanied by several other vessels all out-performing each other by trying to get to the fishing grounds before the sardines or tuna migrate.

By the time I reached Cabo Carvoeiro I noticed that all the fishing vessels had dispersed and I was left on my own which was great; this gave me the opportunity of peacefully selecting a GPS position and I chose the port Poroa de Varzim at the top of Portugal as my next destination; now all I had to do was to give the autopilot the task of keeping a straight line towards this place. I knew that this was going to be a large hop with a distance of 129nm and would take an estimated 16 hours non-stop; I know that's a lot to ask for and... it will also be one of the most boring passages I need to make.

You see, I have done this run many times before and found that it drags on and on; I suppose it's because the coastline is hardly visible and in some cases disappears altogether. Stop complaining! On the plus side, I didn't have to negotiate the fishing buoys and, apart from the occasional fishing vessel and cargo ship, "the coast was clear" metaphorically speaking!

What bliss is modern navigation equipment; it made my life so much easier because if I didn't have this equipment, sailing single handed would have been extremely difficult; however, should this modern system fail then I could always return to the traditional way of chart, ruler and DR (Dead Reckoning) using all possible data - course, tide, wind, depth and speed through the water.

The morning passed by surprisingly fast and as for the weather...? Well, the weather had been superb so far; the sea had been calm with only the large long swell which gave me an indescribable sense of peace and I finally relaxed which was well earned after the incidents of the past few days. Oh yes, although I haven't mentioned it lately I have been checking on my engines and luckily there hasn't been any further deterioration on the exhaust, but I am not sure whether this will last for the remainder of the voyage; anything can happen between here and the south of England and I am always anxious as to what I'll find next time around. Oh well, let's see how it goes...

Midday: just marking off my latest position which is latitude 40º06'090N and longitude 009º11'000W which puts me just about 13.5 nautical miles west of Gabo Mondego.

Marking this position of Gabo Mondego reminds me of the time when I had to run into Figueira da Foz. (Page 208) After a trying day at sea I needed to seek shelter in the Port of Figueira da Foz at the river mouth of Mondego.

I can't help it, but I am really enjoying the peace on the open sea with only a few distant fishing boats to keep me company.

The voyage was progressing well mainly because of the good weather I was experiencing - *as the harbour master of Sines had predicted* - hardly any wind to speak of and the sea stayed smooth with only a very long, but low swell; in fact, I switched-off my stabilizers because they were over-correcting and apart from that, not much else to report.

Late afternoon: I now started to close-in towards the shore which mainly consisted of low-lying land, thus having sandy beaches; beaches are perfect for a holiday but are a menace for navigation because they will generally run into the sea at the same angle, therefore shallow waters. I altered my course near the light of Espinho in order to avoid a particular shallow patch; however, closing-in on the coast presented me with difficulties in avoiding those damn fishing buoys! But luckily, once again, I was able to use the radar to avoid them. I know that I am hammering on about this, but I constantly needed to change the range-setting so that I could keep an eye on the low shore-line too. Having the beach as a coastline indicates that the port was built on shallow grounds.

The shore lights began to blind my vision, big-time, making my eyes sore but nevertheless I had to keep an extremely good lookout and perform some precise and careful navigation in order to reach the port safely.

21:30 - I spotted the port and starboard harbour entry lights flashing amongst the towns' light pollution. So far, So good, I was able to line up the boat with the leading lights and was amazed to see how wide the main entrance was and, from what I could see in the dark, this was a newly built port. Now I just needed to find a suitable place to moor. Earlier in the afternoon I had read in the Almanac that just inside the breakwaters I would find some pontoons on my starboard side; I slowly drifted towards the marina and edged the boat forwards to the nearest pontoon I could find, which happened to be just outside the marked channel, but all of a sudden I found myself in no more than 1½ metres of water under the boat. That's rather odd in this massive port, I thought.

I carefully manoeuvred the boat alongside and threw my first line rather than jumping off the boat because, should I fall or twist an ankle then the boat would drift away and there wouldn't be anyone on board to control her. Securing the boat with the second line was more difficult, so against my own rules, I jumped off and immediately tripped over, and nearly fell straight across the pontoon into the marina; I stood-up and almost immediately tripped again.

What the hell was that? I knew that being at sea for long periods makes you get the land-waddles, but oh no... that was not the reason for my predicament; I had encountered something I have never experienced in the past. This marina had strung numerous fishing lines zigzagging across the pontoon from cleat to cleat. Having thought about it I realized this was to prevent seagulls landing on the pontoons and fouling the place. I seriously think this idea should be given to the harbour master of the Mediterranean port of Caleta de Velez near Malaga which, when I visited, was almost totally white from the seagull excrement. I now began to walk like a duck avoiding the strings and successfully finished off tying up the boat.

Attempted Entry to the Port
May 1992

We had left Bayona (near Vigo in the north) early that morning and made our way along the coast towards my intended destination of Peniche de Cima, but a few hours into the voyage the weather started to change and the wind, which had been coming from the east, had swung around and was now coming from the north-west which made the swell rise into a high but short and uncomfortable wave; in fact it was so high, that a near-empty cargo vessel making her way away from the port of Porto de Leixões – the harbour at the town of O'porto - had difficulty in staying in the water; when we caught up with her I could clearly see her propeller coming out of the water every time her stern was lifted by the waves - It was ROUGH!

We often couldn't see the horizon but I still didn't see the need to run into port because these weather conditions are not unusual and I still had a long way to go.

The problem for me was that along this coast the ports are few and far between and running into them would be a hard task because in this sort of weather these large waves would run onto the shallows making them short, steep and dangerously high.

We didn't cover the mileage I would have liked to have done during the day and as we were passing Cabo Mondego I realised that we still had a good fifty nautical miles to my next destination; I didn't think doing a night passage was idyllic and, as I was near Figueira da Foz, felt that I shouldn't miss this last opportunity of seeking shelter for the night.

Having made my decision, I rounded the cape and ran along the coast towards the port, but the wave pattern changed and it had become almost impossible to navigate this close to the shore so I

208

changed course and headed the boat away from the coast as the waves were beginning to use our boat as an oversized surf board, the difference being that we didn't enjoy this one single bit; little did I know that we had worse to come...

I slowed down so that the waves could overtake me; in this way I was able to keep control of the situation.

I could just about see the western breakwater through the thick salt deposited on my windows and the heavy rolling of the boat from side to side, therefore I needed to stay away from the breakwater for as long as I could because these waves were bouncing back off it, making it impossible to steer the yacht safely. Finally, I arrived at the bar just before the entrance and could see the large waves rolling and breaking over the shallow grounds at either side of me into the relatively small gap of the river mouth.

I could envisage what was about to happen and told my crew to hold on tight; now the boat needed my undivided attention as I had to keep her carefully in line with the markers on shore to avoid the shallow grounds.

I throttled the engines back and drove the boat as slow as possible but still fast enough to maintain her steerage. Although she was 60 foot and possessed two MAN engines with 1000 horsepower each, I still couldn't help feeling that the waves were still playing hell with us by violently shaking the boat from side to side then lifting her high onto the wave, pushing her nearly uncontrollably forward into a nosedive and then mercilessly throwing a wave onto the deck for good measure. This went on repeatedly. I really had my hands full: looking at the markers, waves, steering, controlling the speed and keeping a watchful eye on the depth sounder which showed... Oh no! 14 - 12 - 10 - 8 - 6 feet; every time the boat entered a trough of dirty green-brown angry wave I broke out in a cold sweat and felt almost powerless against the elements.

Luckily it was over in 20 minutes although it definitely felt like hours but we eventually arrived safely on the river and as I hadn't had a chance to obtain any detailed information regarding this port, I entered the first available basin, which happened to be on my port side, and was full of large fishing boats.

I carefully manoeuvred my way into the basin and was guided in by a very friendly fisherman who offered me the space alongside his vessel.

My friendly fisherman took me to the harbour master's office which of course, was closed but the fisherman said, 'Wait here' and a few minutes later a plainclothes officer arrived, greeted the fisherman, unlocked the door and all three of us went into the office.

I handed over my paperwork, which wasn't a normal registration document but a German Customs T1 (Transit1) document; miraculously, the officer understood the implication of that document and accepted it straight away; wasn't that a bit of luck!

He handed the papers back to me and said that due to the high waves the port was closed and he found it courageous that I had even attempted to enter - I am sorry, but to me it was a desperate situation and I didn't see the need for him to give me a pat on the back.

But then, in broken English, he told me that because the boat was over 12 metres and in excess of the permitted horsepower I had committed an offence because I was sailing under the coastline between the hours of 9 pm and 6 a.m. I had never heard of that rule before but thought, Oh well, here we go again!

The next morning, out of courtesy, I asked permission from the harbourmaster to leave the port and, to my amazement, he said that would be alright but not before 11:30 when it would be the top of the tide.

Poroa de Varzim - Bayona
Saturday 23rd March 2002

Having arrived late last night I decided to have my breakfast in leisure, like "the Lord of the Manor". After cleaning the dishes I prepared the boat for sea including my checks in the engine room; everything was fine but I still had to remove the usual 1½ litres of water from the engine sump and, so far, the leak had not worsened.

09:00 - left the Port of Poroa de Varzim. Although I wasn't aware of it, the wind must have increased during the night because the waves are now about 10 feet, but this boat can handle that with no problem and I really want to get away from the Portuguese coast and enter the more familiar waters of Spain.

Immediately after leaving port I turned into a northerly direction and hopped along the coast and tucked myself well inshore. Setting a waypoint target and leaving the autopilot in charge was not an option because, being Saturday, the coastline was littered with numerous boats which, together with the fish farms and fishing buoys, were constantly in my way, meaning I had to alter course frequently in order to stay safe.

The passage planned for today wasn't too far and should only take 4 hours. The sun had finally risen over the hills and was somewhat reddish this morning; this possibly meant that I could expect the wind to change and come from a southerly direction.

12:20 - passing the outlying rocks of Cabo Silleiro; I will need to give those a wide berth in order not to get thrown onto them. Having passed the rocks safely at a distance of 2½nm, I felt ready to change course and headed into an easterly direction keeping well clear of the Las Serralleiras on my port side and now could head into the port of Bayona. This port is well tucked away from the ocean but still susceptible to the large rolling-in swell.

13:00 - rounded the breakwater into the port of Bayona and headed for the refuelling jetty, which I could see was free. Great, that saves me hanging about. I moored alongside and immediately went to task in filling the tanks to the brim.

Whilst I was refuelling I happened to notice a large, fast, modern motor cruiser gently gliding into the marina, but I continued with my business in filling the tanks and hadn't noticed that she had stopped just at my side at the fuel jetty and I heard a loud shout 'Hi Bill! When will you be ready?'

I looked into the direction of the "voice" but the sun was directly in line and I couldn't make out who it was.

I carried on refuelling and paid the bill. Still wondering who was shouting my name, I went back on board, completed the paperwork, stowed my money away, started the engines and slowly pulled away from the jetty.

Whoever was driving that big cruiser knew the harbour well because he had reversed all the way back into a more favourable turning place as it was difficult passing another boat at the fuel pontoon because of the small boats moored nearby.

I finally reached the cruiser and had a glimpse of the person who had called my name and it was Bob whom I have known for years.

Bob was also a well-known freelance skipper with an even greater amount of experience than me.

I moored the boat in a slot near the entrance of the marina which had been allocated to me earlier by the Harbourmaster, then walked back to the large cruiser, where I found Bob filling up with fuel.

'Hi Bob, how are you, I haven't seen you for some time.'

'Yes Bill, the last time we met was four years ago at the Düsseldorf Boat Show; I am fine thank you.'

'Where did you come from Bob?'

'We left Plymouth two, well no, three days ago after waiting a hell of a long time for suitable sailing conditions but finally I managed to cross the Bay.'

'What were the sea-conditions like?'

'The weather was perfect all the way.'

'Are you planning on staying the night Bob?'

'No, I want to continue whilst the weather is good; with this boat I can be in Casçais early tomorrow morning.'

This reminded me of my delivery days, always beating the weather and all the other elements which get thrown at you.

'And you?' he asked,

'I am on my way back to England.'

'Are you alone again?'

'Yes, but this time I am not in any particular hurry' and I hastily added,

'There's no chance that I'll be crossing the bay on my own.'

'How are you planning to get back then?'

'I am contemplating hopping along the coast, but I am not sure which places I'll run into; I am really looking forward to this voyage as I have never had the pleasure of doing the "coast-hop".'

'Well Bill, I wish you a safe voyage back.'

'Thanks and the same for you, Bob'

We shook hands, he started his engines and reversed away from the fuel jetty and slowly left the marina towards the place I had just come from, and me... well, I took a leisurely walk into the town and relaxed a little.

This town wasn't on my list in the early days of yacht deliveries as for the first few years I used to make my way up river to the large fishing port of Vigo. However, in the late 70's it became increasingly more difficult to obtain fuel for pleasure boats as, one by one, the European governments made a new rule in that fuel for pleasure craft was to be taxed. At that time there wasn't a harbour, either here or in the Mediterranean which had made provisions for supplying fuel for pleasure boats. In those days it was a living nightmare searching for fuel; sometimes you needed to carry it in cans, other times you might get some from a greedy supplier who would charge the earth for delivering the fuel in dirty rusty barrels, but I had heard that across the Vigo bay was the fishing port Cangas, where I could get fuel. Well the snag with this port, which was really a pier more than a port, was that it needed to be high or near high water in order to be able to reach the fuel pump. Then one day a fisherman said, why don't you go to Bayona and so I did; and since the early 80's Bayona has become one of my regular fuel stop-over ports along the Atlantic coast.

Anyway, this place is just like any other I suppose, but the main attraction is the Castle Mount protruding from the peninsular directly overlooking the bay.

Although it was only just a few days into spring, the place was buzzing with Spanish people strolling along the endless promenade adjacent to miles of sandy beaches. Whilst walking away from the marina my phone rang and, as expected, it was the owner. I wasn't surprised because I hadn't heard from him for 3 days, since I was in the Port of Sines. I wondered what he had in mind this time.

'Hi Bill, how are you doing and where are you?'

I was pleased to tell him,

'I am in Bayona, just finished refuelling and on my way to get food. I'll leave tomorrow and hope to make my way towards La Caruña.'

'That's brilliant, and how is the boat performing?'

'The boat's good, other than the small problem of water leaking into the engine.'

I felt compelled to tell him today the story of the leaking exhaust, but totally oblivious he said,

'Ok Bill, you seem to have it all in hand, but take care won't you?'

I am sorry to say this, but I was only half-listening to him because I was trying to work out how to ask him the next question,

'Yes... I will... but is there any chance... in you... coming to the boat or... am I to continue on my own?'

'Well, we did have it in mind to come soon, but I am not sure when!'

With those words he ended the conversation and I was left to my own devices once more.

For the first time since leaving Sevilla I had a most enjoyable and relaxing afternoon sitting in the sunshine at a roadside café, watching the world go by but at around five it became cooler so I strolled back to the boat and started to prepare the engines for tomorrow's departure. The engines were fine but following my manoeuvre through the harbour, the water level was a lot higher than the usual 1½ litre. Doubts crept into my head as to whether I really should be continuing on my own and seeing Bob earlier today, complete with supporting crew to help him take his boat down the coast, reinforced my concerns.

Anyway, that's enough of that, I cleared everything away and had a pleasant evening watching videos that my girls had recorded for me so that I didn't miss out on the various "soaps" and documentaries like David Attenborough, my favourite, and watching these programmes erased my earlier worries from my mind.

Bayona - Sangenjo
Sunday 24th March 2002

I awoke to a dark grey overcast sky and couldn't help seeing all the boats dancing up and down, back and forth on their moorings to the same rhythm - *like the Can-Can girls on stage* - and a large number of halyards on the sailing boats were noisily clattering against their aluminium masts, indicating that something was amiss.

I looked into the direction of the harbour mouth where very large waves were creeping very gently, but persuasively, around the breakwater into the port and rolling out all the way to the other end of the marina where they finally came to rest on the beach. I must have been tired otherwise these turbulent conditions would have woken me earlier that's for sure.

I really didn't feel like leaving but staying here was not the answer either and after some deliberation, I plucked up the courage and at 09:30 left the mooring, slowly zigzagging between the moored boats making my way for the entrance; as I was nearing the massive breakwater the boat started to behave like an oversized seesaw. I switched on the stabilizers and gently increased the engine rpm to cruising speed; good, the boat was behaving as she always does, majestically keeping a perfect straight line, almost showing defiance against the waves which were hitting her.

Having rounded the breakwater I was immediately aware of the off-lying shoal near the Castle peninsular on my starboard side which was being bombarded with large breaking waves; having made a bearing on those rocks I needed to take another bearing on the notorious rocks of Cabo Silleiro so that I could stay well clear of both; taking these bearings was easy because the rocks made themselves known by rejecting the deep blue waves and catapulting them high into the air and even from this distance I could hear the thundering noise which these waves produced every time they smashed themselves onto the rocks. Wow, I can't believe this but it is a totally different scenario from that of the previous days and I realized that the harbourmaster at Sines had it right all along.

With the boat moving about so much I needed to drink the remainder of the coffee I had made myself, before it landed onto the deck and whilst I was returning the cup to the galley I thought I would check the boat to see that I had secured everything in all the cabins and that the doors were in the open position, preventing them from slamming and banging about. Then... for the first time since the South of France, I placed the newly designed weatherboards in their fittings at the wheelhouse doors and hoped that they would do the job of preventing the water on the deck rolling into the wheelhouse!

I passed the rocks of Cabo Silleiro to my port, at the safe distance of 1nm, and turned the boat into the direction of Cap Finisterre, some 46 miles away. Just a short run for today but it's Sunday and I was slowly running out of steam, metaphorically speaking of course.

It wasn't long after setting course for Finisterre that the wind started to increase from 10 to 25 knots and changed its direction but unfortunately it was now blowing directly onto the bow and I could bet that the weather was going to deteriorate imminently; the waves were already so high that looking over them was impossible, and medium sized white horses - *white crests* - were beginning to form along the tops; I wondered what next! As you can tell, I wasn't too happy about this situation, but thought I'd better "play it by ear" and try to keep going for as long as it was safe to do so.

A good hour had passed since I had changed the heading and, according to my calculations, the boat had covered a mere 7 miles; this meant that the heavy seas had slowed her down, so much so that I began to question whether I was going to make Finisterre before nightfall.

A little while later I saw a large war ship coming towards me and I noticed how she was ploughing through the waves, rising her bow high out of the water, showing part of her black painted bottom, and then plunging back into the sea, cutting her way through the mountainous waves. Seeing this made me think, what if the engine stops or I need to change a fuel filter - what then... yes, what then?

My main difficulty was that I wouldn't be able to stop without having to drain the water out of the oil again, and I feared that this was no longer becoming a calculated risk but sheer stupidity. No, this is really becoming too risky.

At first, I thought perhaps my nerves were getting the better of me, but after a lengthy five minute discussion with myself, I decided to change course and try to seek shelter behind the first available island which happened to be the Island of Ons.

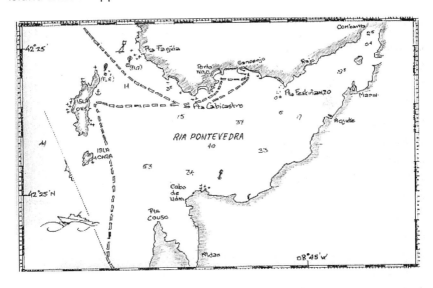

My intention was to anchor in the marked area on the chart and wait there for more favourable conditions, but when I moved closer to the shore I realized that the Atlantic swell had even reached this anchorage; although I crept up to the beach I found that it was still too uncomfortable for a long stay and the island didn't have any other shelter to offer apart from a ferry/restaurant jetty.

Hesitantly I turned the boat around and headed into - *for me* – an uncharted area and my immediate thought was that I didn't want to go back to Bayona but I would have to find shelter much closer.

I looked in the pilot book in search of a port and found Porto Novo on the north side of the Ria de Pontevedra, which is the first main inlet above Ria de Vigo; I now had to find it on the chart and it appeared that this port was neatly tucked away from the Atlantic swell, so my decision was to head for Porto Novo.

It took me a good half an hour to reach Pta Cabicastro and from this point I finally began to lose the Atlantic swell for the first time in four days.

This coastline seemed rather attractive with its lush pine trees and greenery enhanced by small villas scattered against the hillside, just like the French Riviera and for a split second I was enjoying myself so much that I nearly didn't see the off-lying rocks at the Pta Cabicastro which jolted me back to reality. I'd better watch out for any other surprises!

After Pta Cabicastro I turned into the bay and slowly edged my way towards the port of Porto Novo, but I soon realized that this port was not as I had imagined; the place was certainly very pretty with a few houses and a dozen or so small boats on their offshore moorings; it was a fantastic painting scene but that's not what I had in mind and was slightly disappointed that I couldn't find a suitable mooring in this idyllic and panoramic setting; reluctantly, I turned the boat away from entering the breakwater then, over the other side of the bay, I noticed a high breakwater; I followed the breakwater to the east end where I found that I had arrived at the entrance of a marina. I stopped the boat outside and prepared the ropes and fenders. After my preparations I slowly moved into the port passing some low lying rocks just outside the marked channel - luckily it was low water otherwise I could have missed those - and found that I had arrived in the modern marina of Sangenjo.

I moored the boat alongside one of the pontoons near the marina office - all finished for the day. I am glad I had made all those decisions earlier because it wasn't long after my arrival that the wind increased big time.

Although it was very windy aloft I didn't notice it because being sheltered on the south side of the hills made it feel like spring and it turned into a most pleasant afternoon.

It was time to stretch my legs and investigate the town and its surroundings. I found a passage way and walked along the water's edge where there was a magnificent view over the bay. The town was like any other, built around a small village-type town centre which had soon overflowed into this modern 60's type architecture, a bit square and uninteresting, but it was very noticeable that there were an awful lot of people on the move; presumably they had come from the not-too-far distant town of Vigo.

After a while I returned to the boat, feeling a little guilty about my decision to stop here. I was always one for thinking "The show must go on" but it would soon become clear that this was the best decision. All would be revealed tomorrow.

Sangenjo

The weather had worsened overnight which meant that I would have been spending the day here anyway, so I prepared the boat ready for an eventual departure but when it came to my usual check on the port engine I had the shock of my life, because the water I pumped out of the sump was much more than the usual amount and... worse still, the oil was heavily emulsified.

"Well that's it," I thought. This voyage had come to an abrupt end and it appeared that the engine had finally won the day; I knew that this time I wouldn't be going anywhere until a replacement exhaust manifold was found.

I could only assume that this excess water had occurred whilst I was looking for the anchorage and the safe haven and I must count myself lucky, once more, that I had made the correct decision and had found Sangenjo just in time; I just can't imagine what would have happened if I had continued the voyage to Finisterre yesterday; I could have been stranded there and I recall that Finisterre is a small fishing village with hardly any mooring facilities for boats like this one.

I sat down with a cup of coffee and had a good think as to how I was going to handle this situation. "That's it, decision made;" I went to the harbour master and asked him,

'Where can I find a Perkins agent?' he shrugged his shoulders and said hesitantly,

'Vigo!'

Not quite happy with his reply, I tentatively asked,

'You don't have anyone here in the town who would be able help me?'

'Well, we do have a mechanic but I don't know whether he can help.'

'Thanks, I'll see how I get on'.

It's time to call the boss and see whether he can sort out the problem from that end.

'Hi, Bill how are you doing?'

'I am fine, but the boat isn't. You remember me telling you in Bayona that the engine was collecting water in the sump, well... it has become worse and I don't think we should attempt to press it any further until the manifold is replaced'

I received the reply I expected

'I told you we can't get a new one, can't you get it repaired locally?'

'I have already tried, but I am not too optimistic about that; furthermore, should they repair the unit and it fails then we won't have anything at all.'

'Alright, leave it with me and I'll get back to you.'

Now I had to play the waiting game.

Later that morning the boss rang back and said,

'Bill, dismantle the manifold and fly back with the part to the UK; we'll get it repaired here, you can sort out your flight with my secretary.'

'Ok. I'll see you when I get back.'

The following day the secretary called to say that I was to travel from Vigo, via Madrid to London Heathrow where a driver would collect the engine part from me. I took a taxi to the airport, carrying the heavy exhaust manifold under my arm; I must admit this made a welcome break from bouncing about on the Atlantic.

The taxi driver was most informative and told me that this part of Galicia had become popular as a Spanish holiday resort in the last ten years and that, until this present day, not many foreigners came here.

The taxi wound its way through small villages and along the ria - (river) more like a Loch in Scotland but set in a much better climate; I noticed that small houses were springing up like fungus at either side of the road and were positioned like well-spaced seating in a good cinema so that each and every one had at least a small part overlooking the Ria.

At the end of the long winding road we crossed over the bridge and I eventually lost sight of the Bay. We now travelled behind a ridge and slowly climbed the hills then crossed the highway bridge over Ria de Vigo and finally joined the motorway which led directly to the airport.

We arrived well in time for my flight and I was able to check in straight away. The girl at the check-in desk told me that I had a return ticket via Madrid, but the return date was set for a fortnight from today!

Never mind, I thought, that must be a mistake, so I won't query it.

'Do you have any luggage Sir?'

'No thank you'

'Don't you want that - *she pointed at the engine part* - to be checked in Sir?'

'No thank you.' Then the girl said,

'I'll need to weigh it' then,

'Sir, you can't take this as hand luggage; firstly it is overweight and secondly it is in excess of the normal size.'

'Well I'm sorry, but I can't give it up; it's fragile and this is the whole purpose of making the flight to London.'

'What is in the parcel?'

'It's a cast iron engine part and it may get broken or lost in the transfer at Madrid.'

She then picked up the house phone and started to rattle on in Spanish, then said,

'It's our policy not to permit overweight and outsized luggage in the cabin but the supervisor said that they will allow it this time'.

'Thank you' and with a sigh of relief I left the check-in desk.

Upon my arrival at Heathrow I was met by the driver who

exchanged my heavy parcel for taking me home.

The following day I was told that the part would be ready later that afternoon and that "we" would be ready to depart for Spain tomorrow. I did notice the word "WE" and needless to say this meant that the boss was coming out with me. Brilliant, I thought, now I don't have to make the passage across the Bay on my own.

It had also become clear to me that the return ticket was only completed for administrative purposes and bore no relation to my real departure date.

Now, for the second time, I was to fly in the Corporate Jet.

The next day, at the arranged time of 09:30, my wife took me to the small airport a few miles down the road, where we had to wait a little while for the boss and his wife to arrive.

It's not every day that you get a second chance to fly in a Corporate Jet. Now I really discovered the advantage of flying privately: being able to park next to the plane and board her in just a few paces - no queues, no waiting and no fuss.

Minutes later the plane took off at a decent rate of knots, leaving my wife standing there, becoming no more than a pin prick on the ground.

The flight was smooth and it only took an hour and a half before we reached the airport of Vigo.

Back on board the Calypso II I went straight to work and fitted the repaired exhaust, I also had to replace the contaminated oil from the engine; in the meantime the owner and his wife went for an investigative walk around the town.

They returned 2 hours later, having filled themselves with a delicious fish lunch at the nearby harbour restaurant.

The owner stuck his head down into the engine room from above and enquired how I was doing.

'Very well thank you, just a few adjustments then the big trial... That's it, can you please start her up'

The engine made a few noises and finally fired-up but there were a few diesel leaks I needed to tighten and...

'Now try it again.'

This time the engine started and after a few splutters began to run smoothly. I left the engine running for a bit making sure there weren't any other leaks in the system. Inwardly I was really chuffed to bits as I realised that the decisions I had made had paid off big time.

The boat was now ready to go and the weather looked good so we planned to leave in the morning.

I cleaned and cleared the engine room and joined the owners for a meal with the odd glass of red wine of course!

Sangenjo - Camariñas
Friday 29th March 2002

Good Friday! Oh my goodness! I hadn't realised that the time had gone so quickly and had totally forgotten that it was the start of the Easter weekend. I must have been so involved with travelling back and forth to the UK and the repairs that I hadn't put two and two together. So that's why the owner was joining me on this part of the voyage!

I wasn't too sure what to make of the weather because the day started dull and overcast but wind-still which is, as always, a huge bonus of course.

09:00 on the dot - I manoeuvred the boat gently away from the pontoon and headed for the marina entrance; I noticed that the rocks were totally submerged as I headed for the open sea once again, and before reaching the open waters I had to weave my way through a large number of small dinghies which were anchored amongst the rocks, trying their luck at catching some fish and lobsters for today.

This time the ocean was rolling gently on and off the rocks, creating beautiful white foamy patterns around them and onto the unpolluted deep blue sea; a little later we passed between the last rocks to starboard and the Island of Ons to port. Its statue-like lighthouse was balanced on the rocks' edge stating "I am the limit" and symbolically saying good-bye to the seafarers who needed to make their passage into the safety of the ocean depths. Having successfully cleared all these obstacles, I was now able to set a direct course for the peninsular of Cap Finisterre.

The boat was doing extremely well because we passed the southern tip of Cap Finisterre at 14:30; here the weather had changed for the better, still with no wind to speak of but now with some sunshine thrown in for good measure. The sea was so calm and it turned out to be a gorgeous afternoon and a real pleasure to be out at sea.

It was hardly imaginable that this same sea can be so cruel that all you want to do is to say your prayers in the hope that you reach the safety of a harbour in one piece; unlike in May 1991 when I needed to lend a helping hand in bad weather. (Page 230)

After a while we rounded Cap Toriñana not far from Ria de Camariñas, which had become our destination for the day.

The owner requested this particular bay as he remembered being here some years back on one of our previous voyages and I do remember that the area was not the easiest to enter unless you religiously adhere to the pilotage information.

I had deliberately set my course 1nm off Punta de la Barca with its shallow water and the chapel of Mugía on the cliffs' edge and noticed that the car park was overflowing; it looked to me that a church service had just finished and I could clearly see people talking and only then... I was reminded once again that today was Good Friday.

At this point we were 2nm SW off Punta de la Barca which gave me a clear view into the far distance and I was immediately shocked by an awful looking site, because the beautiful hillside was blighted with numerous wind generators which had spoiled this lovely landscape and amongst them I found the two leading lights. The two lights were erected upon two brilliantly white-washed posts, one taller than the other and were needed to guide me safely between the shore and the outlying sandbanks.

The tidal current was coming out of the bay rather strongly and I had a real fight on my hands keeping the leading posts in line to avoid running aground on the sandbank, which had become visible as the swell gently broke and rolled over the grounds.

The second set of leading lights only became visible when I came within a ¼nm from the first set; the second set of lights were mounted way back in the opening of the bay and led me safely onto the home straits.

Once through the gap I noticed that it opened out into a large and beautiful bay with the fishing village of Camariñas and Boria to the north and Mugia and Merejo to the south.

We made the decision to head for Camariñas but before I reached the port I had to navigate my way through some sort of boating regatta and finally - after successfully dodging the boats again - safely reached the floating marina quay.

18:00 - finished mooring the boat and I must say, that this was the most successful and enjoyable day's sailing I have had for a long while and, in addition to this, we had moored in a most beautiful part of this northwest corner of Spain with its breath-taking views of green hills all the way to the water's edge.

Lending a Helping Hand
May 1991

It was early May when I was on a solo voyage delivering a 53ft Taiwanese built boat from Düsseldorf in Germany to Gogolin on the French Riviera. That in itself isn't much, but having another 60ft Taiwan cruiser with an amateur crew "in convoy" makes all the difference and although you cannot be responsible for their actions you do feel obliged to take care of them as much as possible.

We, the two boats, had just come across the Bay of Biscay from Dartmouth and were making for the port of Bayona. We were blessed with reasonable weather all the way across, but this all changed as we were nearing the Galician coast where the wind started to increase making the waves very short, high and confused and it worsened as we were closing-in towards the headland of Cabo Toriñana; in fact it became so bad that I had to slow down, instantly followed by my friends "in convoy" doing the same, but this made the boats wallow about rather a lot.

Sailing along any coast-line can give you a false sense of security so that one is inclined to relax, but past experience has taught me not to let your guard down until you reach the safety of a port because it is under the coast-line where fishing buoys and other obstructions in the water can create unforeseen incidents which perhaps could be avoided by keeping a good look-out.

Suddenly, I received a call on the radio from my friends on the other boat.
'Bill, we have stopped!'
'What's the matter Heinz?'
I could hear panic in his voice and he frantically answered,

'I am not sure!'

'Ok, calm down and slowly tell me what's wrong.'

'We were steering on a straight line behind you, when all of a sudden both engines stopped instantly!'

'Have you tried re-starting them again?'

'No... Oh Bill, what are we to do?'

'Well, for a start, stay calm and make sure the engines are in neutral, then try to re-start them and come back to me to confirm whether they are running.'

'Ok.'

A minute or so later he called back and confirmed the engines were running again.

'Alright, now put one of the engines gently into forward gear.'

Heinz left the phone engaged and I heard him say,

'Oh no' and he immediately came to the phone again,

'Bill the engine has stalled again!'

'Alright, Heinz now try the other engine.'

Heinz tried the other engine and the same happened again.

Having had this situation once before in my life, I feared the worse and said,

'Don't use the engines again, I think you have a rope or fishing net in both propellers; the best thing we can do is to tow you to the nearest port, but first things first, let me organize myself then I will come back to you.'

'Alright Bill, but hurry, because I think we are capsizing!'

I could see that the wind had put the boat "beam-on" - *the full width of the vessel lying parallel to the waves* - in the heavy seas which made it very uncomfortable for the crew but capsizing... that was a little over the top!

As it happened, the owner of my boat had left me all the necessary gear for towing, including a 100 metre towing rope and some primitive breathing apparatus. I imagine that he must have had similar experiences in his past and I must say this was not such a bad idea after all.

I asked John, to keep an eye on the boat and to check that the autopilot was keeping the boat on course, whilst I prepared the tow rope.

John was my crew whom I had borrowed from the other boat with the excuse that if they wanted to sail across the Bay then I would need one of their crew, because I had no intention of crossing the Bay on my own. John was a tall slender thirty year old German who had never been to sea before but his friend, the owner of the other boat, had roped him into joining him on this eventful voyage and now the poor soul had been sick all night and really wasn't much use to me, but for now he did provide me with a little security.

The preparation of the tow lines took me somewhat longer than I thought because the waves were too confused, which made me unstable on my feet and I had to be extra vigilant. I could hear Heinz's voice anxiously calling out,

'Bill... hurry we can't stay here much longer!'

I calmly walked up to the phone and said,

'I am coming in a minute.'

I called John over and handed him a long thin line with a big knot at the end - *representing a weight* - and tried to teach him how to throw the line across to the other boat.

'John, **do not** throw the line across before I give you the command; we don't want to get a line in **our** propeller, do we now?'

I could see that John was very nervous; however, I was able to calm him down by making a little light of his friend's predicament.

John staggered onto the aft deck and attached himself to the life line which I had prepared earlier in the day.

Now it was up to me to get my boat as near as I dared to the limping yacht; I quickly glanced at my watch - it was just after two in the afternoon – that gave me ample time to get us into a port before dark.

Slowly but surely I approached the bow of the other boat and noticed two of the crew hanging on for dear life. I did feel sorry for them but couldn't do more than I was already doing. Then the crew began to shout across,
'Throw the line, throw the line' - but I intervened quickly and said,
   'John, remember what I told you!'
   'Yes Bill I'll wait!'

I heard John shout back at them to shut up and wait; I finally moved close enough and told John to throw the line but, not surprisingly, the first two attempts failed with the line falling in a zigzag pattern across the back of my boat; on the third attempt - I was now getting anxious myself - John succeeded in throwing the line across, but unfortunately it hit the head of one of the crew, nearly knocking him for six; however he did have the sense to stand on the line, proudly stating,
   'I got it!'
   Once I had seen that the line was safely across I ran to the aft-deck and tied the other end of the small line onto the tow rope.
   I told Heinz to pull in some of the line and secure the loop properly on their anchor winch and, with my boat still moving in slow ahead, I automatically fed the tow line into the sea behind me and all I had to do was to wait until the line was fully extended; but to my horror I noticed at the last minute that they were pulling the rope over the handrail and securing it onto the anchor winch; I had to stop immediately because if I had pulled on the tow line, they would have done a lot of damage to their handrail.

I called out over the radio,

'Heinz, get your men to lay the tow line properly **under** the handrail.'

'Sure Bill. Are we then ready to move?'

'Yes, and if you can steer your boat in a straight line behind me then that will help to keep you more steady, ok?'

Then I had a dreadful thought:

'You **can** steer…? You do have steerage, don't you Heinz?'

There was a moment of silence … then he replied,

'Yes we do.'

Thank goodness for that!

'Are you ready Heinz?'

'Ready.'

'Ok, standby.'

I needed to turn both boats into a southerly direction. I stopped my boat momentarily then turned her away from the limping boat, obviously checking all the time that the tow rope wasn't getting entangled in our propellers - this would have been disastrous for all of us.

I had slowed down to a mere drift, but the tow rope still sprung violently out of the water like a catapult; now the stricken boat began to swing around and gently started to follow us in a straight line. I was very glad, and it was lucky for all of us that this boat possessed the powerful engines it needed to do the job properly.

Although the Camarinas were closer to us, I thought it better to head for Finisterre because the direction to the Camarinas was going to be most uncomfortable and it would have put excessive strain on the tow line; furthermore the approach to the Camarinas presented the additional problem of manoeuvring the boats over shallow grounds. Therefore, I had no alternative than to follow the coast down to Finisterre and hoped that the cape would protect us from the heavy beam sea.

I slowly closed-in on the coast but there the waves were bouncing back off the rocks and now I thought it better to steer manually so as to guide the tow safely between the off-lying rocks and the main coast.

The depth under the boat had now diminished dramatically to a mere 20 metres and, just as I thought, the large ocean waves were being replaced by smaller but more dangerous waves; however, we only needed to cover another 3 miles to the cape. The tow line had come under an immense strain as both boats were dancing independently over the waves, pulling and jerking on the tow rope and I crossed my fingers and hoped that we would make port safely.

Thank goodness, Lady Luck was with us and after a painstaking 3 hours, covering a total distance of 8½nm - and without any further mishaps - we rounded Cape Finisterre.

After rounding the cape we entered much calmer waters in the bay of Ens del Sardiñeiro and sailed for 4 miles back up the coast to the small fishing port of Finisterre but this port didn't seem to facilitate hoisting so I carried on until we reached a suitable beach area. I slowly edged my way towards it, where I pulled in the tow rope and left the limping boat drifting onto the beach; as the tide was rising I didn't need to worry that she would be stranded on the beach for long. I then secured both boats side by side and carefully manoeuvred them into a final holding position so that the crew could jump into the water and remove whatever had seized the propellers.

After a good 30 minutes of struggling under the boat the crew reported that they had cleared part of a fishing net, which they stretched a good 20 metres along the sandy beach. There was an air of relief with the lads; now all I had to do was to pull the boat away from the beach. After this I told them that they had to clear everything away, because we still needed to set sail for Bayona.

Heinz started up his engines and slowly moved into the bay and I was given the "thumbs-up" indicating that the operation had been a success.

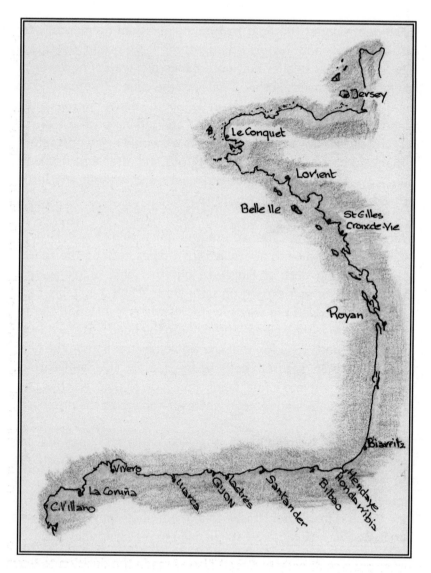

Camariñas - La Coruña
Saturday 30th March 2002

Early this morning I watched the sun rise over the hills on the other side of the bay, indicating that we were in for another glorious day.

The owners went ashore whilst I prepared the engines for the day. The engine check didn't take me long and I am happy to say that the repaired exhaust manifold was working brilliantly - at least this was something less to worry about.

Whilst waiting for the owners to return I made myself a coffee but it wasn't long before I received a call on the mobile asking if I could help them carry the shopping from the village store. Perhaps this meant - *I still didn't have any idea* - that "we" were going across the bay from here.

I walked past the charming small inner harbour, which was totally drained because of low water and I am always fascinated by such a picturesque scene: mooring lines lying criss-cross and disorganised along the bottom; little boats and dinghies on their sides; seaweed covered plastic cans attached to the mooring lines keeping the boats in their positions while awaiting the high tide; screaming seagulls standing on the guard rails and some on the mud trying to catch the worms before the water returns; numerous little fishermen's cottages surrounding the harbour and then the smell of the drying weed arousing the senses and completing the scene.

When I entered the shop I thought we had stocked the boat for a crossing to the Americas, but sadly, I learnt that today the run was only going to be to the large port of La Coruña.

We departed at 11:00 for the high seas again. Although there is a smaller passage directly to Cabo Villano I made the decision to leave the bay in the same way as I had arrived because I wasn't too sure about doing this small passage and I thought it best to use the safer but much longer southern passage; why take unnecessary risks when I had all the time in the world!

The sea stayed calm all afternoon and we made good time for La Coruña; apart from a few dolphins swimming alongside, there wasn't much going on - perhaps because it was Easter Saturday.

16:30 - started the long passage along the endless breakwater and made my way towards the ancient tower and the adjacent yacht club which is located at the port entrance, but the moorings at this yacht club are for much smaller boats than ours so I headed for the local fishing harbour just inside the main port on the starboard side with the "Club Real" Royal Yacht Club building proudly standing on the outer wall.

When I entered this historical basin, I had a nice surprise, because the Harbour authorities had created a proper Yacht Harbour - mind you, that was well overdue.

There wasn't any room for us so I found a pontoon just outside the small port and moored along a very slippery set of steps but at least we would be able to get off the boat when we wanted to go and see the town later this evening.

The port of La Coruña has been, so far, a most welcome and safe haven for me, particularly at the end of some of my most hair-raising crossings but I suppose the most memorable event was a long time ago in a cold February night when I had set off on what turned out to be a disastrous passage and, having fought for our lives, unfortunately lost the boat smack-bang in the middle of the Bay of Biscay. (Next page)

The Miraculous Escape
February 1974

Disaster struck, as the "Christina Claudia" a fast 36 foot Motor Cruiser on her passage from La Coruña to Brest in Northwest France was swamped by a rogue wave in the night of the 18th February 1974.

The 40 foot wave had come suddenly out of nowhere and hit the boat on her port side, but rather than lifting her over the wave it pushed her beam-on for endless minutes, which seemed like hours, then rolled her over onto her starboard side and pushed her helplessly in front of the wave before throwing her into the air - like a killer whale trying to kill a seal - and finally she fell back on her bottom with disastrous consequences: bulkheads distorted, doors flung off their hinges and broken windows; the saloon, aft cabin and engine room were swamped by several feet of water above the floorboards; the engine room was so full of water that the level came dangerously close to the engine air intake. Luckily, we had a most miraculous escape.

This horrific accident is still in my mind as if it happened last night...

Leaving for Portugal

I was watching the evening news when the phone rang. It was John of Moonraker,

'Hi Bill, I was just wondering if you are doing anything at the moment?'

'Well no, it's all quiet.'

I wondered what he wanted me to do. It was a bit early in the year to venture out on the seas for a delivery.

'Bill, we sold a new boat to a Portuguese gentleman at the last

239

London Boat Show in Earls court, but the boat still has to be built. The deal is that we have to get his old boat back to the yard in Brundall, Norfolk so that we can place her on the market to sell. I think you know the boat; if I'm not mistaken you and your friend Jack took her down to Portugal two years ago.'

'I remember...'

Hesitantly I asked,

'When do you want me to get her back?'

'The sooner the better Bill'

"No" not being in my vocabulary, I stupidly replied,

'That's fine John, but I'll have to find crew and that won't be easy!'

I was thinking that no person in their right mind would set out on a voyage through the Bay of Biscay at this time of the year - only mad dogs and a Dutchman!

'Don't worry Bill; we have a young man here at the yard who has been looking forward to sailing with you on the next available voyage.'

'Alright John, you get me the crew and I'll see what I can do at my end, but I don't know how long this is going to take.'

'That doesn't matter, as long as I can say that the boat is on her return voyage to us.'

It took a good two days for me to get things organised: bedding, clothes, tools, navigation equipment, "Sestrel" hand-bearing compass, charts and the long wave portable radio; the food shopping would have to wait for my arrival in Portugal.

Packed and ready to go, I said my goodbyes and left for Heathrow Airport where I was to meet up with my crew.

Richard, a 23 year old, dark haired, tall and slender, softly spoken young man, was waiting at the check-in desk for "TAP AIR". Although I never had met him, I guessed who he was and introduced myself.

He looked a pleasant lad alright and I felt sure we would get on well together; anyway... it was too late to change my mind now!

240

'Have you sailed before?' I asked.
'Yes I have, but not on a small boat across the Bay of Biscay.'

The flight to Lisbon arrived on time and we only had to wait a little while at Lisbon Airport for our internal flight connection to Oporto in the north of Portugal.

The "TAP AIR" aircraft for this domestic run was a "Caravel". It was a very bumpy flight – a taste of what was to come on the Atlantic waves - and as we flew over the ocean, it didn't look too inviting to say the least; on the final approach the plane was shaking and jumping about with the engines constantly altering their pitch, as if the pilot was fighting to keep it level.

Looking out of the window, I could see the wing flapping quite rapidly like a bird, though not as elegantly, and the cross-winds made the landing rather cock-eyed but finally the plane came down with a thud onto the tarmac.   We disembarked with a sigh of relief and were met by a dark haired, well dressed, young person.

'Welcome to Portugal, I believe you are Bill. I am Mr. Sangio, but you can call me Carlos; John told me to look out for a stocky, short, blond Dutchman.'

I am sure that must have been easy for him as most people disembarking were Portuguese with dark hair.

'It's late so I'll take you straight to the hotel where you can freshen-up before dinner.'

Later that evening he treated us to a delicious meal at a popular fish restaurant down at the harbour, which was a very pleasant end to a long day.

The following morning we were taken down to the Marina Porto Atlántico, situated at the northern part of the commercial Port of Leixoes, where we had to wait at the landing stage of the Marina Yacht Club for the arrival of Antonio, the Marinario.

The marina consisted of a large area filled with floating moorings and a small jetty for dinghies for ferrying the crews back and forth to their boats. Looking down into the basin, I noticed that the marina was filled with small sized cabin-top fishing boats and amongst them, well out of place, was a sleek-looking motor cruiser with a white hull and top sides, stainless steel pulpit, all-round wire safety rail and a 18 foot short-wave radio whip aerial.

The cockpit, which was enclosed by a blue zip-up cover, had a hardtop roof with a short mast which had a navigation light mounted on it.

At the other end of the basin was a slipway for commercial vessels and this was fully occupied by fishing boats having their hulls repainted ready for the new season.

Antonio, a middle-aged fisherman, finally arrived 20 minutes later. He took us through the locked gate, but Carlos stayed behind saying,

'If there is anything you need, just ask Antonio.'

We followed Antonio down the numerous slippery steps onto the landing stage where we boarded a dinghy which was just about big enough to hold three persons, but we just managed to squeeze our luggage on too.

With the dinghy well-laden, Antonio started to row us slowly across to the "Christina Claudia"; we climbed on board and luckily the luggage had survived without getting soaked.

My first impression was that the boat looked well-maintained despite the difficulties Antonio must have had in getting to the amenities ashore; he opened the cabin door which led into the saloon with an open plan galley, dinette and two bunks in the bow of the boat.

It had a well laid-out bathroom with toilet, sink, hot and cold shower supplied by a gas fired water heater and a full-length mirror screwed onto the inside of the bathroom door. It was a small bathroom but nevertheless comfortable.

The only source of heating was a truck fan heater and for entertainment there was a car cassette-radio in the saloon.

The centre cockpit was fitted with a dashboard housing full engine instrumentation, compass, speed-log, depth sounder; and on the other side at the Navigator's seat was a short wave SSB (Single Side Band) RT (Receiver & Transmitter) radio. However, the boat didn't have any other navigational equipment, as in those days autopilot and radar were only for the few who could afford such luxuries.

She was powered by two Perkins 6.354T engines which, at the time, were the most up-to-date in turbo-technology. These engines produced a total of 290 shaft horse power and gave a top speed of 17 knots. Batteries, hand bilge pump and a steel container holding two gas bottles were neatly fitted at the rear of the engine room.

This boat also had an aft cabin with a small size double berth and an even smaller bathroom than the one in front; one could use the toilet easily, but having a shower Mmmm...

I opened the engine room hatch and could see that everything looked in order; a bit rusty in places but this was not difficult to understand in this harsh environment of the North Atlantic.

Antonio explained that a full engine service had been carried out not long ago and proudly added that she was ready for sea; I took his word for it as I didn't have any reason not to believe him.

Richard and I made a list of what we still required for the voyage and this included two 50 gallon oil drums which we needed for additional fuel as the boat's own tank capacity of 220 gallons was not enough to make the crossing from La Coruna to Brest, some 360nm away.

The Voyage Home

Eventually, the oil drums were delivered and Antonio kindly ferried them across, one by one, on his little dinghy and we placed the drums at the rear in the cockpit behind the pilot and navigator seats; this happened to be the best place for the displacement of the boat but with one snag: it restricted the access to the rear of each engine, but the advantage was that the hatches wouldn't let any water in.

We were ready to depart Oporto for Brundall in England. It wouldn't have been possible to leave earlier because of the bad weather, but now it had improved, I needed to go for it. As we left Oporto I could see that Richard didn't seemed too keen with my decision but I said,

'Richard, if we wait for the sea to be like a mirror then we're in for a long wait; it's better that we leave now, but should the weather deteriorate there is always the possibility of finding shelter somewhere along this coastline.'

We left the protection of the harbour and headed out in a northerly direction towards Cabo Finisterre. I kept the speed down for a bit in order to settle down the engines - because I didn't know how long they had been laid-up - and match the speed to suit the sea conditions and found that 14 knots was the most comfortable speed for us and the boat. The weather seemed reasonable - grey, overcast with just a little wind, *force 3,* from the west accompanied by a swell between 2½ and 3½ metres from the north-west.

I was glad the fishermen were all painting their boats, because otherwise we would have been surrounded by hundreds of fishing markers which, in these sea conditions, would have been very difficult to spot.

The boat settled down and so far the trip was uneventful but this was abruptly interrupted late afternoon when Richard, who was steering at the time, noticed that the port engine's oil pressure had dropped and there was no doubt that something had seriously gone wrong.

Richard immediately stopped the engines which made the boat roll about endlessly and I had great difficulty opening the engine room hatch but once I was able to secure it I poked my head down and found that a flexible armoured high-pressure hose from the oil cooler to the engine had burst and had left the engine room in a thick oily mess; I quickly closed the hatch, scratched my head and looked over the chart checking exactly where we were. Once I'd established our position which was 5 miles east of Cabo Villano, I chose to make for La Coruña rather than the Camarinas as I thought that it would be much easier getting parts in La Coruña.

I started the starboard engine and moved at a mere 7 knots, which would delay the arrival time at La Coruña by an additional 3 hours. Richard asked,

'Do you think that we are going to have difficulties getting the hose? It's good that the drums are still empty, otherwise it would be impossible to replace that part!'

We arrived totally exhausted in the late evening. I chose to enter the small harbour on my starboard which was especially built for the local fishing fleet; I made this decision because the place allocated for yachts was on the moorings in the open waters just before entering the port, which meant that it would be extremely difficult to repair the engine.

The little harbour was full of fishing vessels rafted - *laying side by side* - together and the only available space I could find was alongside the 12th and last fishing boat.

I wasn't too pleased with this position but, "beggars can't be choosers." This meant that we might have to move very early in the morning.

Some of the boats were occupied by crew eating their home-made fish soup and others having a drink. I wasn't too keen on being woken-up that early and thought it better to investigate what the situation was going to be in the morning, so I went on an obstacle course from boat to boat talking to the crews and asking whether they were leaving tomorrow.

'No mate' replied one. 'Haven't you heard the forecast? It's going to be very rough so, don't worry, none of us will be leaving!'

I did let off a sigh of relief and I told Richard the good news; now at least we could relax and have a late snack before going to bed, knowing we would not be woken early in the morning.

Our Stay in La Coruña

We woke up fairly late and, as the fisherman predicted last night, the weather had deteriorated and I was mighty pleased not to be out at sea; the weather wasn't bothering us for the moment as we had our hands full trying to find and fit the replacement hose. I wasn't looking forward to checking the engine room and seeing the aftermath of yesterday's incident but I would have to grit my teeth together and clean up the mess from the oil spill and whilst at it, I might as well clean the fuel strainers and replace the fuel filters.

It took two days to sort the engine room; then we had to move the boat to the large fishing harbour in order to refuel her for the next leg of the voyage.

We filled the tank and drums and moved back to the fishermen's harbour where we continued getting the boat ready for departure.

There wasn't any let-up in the weather whatsoever, as one depression after another continuously came across the Bay. In the meantime we amused ourselves by tramping off into the town to do some serious sightseeing.

Finally the Day had come

Eighteen days had passed waiting for a gap in the weather. Yes... the end was in sight; a high pressure system, which had dominated the weather over the U.K, had moved south and straight into the Bay of Biscay.

All of a sudden the fishing port became a hive of activity and many of the fishing boats started their engines up, checking them out for an early morning departure.

Various boat crews were arriving on their boats, fishing nets were being prepared and laid out on the deck and the laughing and shouting between the crews made the place come to life again. I could see that they were chuffed to bits to be able to earn some real money again.

'Richard, I think that they are planning to move, we'd better go up to the Yacht Club and check on the latest forecast'

I studied the forecast and could see that the high pressure was extending over France and the Bay of Biscay and it looked like it was going to stay here for at least the next two days; so yes, it was time to leave La Coruña.

'We'll leave at the same time as the fishing fleet, which should give us two days and one overnight run across to Brest.'

Although I went to bed early last night, I couldn't sleep properly and kept waking up; I was excited to leave but at the same time a little apprehensive as I knew, from past experience, that crossing the Bay in a small boat, with only a compass, was going to be long and hard; but time was marching-on and we needed to get moving.

We left on the morning of the 17th February 1974 at 3:30 a.m. Being at the end of the fishing boats gave us the advantage of being able to leave the port first, with the others following close behind; but when we came to the end of the breakwater we soon lost the armada of fishing vessels who scattered themselves into various directions, and now we were the only one left heading into a north easterly direction.

As predicted, there wasn't any wind to speak of unlike the last 18 days when the wind had blown from a southerly to north-westerly direction and surprisingly the sea was relatively gentle with its 6 foot high swell which could hardly be felt; if there was going to be any wind at all today, then it was predicted to come from the south or south-east which would give us a beam or stern sea; this would be very comfortable but to keep an accurate course would be very difficult; anyway a forecast of S to SE 3 - 4 meant that there wasn't anything to worry about - for now.

The sky was deep blue with not a cloud in sight and the sun rising bright yellow made it a real pleasure being out on the sea today.

The weather remained stable throughout the morning, as predicted and the wind came from all directions, but the swell had increased somewhat, and I would say it was now between 12 to 15 feet from a westerly direction, but otherwise the sea was still relatively calm; at 13:45 I estimated that we had covered a distance of 146nm since La Coruña.

Then... without any warning the port engine dropped its revolutions but almost immediately went back to normal and I didn't think anything of it at the time, but soon after it happened again and this time with a sort of stutter, but now the boat had slowed down too, then all of a sudden she increased her speed again, before finally coming to an abrupt stop.

At the time I was trying to pick up the "Five-to-Two" BBC shipping forecast and shouted,

'What the hell is that all about Richard?' thinking that he had accidently knocked against the gear-throttle lever, which was easily done.

'I don't know, what do you want me do?'

'Just carry on - I'll think of something!'

Totally puzzled, I left the radio and walked to the doorway where I sat down on the steps to the cockpit scratching my head and talking to myself, 'what in heavens name can it be? We can't be out of fuel because the tank capacity should carry us at least 250 nautical miles; or, has a cable snapped? No... that's not possible; are my fuel filters dirty already? No, that's unlikely too because the sea has been so calm.' Checking the filters was easier said than done, because now I had to open the engine room hatch and lower myself head first and crawl forward, between the engines, carefully steadying myself with my elbows against the engine supports.

'Richard, I'd better check the fuel strainers and it will take me a little while. Are you alright?'

'Yes I'm fine Bill; it's a little bit more difficult to steer but at least we are still moving.'

'What's our speed now?'

'Mmmm, she seems to hold at around 7 knots'

'That's fine'

I finally succeeded in positioning myself between the engines and started to unscrew the bracket which holds the glass (like a jam jar) and now carefully lowered the glass with fuel onto the engine room floor so as not to spill or break it. I thought: God help us if I should break the glass, then we are really stuffed. Now I carefully took off the rubber seal trying not to drop it into the bilge and finally picked out the fine brass gauze filter.

Yes, the gauze filter had a substantial amount of what I would call fine hairs stuck to it, which could be the reason for a restricted fuel flow. I then examined the glass but the dirt floating about was negligible. Whilst I was reassembling the glass I thought that this would probably be the only time I would need to do this, and with this optimistic analysis, I bled the engine.

> "Bleeding" gets the air out of the fuel system, in order to fire up the engine again after repairing leaks, by means of a small pump.

Thank God this pump was accessible from the centre of the engine room otherwise I would have had a big problem with the other engine because the fuel drum on the deck would have prevented me from getting to the pump.

I climbed out of the engine room and attempted to start the engine, but it didn't want to start and in order not to flatten the batteries I went down and re-bled the engine once more and this time I was successful; half an hour later we were on our way again.

I had to clean myself off in the bathroom and somehow try to get rid of this ghastly diesel smell.

'Are you still alright up there Richard?'

'Yes, I am fine for now Bill.'

Whilst I was washing my hands, I thought that I could hear the engine playing up again. Oh no, not again and fearing the worse I stopped washing my hands immediately.

'Richard, is that the engine again?'

'No, I can't hear anything.'

But then it stalled abruptly.

'Here we go again.'

I was really puzzled with this, because there was hardly any dirt. I lit up a cigarette and thought, at least the weather is good and the forecast, which I was trying to listen to earlier, still gave variable winds for the area, which did put me at ease for now.

All of a sudden the other engine stalled too, and an eerie silence came over the boat.

'What the hell is happening?

'Well... I will have to go down again.'

I was a little deflated with the fact that my last attempt was so unsuccessful and thought, I can't be doing with getting between the engines every time this happens; then I noticed that the set of steps to the saloon was fixed to the edge of the cockpit floor, so I took a screwdriver and began to unscrew the steps then I tried to lift them but they still didn't want to budge. I then noticed that the insides of the steps had sound-proof insulation; well that was easy, I just ripped the stuff off and bingo! They lifted out perfectly and I was now able to get to the jam jars with ease.

'That's funny, both glasses are clear and I am sure the gauze filter couldn't have clogged up in such a short time; I'd better check the fuel pipe lines to see if they are blocked but I can't quite see how.'

I followed the pipes coming away from the fuel filters and noticed that they disappeared under the floor in the galley; I lifted the carpet at the edge by the toilet and found the fuel shut-off valves; it looked as if these were the only obstacle between the tank and the engine; I unscrewed the valve-top and slowly lifted the top away from the base. To my horror I found that inside was a little ridge which had collected glass-fibre hair and a white rubbery substance like thick plastic sheet material from the fuel tank.

I went to the cockpit to show Richard what I had found, holding up the bits in my diesel-covered fingers.

By now the place began to smell of diesel and anyone who has had to deal with diesel fuel at sea will know that sooner or later you begin to feel very queasy, but the sea was relatively calm and the cockpit covers were rolled up so we had enough fresh air not to feel seasick.

I went back down again and carefully picked out the remainder of the plastic bits with the end of a coat hanger; I screwed the valve-top back in its place and then... a light went on in my head. If I take the valve apart and carefully put it back together again then I may not have to bleed the engines.

'Richard, can you start the engine for me and leave her in idle for a while.'

Great! The engine started straight away and leaving her in idle for a few minutes sorted out the bleeding problem.

Having found and solved the problem I was able to move with one engine, but still needed to fix the other one. This process only took me 10 minutes, now that I knew exactly what to do, but the problem of clearing the valves did not diminish; in fact it had become a more regular occurrence and, worse still, the plastic bits also started to clog the jam jar strainers.

I was so busy cleaning the systems that I hadn't realised that the sky had become dark grey and a strong north-westerly breeze had developed at the same time. Because of this, we had to lower the cockpit covers; of course, by doing so we had trapped the awful diesel smells inside the boat and now, with no means for the fumes to escape, our stomachs were turned upside down and we were beginning to feel very sick.

17:00 - 'Richard, don't let me forget the weather forecast, which is due in an hour!'

The last time I checked our position was at 13:45 when I marked the distance of 146nm; since that time we had probably travelled an average of 5 miles an hour which would have put us at around 163nm, but we should have been 194nm, away from La Coruña.

Whilst marking off our position I thought it better to fill in the log regarding the engine problems and fuel situation.

17:50 - the shipping forecast for Biscay and Finisterre gave SW to W 4 or 5 with the barometer falling slowly.

'Richard did you hear that?'

'Yes I did; is that ok for us?'

'I suppose it's not too bad, although I don't expect that change until tomorrow.

It was getting dark and I suggested that we needed to run a bit of a normal watch system; this meant we would steer the boat alternately, and I hoped that when the fuel systems needed to be cleared this would coincide with my hour away from the wheel. We managed to find a system between cleaning the valves and keeping watch, but sooner or later one of us needed to get a rest so at 21:00, after my last time playing with the fuel system, I thought if we slowed down to 1500 rpm giving us 8.5 knots then we might not drag up the dirt so much, thereby giving us longer rest periods between the cleaning.

'Richard, I am going to slow down and try to have a rest, then you can have yours later when the system needs clearing again.'

'OK Bill, I'll manage for now.'

I went to lie in the aft cabin because this was the only place free from diesel smells and much more comfortable with the motion of the boat, but the disadvantage was the engine noise and the constant rumbling of the propellers, which made falling asleep difficult. In these conditions the only way you could really sleep was either to be very exhausted or someone knocking you out with a hammer, but as my mother always said, 'even if you can't sleep, at least you will be resting.'

So, sleeping was a joke; I was constantly listening out for any irregularity in engine noise and after an hour or so I gave up; I looked at the time and to my surprise it showed 23:30, so I must have dozed-off after all without realizing it. Well, I thought I may as well get up but when I tried putting my feet on the deck I immediately lost my balance; I hadn't realised that the waves had become so much higher during the last 2½ hours. But, looking on the bright side, it occurred to me that since slowing down, the engine hadn't required clearing. This was a great improvement; the last thing I wanted to do was to clear fuel systems every half an hour.

'OK Richard, I'll take over from you now'

The poor lad looked really ill.

'How is everything going?'

'It all seems to be fine Bill but I don't feel at all well.'

'Then we'd better leave the engines alone; you go to bed and try to have some rest.'

After Richard went down into the aft cabin I checked on the instrument gauges and the course was 048°, I switched off the cabin lights and settled down at the helm.

Midnight 18th February 1974

I thought I should check on our approximate position and plot this on the chart and to my disappointment I noted we had only covered a measly 21 miles since I went to bed but there was nothing I could do about it. I had calculated that the position was now 195 miles from La Coruña, well over half way; however we should have been 260 miles which would have put us only 100 miles away from the entrance to Brest. Oh well, it was no good thinking "what could have been" - this was the reality.

I was gasping for a hot coffee but this would have been a hairy and acrobatic performance, between steering the boat, steadying myself and holding on to the kettle all at the same time but I was so desperate that I went for it all the same!

After making the coffee, I switched off the lights, and all I had to do was to concentrate on steering the boat whilst leisurely enjoying my coffee; this was short lived as within minutes of settling down the port engine played up again; rather than getting Richard out of bed, I switched off the other engine at the same time so that I could clear both systems. But the minute the boat stopped she rolled about uncontrollably in the now heavy seas. I started to clear the valves and the strainers but was having difficulties in unscrewing the valve screws; not only that, but the lighting in the boat restricted me from seeing properly which made the process of cleaning somewhat longer than I had anticipated.

Holding onto the gear levers I hauled myself out of the engine room and leant over the instrument panel to turn the key but before I managed to switch on the engine I had the most almighty shock of my life. 'What the hell is that!' I shouted out aloud.

'Oh My God...! We are **Never** going to make it!' because I happened to see, in the bright loom of the navigation lights, this horrendous massive wave with a large breaking crest, thundering along at great speed towards us and it was just about in the process of crashing onto the boat; this almighty wave had come suddenly out of nowhere and hit the boat on her port side, but rather than lifting her over the wave, it pushed her beam-on then rolled her over onto her starboard side and pushed her helplessly in front of the wave before throwing her into the air - *like a killer whale trying to kill a seal* - and finally she fell back on her bottom with disastrous consequences; I instantly lost my footing and was just able to grab the steering wheel with the tips of my fingers on one hand and the gear lever with my other hand, while hanging-on for dear life. I waited until the boat had levelled and then I was able to scramble back onto my feet and found that all of the cockpit covers had been torn from their fixings and the zip-up panels were now blowing uncontrollably in the wind. Miraculously, the two 50 gallon drums had not moved an inch which was surprising as they were still full of fuel - *weighing 175 kg each* - and were only strapped on with a ¾ inch mooring rope.

Somehow, still being in shock, I managed to switch both engines on and, as luck would have it, they ran immediately. I heard myself shout with a shivering voice in the direction of the aft cabin,

'Richard, are you alright, come quickly, we have been hit and I think we are taking water!'

Richard came staggering out of the aft cabin moaning that he had been thrown out of his bunk against the bulkhead and said,

'I could see green seawater in the porthole.'

'I am not surprised Richard, the boat was lying completely on her side!'

I had to compose myself but above all, come to terms with this additional most hampering and horrendous circumstance in which we found ourselves.

What a night!

I managed to move both engines into forward-gear and left them in "tick-over" - *the slowest speed I could get out of the engines* - and started to turn the boat away from the waves and the wind, making sure that we were in a following sea, because with the sea and the winds from behind, it would be possible to walk around and inspect the damage.

'Richard, come here and hold on to the wheel and whatever you do try to keep her away from the wind; that should be easy because now that the canopies have blown away you'll be able to feel the wind and water spray in the back of your neck.'

Shaking from fear he uttered,

'OK Bill, I'll try.'

'I have to go below and see what's happened down there.'

I carefully staggered down into the saloon and 'Oh my God!' I stepped straight into a foot of seawater, heavily sloshing about against the cabin furniture and saw the toilet door floating back and forth with the full length mirror face-up in the water, luckily still intact, *thinking in a flash, "brilliant no bad luck."* It was unbelievably draughty and I wondered where it was coming from then, out of the corner of my eye, I noticed that the bathroom bulkhead (wall) had given way at the top and was now held in place by the rear saloon seat.

I slowly waded my way forward into the cabin and found numerous pieces of glass all over the place; it became more draughty further into the cabin and the curtains had blown horizontally which made me realise that a window (or two) might have been broken; but at closer inspection I found, to my great disappointment, that ALL the windows in the saloon had been smashed except for a single one in the front section. Having seen this, I quickly crawled across the wheelhouse deck into the aft cabin and here the water level was at least 18 inches above the floorboards but at least all the windows here were still intact.

Now it was the turn of the engine room and I must admit I didn't hold out much hope and prepared myself for the next shock. I lifted the hatch and saw that the engine room was flooded too and the water level was only inches away from the engine air-intakes and seeing this I wondered for how long the engines were going to run! The 8 batteries, which were placed between the engines in a box, had lost the wooden lid which was now floating about in the engine compartment, hitting both engines regularly.

I jumped down into the engine room on top of the batteries. What a disaster! I didn't know how I was going to get rid of all this water; I cast my eye on the hand bilge pump and said 'What a joke!' I couldn't hear whether the electric bilge pump was actually working because of the engine noise; I knew if I didn't do anything then we were certain to sink. Then, all of a sudden, I came up with an idea; I didn't know whether it would succeed, but what did I have to lose? I shut the water intake for the cooling of the engines and opened the top of the filter housing - about one foot up from the bottom of the boat - so that the engines were now being cooled with the water from within the engine room.

Fantastic, it worked!

This idea turned out to be a most effective bilge pump and I didn't need to worry that the engine pump would run dry as the top of the filters were well below the water line. Very pleased with myself, but soaking wet from the waist down, I pulled myself up by holding the engine room hatch and the pilot seat.

What's next? Now it was time to do something about all those gaping holes in the forward cabin before we were swamped by another wave; should that be the case then I feared that we were destined to sink.

I looked around for something to fill the gaps, and the only thing I could see in my grasp was the bench seat panels. I grabbed one panel and tried pushing it through the broken window but the movement of the boat made it difficult for me to aim it through the narrow gap, but eventually I pushed it through the hole and managed to position it between the safety rail and the window. Then I had to do the same with the other side making sure that I had covered most of the window area. With the panels now lying safely in the gang-boards I just had to find a way of securing them. That's it, mooring rope; I crawled on my knees back into the wheelhouse and grabbed a mooring rope from the cockpit and dragged it behind me into the forward cabin; I looped one end of the rope through the ventilation hole of the panel and did the same with the other; then I pulled the panels as tightly as possible together; all of this was happening while I was bathing in freezing water and dangerously slipping and sliding through the cabin, but I was oblivious to the cold.

The bathroom door with the full length mirror was still floating about in the middle of the floor but as it was not directly in my way I felt this could wait until I could find a more suitable place for it; throwing it overboard was out of the question because you never know, we may need it as drift wood later, to make a raft. I was very pleased to see the gaping holes blocked. Now it was the turn of the smaller front windows; again I grabbed the nearest thing within my reach which happened to be the front bunk infill cushions (these make double V bunks) which were also floating about on the cabin floor. Although the cushions weren't a perfect fit at least they would keep most of the sea out, and as long as we didn't head into the wind we would be safe for the time being.

I carefully crawled underneath the ropes and made my way back to the cockpit where Richard was desperately trying to hold on and attempting to steer the boat away from the waves. I could see him shivering from the cold and I should imagine fear too, but I must admit, it had become a lot colder since the cockpit covers had blown away and the sea spray kept coming into the boat. I could clearly see that hyperthermia was beginning to set-in, but more seriously, and unfortunately, he was unable to keep the boat on a steady course so I had to think of something and said,

'Richard, I'll take her for a while, you take the bucket and get some of the water out of the aft cabin!'

I thought, by asking him to do this he would warm up a little and as he was tall he would be able to reach the water level without standing in the water, and then all he needed to do was to empty the bucket above his head onto the aft deck.

After a while I managed to get the boat back into a safe direction and now had time to send a help message; so whilst steering the boat with one hand I reached across with the other to grab the SSB telephone. I did realise this might be a fruitless exercise because I was well aware that we were 40 miles away from the main shipping route between Spain and the English Channel but 'if I don't try, I won't get.'

Between steering, holding-on and reaching across with stretched arms, I finally managed to switch on the radio and set the needle onto the 2182 frequency then, with a shaky voice, I began to send a "May Day" call, waiting occasionally for a response. I kept repeating my call for help but as I hadn't received any reply, I gave up because I had other major things to attend to, most importantly keeping the boat afloat. I wanted to switch the lights off to save power for when I really needed them; I looked around to see how Richard was getting on; I could see that he was getting very tired, so much so that he was pouring buckets of water more over himself than overboard.

'Are you alright down there?' I asked. Richard couldn't hear me because of the engine noise, water sloshing about in the boat, seas breaking at either side, wind howling through the cockpit and the loose cockpit covers flapping about uncontrollably in the gale. I felt so sorry for him but there was no alternative.

Then, all of a sudden another wave threw itself into the cockpit and momentarily created a waterfall straight down into the aft and forward cabins. 'Oh... No! Not again! Keep your self composed and concentrate harder' I told myself. I had realised that whilst I was looking at Richard, the boat had come off her heading and was nearly beam-on again. I brought the boat back on course and looked down in the forward cabin where I could see that the water level had now risen by another 4 inches or so.

'Richard I am sorry, but I will have to switch off the cockpit lights because I need to keep a lookout!'

I checked the black horizon in the hope of seeing some form of life out there; my eyes had become very heavy and strained by the seawater and I could hardly see but then..., Noooo... No, No, that's not possible! I am sure there was a light on the horizon ahead of me; I had the sense to check my heading on the compass which now showed 180°. I couldn't believe my luck, but just in case these were imaginary lights, which is quite possible when you are staring into the darkness or through tiredness, I turned away from the dark, shook and banged my head with the palm of my hand, as if this would shake my brain back into place, and peered out of the windscreen again. I had to scour the horizon once more, which was "bloody" difficult because the intense searching slackened off my concentration in steering the boat properly.

There... there... It's still there!
I shouted

'Richard, Richard, come here, can you see something out there?'
Richard looked out of the windows,

'I can't see anything!'

'Here!' and I pointed my finger straight ahead into the darkness.

'Mmmm... I'm not sure.'

Never mind, that wasn't a lot of help, but I could clearly see a light which was either flashing or dipping behind the waves, but this could also mean that the light was moving further away. It was time to think what to do next and given the circumstances I said,

'Richard, do you remember where the flares are?'

'Yes, they are behind the seat in the cabin, together with the first aid box.'

'Can you go and get them; we may be able to attract their attention!'

Richard went down into the cabin and a little later came up with a pack of 3 hand flares; He opened the sealed plastic packet, took out one of the flares, read the instructions and with a quivery voice he said,

'These flares are out of date!'

'Never mind, let's just try them; what do we have to lose? If that light is going away we may not see another vessel for some time; you know we are well away from the main shipping route and without our radio no-one will ever know that we exist!'

Richard was standing at my side, looking uncertain.

'Bill, I am really not happy to ignite this!'

'Sorry Richard but we **must** do it; just keep it well away from the cabin!'

I could see that he was unbelievably reluctant but eventually he held the flare away from the cockpit and struck the top once... but it wouldn't ignite.

'You see! It won't even ignite!'

'Oh please try it again!'

He struck it for a second time but again, it wouldn't ignite.

'It won't work!'

'Just try one more time!'

This time the flare ignited and gave off a fierce white light. Richard held the flare as high as possible and started to sway it about; after a minute or so it extinguished. The fierce light had blinded our vision and it took several minutes before we became accustomed to the darkness of the night once more.

'Where is the light gone?'

We had concentrated so much on firing off the flare that we hadn't noticed that the boat was being thrown about again which meant that our half-sinking "Christina Claudia" had turned away from her course once more. I quickly turned her back on course before another wave had a chance of filling the boat. Once back on course I started to search the horizon again,

'There it is, there is the light!'

Unfortunately, Richard still hadn't spotted it, which made me wonder if I was seeing things, but I knew the light was there and finally I spotted it again although this time it seemed to be further away and sadly, within minutes, it had disappeared.

'Sorry Richard, the light has gone!'

I could see the helpless expression on his face – all hope of being rescued now dashed. I started to find excuses for myself, and thought it must have been a French trawler, never thinking it could have been anything else.

'What time is it Richard?'

'Its... 02:30'

Now that this episode was behind us I needed to fully concentrate on steering the boat properly and to try as much as possible to hold her away from the waves. The thought of heading towards Brest had not entered my mind; all I wanted to achieve was to keep the boat from sinking, and "touch wood" the engines were ticking over nicely and still slowly pumping the bilges, which seemed to do the trick because the engine temperature remained at 80°C and the water level had begun to drop, albeit very slowly, but enough for Richard to take a break from bailing out the water by bucket.

Richard had sat down on the navigator seat and just to distract him from his negative thoughts I said,

'While you're sitting there Richard can you try to send a "May Day" again' but after a few times this still seemed to be fruitless. Richard slumped forward and hit his head on the edge of the radio. I think he was suffering from a combination of hyperthermia and nervousness, which made him shiver uncontrollably and he couldn't seem to stop.

'Go and get my sleeping bag and put it around you Richard.'

What a situation; now for the first time since the disaster I felt around in my wet trouser pocket and searched for a cigarette; after struggling to get my hand out of my soggy, tight jeans I took a squashed and partly wet cigarette out of the packet, but I didn't care, anything was better than nothing. I needed it to make me think more clearly - that was my excuse and I am sticking to it!

We both sat quietly in the cockpit: exhausted, wet and unable to change into dry clothing. I hoped for two things to happen: firstly, that the engines wouldn't stall because this time we wouldn't be able to clear the valves as they were now well below the waterline of the flooded cabin; secondly, I really hoped that we would be rescued soon but I wasn't too optimistic about the latter.

'Bill, shall I try to send a "May Day" again?'

'Yes, why not, it can't do us any harm.'

I must admit I didn't sound very convincing. Richard picked up the phone again and called "May Day" but after repeating the call several times,

'Oh No, that's all we need!'

I am sure that all the lights started to dim which meant that it wouldn't be long before we ran out of power.

'We'd better stop using the RT Richard because we need to save power for as long as we can, otherwise we won't have lights to see our way through the boat; after all, we haven't had much success with the RT so far!'

Richard couldn't argue with that and stopped calling for help.

The wind had become near storm force and the waves were now bigger than before, but at least they had become a more even length, which made steering our limping boat manageable.

'I hope the weather is not going to deteriorate much more, otherwise we will have REAL problems Richard.'

'I hope so too, what are we going to do?'

'At the moment… all we can do, is to save our energy, ride out the waves and wait for daylight.'

We were now smack bang in the middle of the Bay of Biscay, which meant that we were at least 160 miles away from the nearest shore; this thought didn't give me a lot of hope of being rescued soon and I wondered whether we were ever going to see our folk back home again.

'Bill… what are you thinking?'

'Well I just hope that the engines don't fail on us and the weather doesn't get worse, then we should manage to keep her going until we get help!'

I had come to the realisation that we would never be able to make it safely without help.

In the meantime, we were getting hungry and thirsty and, in my wisdom, I always carry a collapsible container with drinking water for the "just in case" of an electrical pump failure and right now, the canister came in very handy.

The water level in the boat didn't seem to have dropped anymore and I asked Richard to steer the boat again whilst I went to investigate why this was happening. I discovered that the water was sloshing about in the engine room to such an extent that the engine cooling intakes weren't picking up the water any longer; I'll have to change-over to the normal system before the engines run dry and overheat.

Coming to the Rescue

Some distance away from the "Christina Claudia" was the 500 ton cargo vessel "Trader I" which was Panama registered and carried a German crew of eight.

The freak wave which had struck the "Christina Claudia" had also hit several other vessels in the vicinity including the "Trader I", causing her cargo of orange pulp to move over to one side. Captain Günter, a stocky person of around 40 with a slight beer belly, short curly blond hair and a calming demeanour, decided to change his course away from the main shipping lane in order for his crew to secure the drums again.

Captain Günter was on the bridge, when he heard the call from Land's End Radio.

'All Stations... all Stations... This is Land's End Radio. We are receiving a May Day call from a station somewhere in the Bay of Biscay, but it is extremely weak and we do not have their position; please listen out on this frequency for any information, and in the meantime, please keep a look-out for this vessel and report to this station; Out!'

Captain Günter said to the helmsman

'We'd better keep a sharp look-out just in case; but if it is a small vessel it will be very unlikely that we will see her in these waves.'

The Boson, who was much older than Günter, was a big, strong, dark haired person with a weather-beaten face; he came to the bridge and said,

'Günter, we are not doing well, can we get the vessel more stable?'

'Well, we can turn away from the waves and try to hold her with the stern into the seas, but I will have to be careful that we don't get "pooped" *meaning, the waves running from the rear on to the vessel which could swamp and possibly sink her.*

'I'll appreciate it if you can make it snappy!'

Now, another call came through the RT, this time from a 10,000 ton Greek cargo ship who were asking for immediate assistance and gave their position as 20 miles west of the "Trader I."

Günter took note, but had his hands full in keeping his own vessel safe.

'I don't know what's happened tonight, but it sounds much more serious than just bad weather.'

'What are we to do, Skipper?'

'We'll continue as we are, and see how long the boys need to secure the cargo!'

The Boson came up to the bridge from the cargo hold,

'We are ready Skipper!'

Günter looked at the ship's clock; it was now 03:30; he walked over to his chart and marked off his estimated position, which was showing that they were 169 nautical miles SW off Queasant.

'Right boys, we are going to change course and head for the inshore shipping lane at Queasant!'

The Captain switched off all the deck lights and sailed at a reduced speed into a north-easterly direction.

-o-

I asked,

'Richard, what time is it?'

'Ehhh... It's five past four!'

'Oh Good, then we only have another 3½ hours to wait for daylight'

I was now really getting tired but daylight would help me to stay awake and make steering the boat a lot easier too.'

Fairly nonchalantly Richard said,

'Bill... I am not sure, but I think there is a light over there!'

Hastily, and almost not believing it, I said,

'Where?!'

'There, way over there on the starboard side!'

'Alright, I'll take a quick bearing on the light, so we can keep an eye on it.'

I turned the boat directly towards the light and established that they had come up from behind our original course.

'Richard, just keep looking at the light for me will you! I'll have to get back onto our heading before we get swamped again!'

'Do you think she will see us?'

I hesitantly answered,

'I hope so, but I am not sure, she's only showing a single light, therefore she's either: a small vessel, perhaps a French fishing boat **again**, or she is still in the far distance. Do we have any flares left?'

'Yes, we have two!'

'Alright then, we'll save them until the very last moment - this will be our last chance.'

I nervously kept looking at my watch but the time seemed to go so slowly.

'How is the light doing?' I asked - *Hoping that this time the light would be coming towards us and not dimming over the horizon again.*

'It looks like it might be getting brighter.'

I took my eyes of the compass and looked at the light myself and was thrilled to see that the single light had become two, one to the right being higher than the other, which meant that the vessel was moving from far over on our starboard to the port side, crossing over our bows.

'Bill... is she's going to pass in front?'

'It does look like it.'

My tiredness momentarily hampered my decision making.

'We'll wait a little longer, Mmmm... or perhaps we shouldn't, on the other hand, I can see her red light too; this indicated that she was showing her port side and also meant that she couldn't be too far away from us. Well..., I have made up my mind; it's now or never. Let's light a flare and hope that they can see us and God be with us.'

-o-

Meanwhile; the crew on the "Trader I" had come up to the bridge to give their report on the status of the cargo and Captain Günter enlightened them as to what had been happening in the past hour. Their conversation was abruptly interrupted by an urgent SOS message coming from the Greek cargo vessel, which said that they were sinking fast. Captain Günter answered the call, saying

'We're on our way!'

The Boson, who was leaning against the wheelhouse door said,

'Skipper…, I have just seen a bright light over there!'

'Where' Günter asked,

'There, on the port side; it can't be too far, I guess 2 miles at the most.'

A minute later, he said,

'There it is again.' and pointed into the direction of where he had seen the light the first time.

-o-

Richard had just struck a flare, but the light didn't last long; and I reluctantly suggested that we let off our last flare anyway.

'Well that was it.' mumbled Richard as the bright light from our last flare slowly extinguished and we were plunged back into total darkness once again.

Then… the vessel which had shown her navigation lights had now become brightly lit, and at the same time she seemed to have changed her direction and was now heading straight for us.

-o-

Captain Günter said,

'Boson, whatever you do keep an eye on the location of that vessel; I'll call Lands End Radio and ask permission to investigate what this is all about; it might be the vessel they mentioned earlier!'

'Lands End Radio; Lands End Radio this is "Trader I" come in please!'

"Trader I" this is Lands End Radio what can we do for you?'

'We have just seen a flare being fired not far from our port side. May we investigate or do you still prefer us to head towards the Greek cargo ship?'

There was a short pause and then,

"Trader I" this might be the station who called for help earlier in the night. Go ahead, good luck and please call us with an update; thank you Captain, standing by on 2182.'

'OK lads,' said Günter 'let's go and investigate. Helmsman, turn to port slowly but be careful, we don't want to get swamped ourselves, then head into the direction where the light was seen; Boson where was it?'

'Over there, Skipper!'

'Just slow down to half speed now'

'Will do, Skipper.'

It didn't take long for the "Trader I" to cover the distance to the "Christina Claudia". Now, lying almost alongside her, Günter said,

'Oh my God, I'm surprised they are still afloat!'

'How are we going to handle this, Skipper?' the Boson asked.

'To be honest, I am not quite sure; our difficulty is that we are unable to communicate with them, but what I have in mind is to "heave-to" *(bringing the "Trader I" to a standstill)* and make a lee *(a shelter)* and hope that we can create a smooth sea for them, but until then... all we can do is wait and see what they are going to do themselves!'

The Boson went with some of his men onto the starboard foredeck and tried to communicate by shouting across, but this was to no avail because his voice was being drowned out by the extreme deafening noise of the howling wind and the breaking seas over the vessel; he needed to find out what the skipper on the yacht had in mind so he cupped his hands around his mouth and shouted,

'What… are… you… going… to… do?' but still he couldn't get any response. He looked up at the bridge shrugging his shoulders in a form of sign language "What now Captain?"

-o-

I, on the other hand had to make some difficult but concrete decisions now that rescue was within our grasp. All sorts of thoughts rushed through my mind but being cold, wet and exhausted made it very tough to make snap decisions and I desperately needed a bright idea as to how I was going to make this rescue work, but above all, I could **NOT** afford to fail!

I had now become accustomed to the high waves, but I hadn't quite realised their enormity until I saw the larger vessel heavily rolling. This made me realise that this rescue attempt was going to be a lot more difficult than I had ever imagined and the thought of ending up in the ocean at night was frightening; the way things looked right now, I can tell you that this thought could easily become reality.

My mind started to work overtime but somehow, I became very calm; I am sure this was because we **HAD** to get off this sinking ship. Richard knew the difficulties we had to overcome and thought it better not to say a word, which helped me to organise my mind. The main question was: how do we get across onto the other vessel without falling into the ocean?

That's it; I have a plan "A". But what's your plan "B" I hear you ask. To be honest, I couldn't see a plan "B" as yet, but if there is a need for plan "B" then I will think of it when the time comes.

'Richard, I am going to try to manoeuvre alongside the vessel and when we get near, prepare yourself to jump across'

I could not believe that I was saying this, because it sounded a hell of a lot easier that it was likely to be.

'What about you, Bill?'

'Don't worry about me, I'll sort myself out when the time comes and listen carefully, we **won't** get a second chance at this!' and with panic in his trembling voice he said,

'I can see that, Good luck Bill.'

Now it was time to set my plan "A" into action. As I started manoeuvring the yacht towards the vessel, it suddenly began to dawn on me that this looked an impossible task, but I needed to have a go at it all the same; I edged closer and closer to the vessel until there was only a matter of metres between us. I couldn't help but noticing that as the "Trader I" was being picked up by each wave it seemed to send us into the trough and the only time we were level was when we passed each other on the way.

It was unbelievably scary. At a glance I could see the crew waiting for us in anticipation of what I was going to do next. I must admit, that this attempt didn't look promising because I was hampered by the limited manoeuvrability and could only use the engines in either tick-over, ahead, or stop; I daren't attempt to go astern just in case the water in the engine room sloshed into the air intakes. I also had to watch out that the boat wasn't going to be swamped or smashed against the hull of the other vessel. This didn't leave me with a lot of options but I had to make every effort to stay alongside; now the wind and waves played havoc with us and had moved the boat further away from the vessel, in fact so much so that I was left with no other option than to make a full circle in order to have another attempt at this; I knew that this had to be done with extreme care because the water in the engine room was still at danger level and could be sucked up into the engines, or worse still, the boat could easily capsize.

I had a quick look into the forward cabin and 'Oh No' that is all I needed, we were filling up again; this must have happened when I was manoeuvring alongside the vessel.

Richard was still standing silently on the aft deck; I called him,

'Richard, come down, it's not working, there's no chance in hell that we'll make it safely across; I'll have to find another way of getting us off this boat.'

Now, for the second time I was feeling in my pocket for another cigarette and with frozen fingers I finally managed to pull-out the shrivelled packet. I took out a cigarette, straightened it out as best as I could, lit it and slowly inhaled, holding my breath momentarily then even more slowly blowing out the smoke, which seemed to calm me down; and after several long puffs I said, with renewed confidence,

'Richard! We are going to make it!' and with a little bit of sarcasm he replied,

'I suppose the cigarette has made everything fine again!"

'Yes, now it's time to think of a plan "B".'

To which he replied,

'I didn't know you had a plan "A" in the first place!'

'Yes, I did, but it didn't work.'

In the meantime, I had nearly completed the full circle and was now coming up from behind the vessel when I noticed a great opportunity and decided to make an attempt to come alongside at the rear of the vessel because I could see that both the "Trader I" and the "Christina Claudia" were riding on the same wave.

'Richard, I am going to have a go at this; will you take my briefcase and get off the boat as soon as possible; climb onto the roof and standby to jump across as soon as you get a chance; and this time don't wait for my instructions.'

'Are you alright Bill?'

'Yes thanks, don't worry I will get off as soon as I get an opportunity but you first; **GO**!'

Now the adrenalin had set in "big time" which gave me all the additional mental energy needed to concentrate on getting the boat safely alongside the vessel; I hoped to hold her there long enough for Richard and I to jump ship. I knew that in the next few minutes everything would get extremely dangerous and nerve-wracking.

Slowly but surely I was able to manoeuvre our limping boat towards the rear of the vessel, then... the waves became turbulent and confused but, at the very last moment, I succeeded in getting us within 3 feet of the vessel; I knew that this couldn't last because as we were closing-in on each other the handrails and hull were in imminent danger of crashing together and the vessel was heeling-over towards us dangerously.

The minutes that followed seemed like hours, and being this close to the vessel must have given Richard several opportunities to jump off safely.

While I was concentrating hard on keeping the boat alongside, I couldn't hear anything other than our engine noise and the waves crashing between the boats but then, I am sure that the crew were shouting,

'Come on... Come on... get off that boat!'

I wasn't sure whether they meant Richard or me. The crew on the vessel kept shouting louder and louder, almost screaming which made me think that this was meant for me! But if not, and should Richard still be on board, then I needed to try and hold the boat for a little longer just to give ourselves a little extra time; but looking at the state of the boat and its precarious position, I needed to make another snap decision and this was it! It's now or never, this situation cannot last much longer before we get smashed against the vessel.

Right; final decision made; it's time to get off. I left the engines running in "tick-over ahead", turned the steering wheel slightly towards the side of the vessel and secured the steering friction nut. I quickly scanned around to see whether I had a clear passage to the aft deck, I certainly didn't want to break my neck and miss the chance of getting off the boat by stumbling over debris left behind from the initial wave smash. As soon as I saw a clear passage I ran outside, jumped onto the top of the cockpit roof and... was miraculously at the same height as the vessel's deck. **NOW...** this was it!!! I was either going to fall between the vessels and drown or be rescued and without any further thoughts I jumped. "God Help Me Please"

I took a giant leap of faith towards vessel and felt myself holding onto the ship's coaming cap - *vertical surface preventing the entry of water onto the deck* - and immediately was pulled on board by two strong sailors who lowered me carefully onto the deck. "Thank you Lord for saving me" But whilst I was trying to get back on my feet I still heard the crew shouting; I looked back onto the "Christina Claudia" and... 'Oh Shit! To my horror I spotted Richard still sitting on the roof holding his arms around the little flag mast and his knees pulled-up under his chin; he was definitely in a state of shock.

I was totally puzzled and couldn't understand why I hadn't seen him, the roof wasn't that big!

I began to shout and scream with all the others,

'Come on Richard!!! Come off that boat, Get off NOW!'

We all kept shouting in the hope that Richard would come out of shock. Luckily the "Christina Claudia" stayed near the vessel but I could see that this wouldn't be for much longer, so I shouted in an angry tone again **'Richard...the boat is going to crash, get off quickly; quickly, GET OFF, GET OFF NOW!** Then... in slow motion Richard started to move from his position and tried to balance himself at the edge of the roof; thank goodness he was tall and was now within easy reach of the sailors who were able to grab him by the scruff of his neck and shoulders, waiting until the vessel heeled-over to the far side before they pulled him on board; then when the vessel heeled back over towards the "Christina Claudia" I heard the cockpit roof crash against the side of the ship.

I looked at the now half sunken "Christina Claudia" lying helplessly whilst she was being violently thrown about as the waves were relentlessly smashing against her sides - *like an animal being shred to bits by a predator* - and slowly being filled with water to a dangerous level .

I could hear the engine of the "Trader I" being started-up and we began to pull away from the "Christina Claudia" leaving her half-submerged and swallowed up into the total darkness of this dirty, February night and I hoped that no-one would accidently sail into her before she went to her grave in the depths of the ocean.

The crew touched us on the shoulders in a friendly manner, as if to say "Welcome on board, you can relax now!" They then took us to the messroom, threw some blankets around us and handed us a hot cup of coffee with a stiff brandy. I thanked the crew profusely for their patience and rescue. The deck officer said,

'I don't think you had a lot of time left before you were going to be in "real trouble", which I thought was definitely an understatement. Richard stayed with the crew until he finally went to bed.

My adrenaline was still running high and I needed to calm down before I could contemplate sleeping. Leaving the ship's crew behind, I went upstairs to the bridge and stood still in the opening of the door to adjust my eyes to the darkness. After a while I began to see the dimmed red lights of the necessary instruments and I could also make out the outline of a person behind the wheel and another leaning against a window frame looking out over the foredeck.

The vessel was heavily pounding the waves, each one of them landing on the deck heavily sloshing about from side to side before rolling over the edge back into the sea with the spray blowing high into the air before hitting the wheelhouse windows.

The person standing at the window had waited until I found my way there. I carefully stepped forward onto the bridge and was greeted,

'Good morning sir welcome on board, who are you?'

'I am Bill and my crew is Richard. I apologise that he has not come up to see you but he is in a state of shock and has hyperthermia and your crew are looking after him, but we both thank you so much for rescuing us Captain.'

'That's nothing, but please call me Günter' he answered humbly.

'I'll just have to make a call to Lands End Radio to tell them that you are safe and well.'

Of course, Günter wanted to know exactly what had happened and listened intently to my account of our horrendous adventure, when he said,

'Well, all I can say, is that you have both been extremely lucky to survive such an ordeal because, in the first place we had some difficulties ourselves with the cargo that had shifted and I needed to "heave-too", which made us slowly drift towards the inner traffic zone, leaving the main shipping route miles away to the west. Secondly, we were asked by Lands End Radio to assist a 10,000 ton Greek cargo ship in difficulty twenty miles from our position, but when our Boson saw the flare I asked permission to investigate. They told me that they had received a May Day message but you were unable to communicate with them.

'Yes Günter, that must have been us, but we had to stop sending May Day calls as we were running out of power because the alternators stopped functioning; furthermore the batteries themselves were submerged. We really can't thank you enough for coming to our aid and I hope that everything worked out on the cargo liner?'

'Yes, I heard that the vessel has not sunk but a tug from Brest is on her way to tow her to a safe location and most of her crew have been transferred onto another vessel nearby.'

I wondered where the "Trader I" was bound for and, because the ship had a German crew, I assumed she was perhaps heading in that direction, which could present difficulties for us, because Richard and I had left all our possessions behind on the yacht, including our passports and money; I hesitantly asked,

'Günter, where are you bound for?'

'Southend on Sea in England, do you know this Port?'

I softly smiled and said,

'Yes, I do Günter?'

Unbelievable, and what a lucky escape; but this misadventure could so easily have cost us our lives.

La Coruña - Rio Vivero
Easter Sunday 31st March 2002

We didn't make a great effort getting up this morning after having enjoyed ourselves in the town last night, but then… who would want to get up; after all, it was Easter Sunday! The owner and his wife went into town looking for fresh bread, which gave me, time to tidy up for our departure.

Jumping ashore was not without difficulty; being the bottom of the tide made it a bit tricky for them to jump onto the very slippery set of granite stone steps and with nothing to hold onto made it somewhat dangerous; fortunately they succeeded without any major incidents, just dirty hands, knees and clothing.

When it came to paying for the overnight mooring the owner was told, 'This is on us, sir. It was a pleasure having such a beautiful boat alongside the Clubhouse. I wish you Bon Voyage'

We left the mooring and slowly made our way to the end of the 1¾ mile breakwater and as I was nearing the entrance I could see that the ocean didn't have any noticeable waves and it seemed that we were in for a very pleasant day. I did some wishful thinking and hoped that the owner was going to suggest crossing the bay to Brest, but this was not to be… at least not for now.

'Where are we going to today?'

'Well, as it is such a lovely day let's run along the coast and make our way to Bilbao; there are some museums my wife wants to visit!'

I was a little perplexed - I am sure it must have been noticeable as my eyes felt as if they were bulging out of their sockets - and I diplomatically replied,

'That's quite far from here, but we can make our way towards it '

'How long will it take to get there?' I gave it some thought and replied,

'With the rate we are going, it could take three days.'

'Oh well, never mind; let's go along the coast and see how far we can get today.'

I laid the courses necessary for Cabo Prior, passing the port of Cariño.

> Looking on my chart at this part of the coast jogged my memory regarding some scary moments from the past like the time we got "lost and low on fuel" (Page 280) and another story which came to mind was "we needed to seek shelter" (Page 287)

I made a point of running as close as I dared under the shore. The sun was shining brightly on its steep, rugged and lush green coast with the Atlantic rollers bombarding the rocks before being instantly rejected and tossed back with great spectacle; I could easily have watched this for hours.

The afternoon was uneventful and we made our way to the next headland at Pta de Los Aquillones; at 17:00 we passed the headland and I suggested that we should be looking for a port. We looked at the chart and noticed a port called Barquero which seemed to be tucked away from the Atlantic swell, but when we moved closer we found that this port wasn't suitable for us. We turned around and headed out of the bay, hugging the coast between a small island and the headland, and moved into the next bay which had a well-marked channel which meant that there was a suitable port for large vessels.

We navigated at the outer edge of the channel and spotted a sailing boat under power; we followed her and she eventually led us into a medium sized yacht harbour just off the river Vivero.

The town looked a reasonable distance away from the marina and I suggested staying behind with the excuse that the marina didn't seem to have proper security, although it certainly didn't look like the place was inundated with crime. I simply just wanted to chill out.

Lost and low on fuel!
March 1971.

I prepared "La Princess", a twin screwed Moonraker 36, for her maiden voyage from Great Yarmouth to Marbella Spain and Mike and Dany Sullivan, the owners of the boat, joined me to experience first-hand this great venture in crossing the Bay of Biscay and the Portuguese coast.

We left on a bright sunny Saturday morning and soon after we cleared the piers, I gently coaxed "La Princess" up to cruising speed but found that she was rather slow, probably because she was fitted with a fly bridge which made her a lot heavier than her forerunners; anyway, there wasn't much I could do about it but this meant that I would have to consider carrying extra fuel for the 360 mile crossing of the Bay of Biscay.

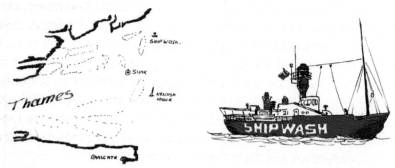

Just after passing Lowestoft, not long into the voyage, we were consumed by thick fog which lasted all the way to Ramsgate. Sailing in fog is scary at the best of times but only having a compass, speed log, depth sounder and Dead Reckoning navigation, kept me well on my toes; I hoped that the compass had been adjusted properly, as the only visual or sound fixes I could expect were the manned light vessels "Shipwash" in the north of the Thames Estuary and "Kentish Knock" at the middle entrance; their powerful foghorns would give away their positions.

After eight strenuous hours I found my way safely into Ramsgate Harbour. I manoeuvred to the fuel barge and as luck would have it we were able to refuel immediately but it seemed to take so long that for a horrible moment I thought the fuel tank had a leak but thank goodness the fuel finally spilled over out of the tank breather. Wow! This boat is really guzzling fuel; we will have a hard time making the passage across the Bay even carrying extra fuel!

After refuelling I made some calculations and found that the boat had consumed 100 gallons (454 litres) over a distance of 86nm. This was totally unexpected. I was completely flabbergasted and suggested that we would have to run the whole of the voyage to Marbella at the displacement speed of 8½ knots which should give us the fuel needed to make the crossing.

The next morning we left Ramsgate and sailed for Cherbourg, our next refuelling port and from there we marched on for Brest. Just short of Brest we found ourselves in thick fog once more; this time, I wasn't so optimistic with the accuracy of my navigation because we were entering the notorious Channel du Four - *the channel between the island of Queasant and the main coast of France* - although I did have Mike and Dany's help in looking out and listening for the fog-bells chiming on the tall channel markers; I am happy to say that after a few hairy hours we arrived in the port of Brest.

We spent two days in Brest: firstly, to rest from the stressful voyage and secondly to await a reasonable weather window for our intended crossing. I estimated that we needed 42 hours - two daylight days and one night - in decent weather. Luckily, Dany, being French, was able to obtain a full weather forecast from the naval vessel moored just ahead of us.

I refuelled the boat plus eight 20 litre plastic cans, which I carefully lashed to the handrail on the aft deck. We didn't have to wait long for suitable weather and left at 04:00 the following morning. We sailed the first 12 hours with a dark grey, overcast sky, wind still and only a long low swell but it didn't last because later in the afternoon the ocean became increasingly larger and soon Mike's & Dany's stomachs didn't like the wallowing motion but I had to reassure them that it could take a little while before they became accustomed to the swaying of the boat and offered them the usual dry biscuits and toast for now.

The night was unbelievably long, especially as Mike didn't get the hang of steering the boat properly on a course and in order to reach a target, good course-keeping is a must. During late evening the waves had started to increase dramatically and often we were looking against massive walls of water.

I worked out that we had been at sea for 28 hours and would soon need to consider refuelling from our spare fuel; filling diesel out of drums into the tank by deck filler was a non-starter as I would throw more on the deck than in the tank so I had to improvise by taking the hand bilge-pump to pieces and adapting it for siphoning so that I could fill the fuel through the fuel filler cap in the saloon floor. Although this was working beautifully we did have to endure the stench of fuel which made us all rather queasy. I had to hand the wheel over to Mike during this process, which took a lot longer than I had anticipated but finally, after 2 long hours, I was able to stow the empty cans back in their places and refit the smelly hand bilge-pump in the engine room. Having cleaned the fuel spillage on the floor in the saloon, Dany went down into the cabin for a while with the door closed, which I thought was a brave thing to do!

Later, she started to get a little apprehensive and asked me how long she would have to endure the motion and these atrocious seas. I checked the chart and estimated that we were about 15 miles off the coast so I tried to reassure her that we should be seeing land soon.

At around 14:00 I sighted a plume of black smoke rising up from over the horizon and knew that this could either come from ashore or fishing boats. Yes, you **DID** read that correctly, because a large number of Spanish and Portuguese fishing vessels were then still driven by coal-fired steam engines!

It wasn't long after seeing the first plume of smoke that several other plumes of smoke appeared on the horizon; so... this was not land, but definitely fishing boats.

I now realised that we were still well away from La Coruña.

15:00 - Still no coast visible this is now beginning to worry me; how much further? Will I have enough fuel? I reduced the speed to 7 knots hoping to stretch the fuel.

What now! Yes! I was sure that I could see the coast; or was I looking at clouds just above the horizon; no! In the glare of the afternoon sunshine I could clearly see that it was the coast on our port side; at least the end was in sight, or so I thought!

I went to recalculate our position and estimated that we may have overshot our target to the west, which made me think that I was looking at the coastline near Cabo Villano, but not being sure I continued on this course for a little longer and at 17:30 we were about two miles off the coast; I scanned the coastline and spotted a lighthouse halfway up the cliff, hoping this was Cabo Prior (the cape I had aimed for), but which lighthouse was it really? Then I had a thought and suggested that we should wait until evening when the light would start to flash, in order to confirm our position but Mike and Dany preferred that I took a chance and got them into port – any port - as soon as possible.

Thinking logically, I turned back and sail eastwards up the coast, but that decision turned out to be a huge mistake.

We spent several hours sailing very slowly looking for La Coruña.

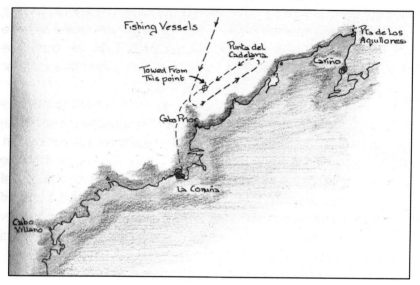

As the night fell I saw, in the distance, flashes of light ahead of us. I started to count the flashes - "One, two, three and a few seconds later another flash" and counted them again just to be sure. I ran my finger over the chart and found that this lighthouse was Punta Candelaria, well east of La Caruña; this meant that the lighthouse we'd seen in the afternoon **was** Cabo Prior after all and I had been totally on target, but tiredness and the hazy visibility had prevented me from seeing La Coruña in the first place.

Unbeknown to me, I then made my second mistake; seeing Punta Candelaria made me turn around to head for La Coruña but little did I know I could have gone for the port of Cariño only fourteen miles from there. But in my defence, the Pilot books and Reeds Almanac only described the larger ports in detail.

The evening dragged on with still no end in sight so I had to shut down one engine to save the little fuel I had while still maintaining a speed of 5 knots.

Mike and Dany had settled themselves down in the saloon, leaving me in the cockpit to concentrate. I estimated that we had sailed a total distance of 372 miles and realised that soon we would be running out of fuel; I went into the saloon and dipped the tank for the umpteenth time.

The palms of my hands began to sweat and I started to get very shivery too. Now it began to dawn on me that things were not going well and I could only hope that we weren't going to run out of fuel. Some time had passed when I noticed a large fishing vessel bobbing up and down between the waves and it seemed to be on a potential collision course with us; this gave me a brain-wave and I headed towards her and now I was just about to do something I never thought I would do... I turned parallel to the fishing vessel and called Dany, who also spoke Spanish.

'Dany, can you ask them how far we are from La Caruña!'

'Bill, they said that La Coruña is about twenty miles from here in that direction' and she pointed her finger into the direction of our heading. In a flash I thought that will take us well over 4 hours and although we may have had enough fuel, I wasn't going to take any more risks.

Inwardly, I was now really worried and in a panic, asked Dany,

'Can you ask them whether they are going to the port?'

'They are going to La Coruña in about 2 hours Bill'

'Oh that's fantastic; please ask whether it is possible for them to tow us in?' Dany asked them

'Yes, they said will tow us for a small fee.'

'Dany, can you tell them that we would like to take up their offer and will wait for them here.'

Now I was able to relax a little and all I had to do was to wait for the fishing boat to collect us.

Two hours went by and the fishing boat's lights began to sink in-between the waves and I had this awful feeling that they had forgotten us but then... all of a sudden, they turned around and sailed directly towards us; they threw a line across and towed us to the safe haven of La Caruña.

Sometime later I stumbled upon an idea which would help me to navigate across the Bay of Biscay more accurately. I always carried my Gründig hand-held long and short wave transistor radio for the shipping forecast and discovered that some of the Radio Direction Finding (RDF) frequencies were to be found at the top end of the LW dial and with the built-in aerial I was able to locate (albeit roughly) the direction of the station. I can truly say that since then I have never had to endure such a dreadful and embarrassing situation. But Mike & Dany frequently used this incident as dinner table entertainment!

We'll need to seek shelter!
19th April 1996.

I skippered the TSMY Lancetta 680 called "Queen" on her voyage of around 3350 nautical miles from Düsseldorf via Rotterdam, Dartmouth, Lisbon, Gibraltar, Palma de Mallorca, Messina, Otranto and Portoroz.

This voyage was to be in two legs: firstly from Düsseldorf to Palma where the boat was to be exhibited at the show and then the second leg from Palma to Portoroz.

From the outset it had its minor problems like the time when short steep waves created by the over-falls just off the headland at Portland Bill had pushed in the seals of a porthole in the forward cabin. Unfortunately, portholes in the front of a vessel often had to endure large quantities of water thrust against them and it always reminded me of a washing machine in motion.

In Dartmouth I made porthole weather blinds from thick marine ply to block them off for the remainder of the voyage.

After Dartmouth the voyage progressed well and we travelled at the speed of 10.5 knots: firstly to save fuel and secondly to save the boat from structural stresses encountered by travelling too fast through the waves.

Then, during the first evening things started to go dramatically wrong because the electronic engine control system began to fail;

287

I am not sure why, but the boatyard in Taiwan had positioned the electronic gadget box for the controls near the heat of the engine and now the RPM equalizer had to work overtime but eventually had to give up the ghost.

Here we were smack bang in the centre of the Bay of Biscay in the middle of the night with a strong headwind and waves building up every minute when I totally lost control of the starboard engine.

"Oh no, now I'll have to do some quick thinking!" That wasn't easy but after several minutes I came up with an idea, not a conventional one, but I thought that if I disconnected the levers from the cables then I could improvise a string mechanism so that the throttle lever could be set to the required 1000 rpm. After messing about in the engine room between the hot engines I succeeded in attaching a string to hold the lever in place. I must say it worked rather well, but the weather started to deteriorate further and the waves had become at least 4 metres in height. This in itself wasn't a hazard, but not having full control over the throttles created a **real** problem, because every time the boat was about to hit a wave I should have been slowing her down momentarily but now this was not possible and being night-time it was difficult to judge the waves, which exacerbated the problem.

It was just about getting daylight on our second day of the crossing and not having slept since leaving Dartmouth, I thought it was time to have 40 winks; but firstly I went to check on the engine room with the sole purpose of resetting the throttle string to a lower setting but I found, to my horror, that the engine room was flooded and seawater was sloshing about at ankle-height above the floor plating; where in heavens name had this come from! I then saw that every time the vessel's bow dived down into a wave it scooped up a large quantity of water which ran all the way down the side-decks and finally found its way through the nearest escape route, which just happened to be the engine room ventilation cowlings.

So not only did we have the problem of a failing engine control but now we also had the additional hazard of water relentlessly bucketing into the engine room; as if this wasn't enough, I now began to feel the boat juddering under my feet which didn't feel right at all! I have experienced this type of motion previously when a boat was filling up with water. Oh dear, there seemed to be no end to my problems; minutes later, whilst inspecting the forward cabin for water ingress, Martin, my crew, called me and said,

'Bill, I think we have a problem with the tender!'

The tender had broken loose from its platform and was now partly submerged, trailing uncontrollably behind the vessel. This was the last straw! Now I would have to stop the vessel and somehow pull the tender back on board. Easier said than done! Firstly, I went back to the engine room and disconnected the throttle cable. I opened the engine room door and luckily the water hadn't risen since the last time I had looked and I hoped that the bilge pump would hold out. I waded through the water and disconnected the throttle cable and almost instantly the boat stopped in her tracks; now the waves started to play havoc with her and made her violently roll from side to side whilst being tossed up and down, like on a rollercoaster ride, but we would just have to endure this while we pulled that wretched tender back on board.

Holding on for dear life, I carefully lowered myself down onto the platform hoping not to slip into the sea; I wedged myself in the corner and managed to get rid of the two broken straps which had secured the tender. Next I started to pull in the boat and was occasionally assisted by the waves which, after some strenuous fighting, lifted the tender up from the sea and plonked it back on the chocking blocks. Now I needed to find a way of fixing it down but this was an impossible task as every time I tried to throw the line around the boat, a wave landed with full force onto the platform and started to shift the flipping tender from its position again. This went on for some time but the sea won on every occasion; then... I had a brainwave which was a miracle considering I was extremely tired: if I could only push the hydraulic gangway down into the bottom of the tender then my problem would be solved. I grabbed the remote control and... Bingo, this tender was not going anywhere!

08:00 enough is enough; overtired, cold, soaked to the skin, I decided to abort the crossing to my intended destination of Vigo and started to look for the nearest safe port. I looked on my chart and found the Port of Cariño; I changed course onto this new direction, almost at a 090° angle from before; thankfully this did stop the seas from breaking over the bows which also gave the engine room a break from flooding.

Now that the vessel had settled down I thought I would have a general look around, including the foredeck. I looked over the bow - *which I did sometimes, hoping to see dolphins* - when to my horror I found a large crack in the hull near deck level. This is it! Whatever I had planned had now gone out of the window.

Eight hours later we entered the bay of Cariño. I instructed Martin to take up the floor board so that he could operate the gear-lever manually and we finally anchored the boat in the large, but well protected bay. We never had the pleasure of landing there, but at least we were able to mop up the water and make the boat safe for sea again; then we had a rest until the following morning.

Rio Vivero - Luacra
Monday 1st April 2002

Yes it's April Fools Day, little did I know! This morning we were presented with a miserable, grey overcast sky; in fact it was drizzling but luckily wind-still. We cleared up our breakfast and departed for our next destination of Luacra.

Luacra looked to be a very pretty little port - *on the chart that is* - but I needed to be sure whether it was big enough for us, so the best thing I could do for now was to read about the place in the Almanac.

The reason for my apprehension was the way in which the port was drawn on the chart, which made me think that it was a difficult and a tricky place to enter; added to that, it will be low water when we get there, therefore leaving very little depth at either side of the entrance; it was also noted that the place was littered with numerous rocks, which are exposed at low water in the outer bay and these could be a potential hazard to navigation; luckily they had provided the navigator with two large leading markers, which guide you between the breakwaters and once this hurdle has been overcome all that is needed is to find a free mooring place in the fishing port because the yacht moorings are only for small sized boats.

The morning went well and the sky started to clear as we moved further away from the coast, leaving drizzle hanging over the foothills. I know not to mention the weather but the sea had been, and still was, fantastic and I couldn't believe that we were actually running into the Bay of Biscay. We made good headway and passed Ria S Augustin a little ahead of time.

16:10 - changed course and started to close-in on the coast but -*and perhaps I was getting impatient* - I still was unable to see the Port of Luacra, then all of a sudden I began to notice a small gap in the cliffs which eventually opened up enough for me to see a picturesque village against the foothills. I also spotted my leading markers, freshly painted, which could clearly be seen against the dark shadow of the cliffs surrounding the fishing port.

Bill, you'll have to concentrate; although the sea was relatively calm, I still had great difficulty keeping the boat on the leading-in marker; goodness knows how I would manage in bad weather! Perhaps in those conditions they might close the port, as they do in Portugal. Brilliant! I made it and found a place alongside the quay by squeezing in between two fishing vessels and hoped that I hadn't taken someone else's place. Oh well, I will have to wait and see.

It was 18:00 when I finally finished mooring and cleared the boat. I was offered a cup of tea which I drank sitting in the wheelhouse while admiring this quaint and picturesque port. It seemed to be developed around a natural bay, with a backdrop of a sandy beach and sloping hills on the far side, and on this side a steep hill littered with small dwellings overlooking the harbour.
The quayside was surrounded by several restaurants specialising in guess what? Seafood!

Later in the evening we had a look around the village where a clear freshwater stream coming from the Cordillera Cantabrica Mountains found its way into the Atlantic. After our early evening stroll we wandered back into one of the restaurants where we had a delicious meal and chilled out with a glass - or two - of red Rioja.
The spell was broken by a few phone calls to the boss who then said, not surprisingly, that sadly they had to return back to England in the morning. I thought that puts pay to that; here we are, well into the Bay of Biscay and... I am being left on my own once more!
Being very disappointed with the news, I had to say something:
'Now that you are going back what would you like me to do? I

can't stay here.'

'No, but can't you continue?'

'Yes... of course, but I hoped that "we" were taking the boat across the bay and I am not sure whether I can manage that on my own!'

'No Bill, you don't have to do that, you can go around the coast and take your time if you like!'

Great! Now I had something else to worry about. Now all sorts of thoughts went through my head as I tried to visualise where to go next and the length of time it would now take. I had always promised myself never to attempt the Bay of Biscay on my own and here I was..., still having to venture solo into these - *sometimes atrocious* - seas and I couldn't help thinking "what if" but finally, totally exhausted, I went to bed, but sleep did not come very easily.

Luacra - Lastres
Tuesday 2nd April 2002

Having had a very disturbed night I woke with a heavy head, as if I had been out on the town. The owner and his wife were busily preparing for their departure and at 09:45 a taxi drew up at the edge of the quayside to take them to the airport at Gijon where, for the third time this voyage, the corporate jet was waiting to take them back home.

It was a real performance climbing up the rusty and slippery integrated quayside ladder at low water, while having to let go momentarily with both hands in order to grab the next rung with one hand while balancing the suitcase with the other.

After waving them off, I had a leisurely breakfast and cleared the boat of the accumulation of clutter. Although I didn't expect any bad weather, this is after all the Bay of Biscay and anything can happen, especially this early in the year, so it's better to be prepared for all scenarios.

I simply can't get my head around the fact that I am on my own again and I will have to change my mind-set to thinking that I am on a "boat delivery" rather than being the skipper /engineer. Right, snap out of it and get on with the job! I finally summoned up the energy to set off for the next and final section of this voyage; only 869 nautical miles to go.

I left this pretty port at 10:37 ready for the next port of call but, in fact, I hadn't even planned the next port of call as yet and I didn't really know how far I could get today; that's fine because I always believe that if you don't have a plan then nothing can go wrong! Past experience has taught me that when you plan too far in advance and try rigorously to adhere to your plans then it can often be disastrous. "Flexibility" is the key answer.

I was pleasantly surprised to see a calm blue ocean and a brilliant blue sky with some high cirrus clouds; this meant that I was in for a glorious day. Just ahead of me I noticed a flock of seagulls which made me think that they had spotted shoals of small fish in the area; this in turn could mean that dolphins wouldn't be too far away. I kept my eyes focused on the sea and this paid off, because just ahead the sea began to boil with small fish jumping high out of the water and yes, I couldn't believe it, but there were about a dozen dolphins encircling the fish and enjoying their brunch for the day - what a sight.

It was just after midday when I passed the cap of Vidio which is also the entrance to the bay at Gijon. Seeing the town on the horizon made me momentarily wonder if I should run into Gijon's old port; then again it was far too early in the day to pack up, although I noticed that the seas had started to build up but they were still no threat to me because I hadn't had to switch on the stabilizers just yet.

Passing the large commercial port of Gijon made me think of the numerous times I have used this place as a refuelling stop for the smaller vessels, when coming from the port of Le Palais on the Belle Ile across the bay. Choosing this route was not for economical reasons because it added another 90 nautical miles to the voyage, incurring the cost of additional fuel, but this was the safe option.

The afternoon went extremely fast and I have to admit that I began to enjoy my own company again. I looked at the chart and tried to find a port for the night; there was a little place around the headland called Lastres, which might well be the chosen one.

Lastres is another steep hillside fishing village with a small harbour protected by a massively high breakwater and surrounded by sandy shoals; I would have to watch out for a few off-lying rocks just before entering the port. I was just off the Pointa Misiera and yes, I just spotted the rocks being washed by the waves but whilst I was concentrating on keeping an eye on the rocks, all of a sudden I lurched forward as the boat came to an abrupt stop with both engines stalling at the same time. 'Oh no what now?!' My initial thought was that I had ran onto a sandbank, which wasn't the case, but I found that I was surrounded by loads of fishing buoys. I can't believe they would lay their nets so close to the harbour entrance. I don't think I was less than 200 metres away...

I started the engines again and tried to put the starboard engine ahead only to find that it stalled again. I crossed my fingers and gently moved the port engine gear-lever into forward; the revolutions dropped, almost stalling, but then picked-up and the boat started to move slowly forward although she began to shake uncontrollably; never mind at least I can enter the port under my own steam. Rather than mooring in the allocated visitors' mooring at the end on the inside of the outer breakwater, I moved further into the port and clumsily moored alongside a fishing boat whilst being watched by a fisherman. He asked me why I had parked the boat there and I told him about my predicament; luckily he knew of a diver who would be able to investigate the problem for me.

The diver agreed to take a look for 350 Euros which I thought was a very good deal. He was under the boat for sometime but eventually surfaced with 10 metres of fishing net in his hands! He must have enjoyed diving because he also offered to clean the barnacles from the propellers and I thought that was really good of him; of course I gave him something extra and thanked him profusely.

After the diver left I went to have a look ashore and ended up in the local restaurant half way up the hill where I took time to relax after an emotional and adventurous day.

Lastres - Santander
Wednesday 3rd April 2002

I don't know why, but surprisingly I woke up feeling well rested for a change and was happy to have an early start this morning. But it was a dull day and I could hear the wind howling and clattering away through the tackle on the sailing boats which were tucked away in the inner harbour; looking into the other direction I noticed the sea spray coming over the harbour wall.

Now what shall I do? Oh dear! I found myself having an intense argument as to whether I was going to sea or staying in the harbour; the adventurer in me won the argument. Ha, ha! For the first time since Sangenjo it seemed that I was in for some real Biscay weather.

I stowed all loose gear, checked the engines and bilge pumps, closed all portholes, made sure the seawater filters were clean, started the engines and departed Lastres' breakwater at 07:00; but the minute I left the sheltered harbour, the boat was violently thrown about and I just managed to switch on the stabilizers to full power; she then settled down quite quickly and now I needed to concentrate on avoiding the fishing buoys which I had encountered last night and I also noticed, further along the coast, a large fish farm. The poor daylight and large waves made it impossible to spot the fishing buoys easily and unfortunately, this time, my radar wouldn't pick them up; I suspect they were too small and couldn't provide the necessary echo.

I had set course first to the north to make sure that I was sailing well out of their range, and after a strenuous 5 miles I changed to an easterly direction and hoped to make Santander today. Luckily, the wind, although gusty, came from the SW, therefore running from behind, which was fine but a few hours into the run, the wind started to increase and became a full blown storm force 8 with gusts up to 43 knots and I estimated that the waves were now between 4 - 5 metres; now I wished that the other imaginary guy, the more sensible one with whom I had argued earlier, had won!

It also started to rain heavily which hampered my visibility no end. Anyway, the show must go on. Now I definitely had no alternative than to go for Santander because changing direction would be unwise as I would be beam-on or worse still head-on into the waves; also, as the waves were coming from behind me, I was going faster by 1 knot and every little helps, so why change.

It was a long, long morning, but at 14:00 I passed the first headland off Pointa Del Dichoso at a distance of 4½nm. I thought it wise to stay well off the coast just in case the boat gave me any trouble. The autopilot decided to play havoc with me as it started to steer like a swaying ski slalom on a mountainside; now I had to take over and steer by hand, that's all I needed. However, steering by hand was even harder but now that the end was in sight I let the autopilot take its turn again so I could make myself something to eat.

15:20 - finally my plotter told me that I had arrived at my waypoint which was set 1½nm off Cabo de Lata and the wind had dropped to a force 4 making my life a lot easier, but I still needed to concentrate because I was planning to take the short cut between the Isle of Mouro and the headland of Palacio in order to avoid the waves running beam-on.

At exactly 16:00 I stopped in front of Santander's town Marina but found that it was for local boats only; what a shame because this little harbour was in the centre of the town, never mind.

I checked the Almanac where I found the description of a new marina which unfortunately was built well outside Santander. Blast what a nuisance. Anyway, I slowly made my way up the channel and finally arrived in the new Marina de Santander and stayed here for a few days waiting for the weather to improve.

Santander - Hondarribia-Hendaye
Friday 5th April 2002

The weather was awful yesterday, still blowing a gale like the day before, but this gave me the excuse of having valuable resting time besides getting the boat ready for the next leg. I have to admit that since passing Gijon I have felt well out of my comfort zone and although I don't like planning I was now eager to suss out what was ahead of me. Since I have never been along this part of the Bay before, I studied the Reeds Almanac in detail to see where to head next; after some deliberation, I decided to choose the port of Hondarribia-Hendaye - *weather permitting* - which is in the far corner of the bay and not far from Bayonne in France, on the border between the two countries.

I refuelled - 1270 litres - just to keep both tanks topped-up, which can be extremely helpful in these sea conditions. I also checked the engine room and I didn't have to do a lot to the machinery except for the usual topping-up of oil and cooling water; the repaired exhaust manifold was doing its job perfectly; mind you, I mustn't speak too soon, you never know!

Whilst I was in the marina office to pay for my fuel and two night's mooring fees, I asked what the weather was going to be like and to my surprise, the depression of the past few days was going to move away overnight giving me a clear spell for at least three days. Fantastic! That's just what I needed and I hoped that the predictions were accurate!

I didn't have a chance to visit Santander so I can't say much about the place other than it looked alright from a distance, but I did have my long walks to exercise my legs.

I spent last night resting and watching TV and went to bed at a reasonable hour because I wasn't sure what today would have in store for me.

The sun had shown its face at 07:30 and the day started wind still with a blue unblemished sky. Wow! This is a fantastic start to the weekend; now all I can hope for is that the forecast of a force 2 and a maximum wave height of 2 metres is spot-on.

Unbelievably, I didn't depart until 08:32; after leaving the marina I gently meandered my way down the fairway, passing dozens of weekend fishermen angling and enjoying the crisp and early morning sunshine on the river.

My progress down the river was very slow but that was purely because I was pushing the incoming tide; but this would change when I was outside where I should enjoy an easterly push from behind. Finally I passed the Isle of Mouro at 09:13 and from here intended to hug the coast to the next cape called Cabo Ajo and then onward into an easterly direction for Cabo Villano - that's strange, they have two capes with the same names along this coast.

The weather developed an easterly breeze but nothing to write home about and I couldn't believe that it was only just into April. 13:00 - I could just make out the west pier of Bilbao 7 miles away on the radar. This reminded me that it was in February 1961 when, as deck boy, I came here on my first ever round-the-world trip on the Dutch cargo ship "Schelde Lloyd", nearing the end of the voyage.

The afternoon was uneventful and I couldn't believe that the weather was so lovely. I didn't feel at all bored because for the whole of the day I had to either pass or avoid small, large and very large vessels; it was as if all the boats had come out of hibernation. I was making good headway - I hadn't planned my arrival time - although I had an easterly wind to contend with.

It seemed to have taken for ever but I finally passed Cabo Higue at

19:55 and from this point only had a short way to go before reaching my destination for the day. I don't know why, but I went up the river and turned to starboard into the Spanish side of the imaginary dividing line between Spain and France.

20:35 - moored at the first available pontoon and went straight up to the office which, not surprisingly, was closed so I was excused from having to pay the mooring fee for the night. I climbed back on board and made a quick microwave meal - not my usual or favoured style - and reminisced over a glass of wine on the lovely day I had enjoyed.

Hondarribia-Hendaye - Royan (River Gironde)
Saturday 6th April 2002

I must be honest, I am not looking forward to this part of the voyage at all because for the past week I have had to occupy myself endlessly by reading the chapter in the Almanac regarding this section of the coast; I had to read it over and over again before I came to the definite conclusion that this section between Cap Breton near Biarritz up to the entrance of the River Gironde, covering an approximate distance of 100nm and a bandwidth of 48nm, was a "No-Go" area from Monday to Fridays during daylight hours; I noticed that along this stretch of the coast there was only one port called Arcachon to run into; this meant running through this restricted zone would take more than the overnight period. So sailing weekdays was not an option because I did not intend to travel through the night unless I was forced to. Like Victor Meldrew would say, "I don't believe it!" I must be the luckiest person on earth because I just happened to be in Hondarribia-Hendaye at the beginning of the weekend. Yippee! What great timing; this gives me two full days to reach the river Gironde.

The weather forecast last night read, 'variable wind force 3 at first perhaps NE 3-4 later' and as predicted I woke up to a misty but calm morning and although I hadn't slept well, I felt perky and in good spirits.

04:30 - boiled the water for a coffee and ready to move, slipped the moorings and nosed my way out of the marina. Everything was quiet and I seemed to be the only boat on the move; I pressed the button to "auto" on the autopilot, then to "track" and hoped that it would follow the path to the waypoint, which I had set earlier, for the SWM entrance buoy at Pass de Sud Gironde.

I am afraid I spoke too soon about being the only boat around as I detected a vessel on my port quarter and the way in which her running lights were displayed showed that she was making her way to the east, on a potential collision course with me; should she miss, then I think she could be heading for the Port of Anglet/ Pyrénées Atlantique - although I couldn't be sure; her speed seemed well in excess of mine and although I had the right of way, it was prudent on my part to keep an eye on her and avoid a collision.

06:30 - the first signs of daylight and it looked like I was going to have a day with thick low clouds and an easterly wind, just as predicted.

The ship I had spotted had changed course and safely passed behind me which gave me some peace of mind because I was now in desperate need of the loo. A little later I saw an orange light flashing on the horizon ahead of me, or was it? I waited a little while but now the light became bigger and so did the boat showing it. Mysteriously, this light began to show itself at the edge of the marked Military zone and I had this horrible feeling that it belonged to a naval vessel patrolling the area.

It can't be true, I thought, and grabbed the Almanac to check the pages again but found no restrictions for the weekend. Well I may as well continue, let's just wait and see. The boat moved closer and closer but... what now? She is turning towards me! All the enthusiasm from first thing this morning had now been deflated and I wondered if they were going to tell me to make the 48 mile detour after all.

With the binoculars literally glued to my eyes I tried to make out what kind of boat it was, but I couldn't hold the binoculars steady enough and gave up my attempt at "boat spotting".

Before I lose my patience altogether, I thought I would brew a coffee and chill out a little; the day was going to be long enough as it was and I needed to save every ounce of energy for later. As it turned out, the boat with the amber flashing light was a French fishing vessel; in fact she was at the head of a fleet and ironically all of them were fishing in the Military zone! This gave me confidence again and I was so glad not to have misread the notes so I celebrated this fact with a good breakfast.

The morning went extremely well and I made steady progress towards my "escape port." I call this an escape port for the simple reason that should something happen to the weather, boat or myself then I wouldn't have far to go before reaching a safe haven.

By midday the sun started to pierce through the grey clouds, and slowly produced full sunlight, giving me a very pleasant afternoon on the deep blue ocean, passing the occasional small fishing boat trying her luck, surrounded by large gannets hoping to catch a meal in the turbulence of my wake.

After passing Cap Ferret - *my escape port* - I began to close in towards this lovely coast with its hazy sun-baked shoreline and pine trees, divided by the golden sandy beach on which the Atlantic breakers found their resting place. If anyone had told me that the sea and weather conditions in the notorious Bay of Biscay could be like the Mediterranean then I would never have believed them, but the truth was here to see. Oh boy! Was I a lucky lad!

During the afternoon I read the Almanac again and used my photographic memory to memorise the lay of the land in relation to the lights etc., in order to prepare for the possible difficulties I may encounter during the coming night passage. I noticed that there was the possibility of entering the river via "Pass de Sud" or the main "North Channel" and never having been there made me a little nervous but the weather and the sea conditions were perfect; however this is the time when the help of a crew would have lightened the load. But having a crew can also be a handful, which was why I had made the decision for "Going Alone" most of the time. (Page 309)

I had my dinner whilst it was still daylight so that I was ready for anything that came my way later on. Thank goodness the ocean had been calm all day and just before sunset I noticed that several fishing boats started to occupy the northern section of the military zone and I knew then for sure that the weather was going to remain reasonable - at least for tonight. The sun was setting as a large dark reddish ball slowly sinking into the sea, leaving behind a dark grey haze above the waterline and above this was a red/yellow glow which slowly gave way to a deep blue sky and eventually pitch black, with a star or two twinkling away over the Gironde.

Although it is quite romantic seeing a sunset like this, it also plunges you into the silent and mysterious world of the lonely sea. All of a sudden the light beacon on the coast began to flash its hazy yellow light on my starboard side through the darkness, and ahead of me was the flashing light on the tall marker buoy bobbing gently over the long calm swell.

19:45 - it was decision time: either to continue north and choose the "North Main Channel" or the sparsely lit "Pass de Sud"; typical of the French, they do know how to mark their channels - *at least on the Atlantic side.* So having studied the book and the chart once more, I opted for the "Pass de Sud" and seriously needed to prepare myself for some real navigation.

21:10 - abeam of the first headland at Pte de la Négade. Strangely I began to notice that the boat was being pushed by a powerful current and I had to make a large correction in order to keep my heading straight for the SWM buoy at the entrance of the south channel.

20:40 - turned onto the new course of 063° towards an intense green light standing at the edge of Pte de Grave; but what's that... I suddenly lost the light; the visibility had diminished to less than a mile - I suppose that's the price I had to pay for the fantastic weather I had experienced so far today.

That's all very well, but I was just about to head into the narrow channel and not far from the shallow grounds I began to notice that the swell had started to come in from behind, lifting the boat up at the stern and making her surf down the wave; not being able to see the leading lights and unlit channel markers made me somewhat apprehensive.

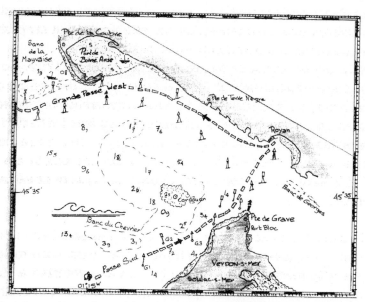

Now I was in real trouble, the only consolation being that I had the radar to pick up the blind markers; I noticed on the chart that the heading for the narrow channel was almost in line with the edge of the coast at Pte de Grave, which gave me a fair indication as to where the channel was; a little later I was able to make out the dark outline of G1, the first starboard hand buoy, which looked a reasonable distance away from the boat and immediately I began to search on the radar for G2, the port marker, but my eyes caught the white foamy outlines of the big Atlantic rollers running over the sand bank of the Banc du Chevier.

The depth under the boat began to decrease rapidly from 30 feet to a mere 7 feet; I now had to keep a cautious eye on the depth sounder and hoped that it didn't drop any further than 6.6 feet; I also had to look on the radar to see whether I was still in the channel while, at the same time, keeping a look-out into the darkness around me. After a few heart-stopping moments I could see that the depth was slowly increasing to a healthy 21 feet; now I knew for sure that I was heading into the right direction and established that my position was between the Island of Cordouan and the mainland.

Finally, the waves had settled down to a short chop, which allowed me to keep a straight course. It didn't take long before I reached G3 where I had to alter course so as not to run aground on my starboard side then all of a sudden the visibility cleared and I detected the leading lights of Royan, the port I was heading for, on the east side of the River Gironde. I called that a stroke of luck and breathed a sigh of relief. Believe me you don't want to be in that type of situation too frequently!

22:00 - passed the headland of Pte de Grave and now I had to dash across the river entrance; although there wasn't any wind to speak of, I encountered waves on my port beam and detected a strong current from my starboard which meant that the river was ebbing in full flow and, you wouldn't believe it, but I needed to adjust the course by at least 30° in order to keep the boat on track for the leading lights of Royan.

I desperately needed to go to the loo but didn't get the chance because, as I was edging away from the headland, I seemed to have entered a hive of activity: ferry boats crossing, three ships crossing over my starboard bows running downstream and one large vessel against the shore lights making her way upstream towards Bordeaux. But nature called - I DO have to go now! So I went outside, which is totally against my principles but that's how desperate I was and now, being relieved of this heavy burden, I carried on crossing the river Gironde!

22:40 - reached the other side of the river entrance and was lucky to see a small vessel heading into the same direction. I followed her as the shore lights had become very confusing but doing so might take the edge off the intensity of keeping course and finding the port entrance of Royan. You see, on the chart it gave the fairway as a narrow band running parallel along the beach with only a single starboard hand-lit marker at the beginning of the channel; with all the confusing shore lights I did succeed in finding the channel and now entered the fairway together with the small fishing vessel; wasn't I lucky meeting up with this boat because it wasn't just the confusion of the lights but I also noticed that the depth of water in the fairway reduced itself to a mere 12 inches under the boat and even the fishing boat in front began to slow down and completed her last few hundred metres at a very slow crawling pace.

I must say, if I had entered this section by myself then I would have had serious doubts as to whether I was in or even near the channel!

Finally, coming to the end of the channel, I had to make a near 180° turn back on myself where I noticed that the glitter of the promenade lights - now not too far ahead of me - shone on a large mud bank stretching from just outside the channel all the way back to the beach.

I slowly entered the Port of Royan. That's funny but the fishing boat, who had guided me in, had suddenly disappeared and left me to find a suitable mooring; I really had no idea where to go but then I spotted a Coastguard Cutter and moored just ahead of her thinking, if it's good enough for her then it's good enough for me. Then after a very successful 18 hours at sea, as usual, I poured myself a well-earned drink!

Going Alone
April 1974

This was the year which changed the way I delivered boats forever. It was this single incident which changed my mind about ever having crew on my voyages.

I couldn't say this was the **best** decision I ever made, but it worked for me, and by doing this I increased my self-discipline and kept the risks I took to a minimum; in fact, I would like to believe that they were "calculated risks" and as for overstepping the mark!

It all started when I found that I had to deliver a boat from Brundall, Norfolk to the port of Glyfada just south of the old Athens Airport. This voyage was going to take 3 weeks and finding a crew for that length of time was simply impossible; in the past I had my friend Jelle, who had sailed with me some years ago, but he needed more security and went back to Smit Lloyd; then I had the pleasure of Richard but he went to work for the Moonraker boatyard after the affair in the Bay of Biscay.

I went to see my friend Jack - *whom I have to thank for introducing me to this newly found work in boat deliveries by sea* - and although he didn't know of anyone at the time he had heard a rumour that Albert, a radio operator who worked on the oil-rig "North Star", might be interested.

Well... I knew Albert too, but only through speaking to him over the VHF radio whilst I was at Smit Lloyd a few years ago. So Jack and I went to see Albert's friend Bill who lived across the road; he also worked on the oil rigs as a radio operator but came ashore and started a radio repair shop.

Jack introduced us.

'Hi Bill, this is Bill who is delivering a motor cruiser to Greece and didn't you say that Albert wants to do something like that?'

'Yes, he keeps mentioning it and he'll be thrilled to bits to have the opportunity, but beware he likes a pint, in fact he likes a lot of pints, otherwise he's alright.'

'That shouldn't be too much of a problem as most of the time we'll be in the middle of nowhere.'

'When are you planning to leave?'

'All being well I plan to leave next Wednesday from the town hall quay at 06:00.'

'I'll make sure that he gets there ready and packed.'

'Thanks Bill.'

The following Wednesday, as planned, we departed from the town hall quayside. Albert was a slender 5' 9" person with curly thick black hair, slim face and a thick bushy moustache. The moustache had long pointed hair sticking out like cats' whiskers, similar to that of the Spanish painter Salvador Dali, but Albert's whiskers were pointing outwards rather than the curled type of Mr Dali.

The voyage started well, although I had to do most of the steering across the North Sea and English Channel to Le Havre but then I was used to that because most of the crew I was able to find were inexperienced except for Jelle, Jack and Richard.

We made good time and I moored as much as possible in places where going to the pub would be difficult, mind you this didn't mean that Albert didn't have anything to drink - he brought enough booze to sink a battleship but at least I could keep him on board where he wouldn't be able to get up to any mischief. So I thought!

The following days we travelled through Rouen, Paris, Epernay, Shalon-sur-Marne and Vitry le-François where we joined the Canal de la Marne a la Saône. It was late afternoon and we had already been through locks 71 down to 67 where we laid-up for the night in between locks 67 and 66 - *Lock 66 was still a good kilometre away from the boat.*

As usual, I made the dinner with a beer or two and after dinner washed-up; Albert went to stretch his legs for a while and said

'I'll see you later.'

I went to bed and as always, it didn't take long for me to fall asleep.

05:45 - and I was ready to go, so that I reached the first lock of the day spot-on 6:30. When I looked into the forward part of the boat I found to my astonishment that the bed had not been slept in and thought: I hope he hasn't fallen over-board! As you can imagine, I didn't want to leave without him but I did need to move from here just in case a barge caught up with me, so I had to move on.

Still in a mode of apprehension I carefully entered lock 66 and carried out the usual procedures of tying-up etc. When the boat reached the upper level, I jumped off and had a word with the lady lock-keeper; this was great because she recognised me from earlier voyages. I was still puzzled where Albert had gone; I had deliberately stayed away from any villages and pubs, so where in heavens name was he? I asked the lady in my poor French whether there was a village nearby, to which she replied 'Non'. Then I asked if there was anywhere where you could get a drink like wine or beer? She said 'Oui' and pointed across the fields into the far distance saying there was a road called Route National RN 4.

'How do I get there' I asked in my clumsy French. She pointed to a bike standing beside a small wooden shed where she also had some chickens and turkeys roaming around, and said

'You can borrow the bike.'

Now I had another problem because the boat was still in the lock but she calmly said,

'That's ok.'

Not having been on a bike for some time, I was a bit wobbly as I raced through the fields and headed towards the main road where I found the roadside café. I parked the bike against the wall and went inside where the smell of French cigarettes was so thick that you could cut the air; there were a large amount of tables occupied by early morning drivers having their breakfast and, through the smoke in the far corner on a bench, was Albert and a few French guys with at least a dozen empty beer bottles in front of them. Albert looked wrecked and probably hadn't had any sleep last night; he spotted me at the doorway, greeting me loudly, with a slur in his voice:

'Hi Bill, come and sit down, these are my friends come and have a drink!' I am ashamed to say I was very abrupt with him, but then what do you expect at 7:30 in the morning with an expensive boat left unattended in the lock. I angrily chastised him, like a naughty boy:

'Albert, I have to go back, the boat is still in the lock and I **have** to move her **now**! You can get yourself a taxi to catch up with me and I hope to see you later!'

I was so worked up about it all that I never thought whether he had any money on him or would know where to go, but that wasn't on my list of priorities; now, for the first time in my life, I had to re-think the process of working the locks by myself and was pleasantly surprised that, after a while, I was fully in control and even began to enjoy it.

Albert turned up alright, in the middle of the day outside lock 59 in Saint Dizier and, as you can imagine, he was so drunk that he flaked out on the bed and fell asleep for the rest of the day.

"Therefore I can announce that today, 11th April 1974 I managed successfully to navigate a total of 27 locks single-handed for the very first time in my life."

Royan
Sunday 7th April 2002

I did have a fantastic deep sleep last night, probably because of the amount of wine I had drunk to celebrate my safe arrival and finally being able to relax after several days of anxiety regarding the stretch of water I had now successfully completed. After breakfast I left the boat to investigate where I had actually ended up and found myself to be close to the marina office which, to my surprise, was already open. I walked in and was greeted by a chirpy young lady, who said in perfect English

'Good morning sir, what can I do for you?'

'Good morning to you too; I arrived last night from Spain and moored the boat on the Coast Guard pontoon and I would like to stay today.'

'That's not a problem, but you will need to move into the marina and moor here.' She pointed her finger at the marina layout on the wall behind her desk.

'Just one more question, is your fuel station open?'

'Yes but only this morning we're off at midday.'

I looked at the clock on the wall. 11:30 I hadn't realised that it was so late already. So I moved the boat to the fuel station and topped-up the tanks, possibly for the last time on this voyage and was able to squeeze in 759 litres; I paid € 668 and thought that's not too bad.

After paying the fuel and the overnight mooring fee, I moved the boat to the inner basin where I did my usual engine checks and replaced the fuel filters; although I didn't have a problem I felt it was better to do it now, rather than trying to wrestle with them out at sea. You see, I had already been running on these filters since Sangenjo, a distance of 500 miles (60 hours), so it wouldn't be long before they needed replacing anyway.

It was 16:00 when I finally closed the engine room hatch and made a brew; looking out onto the marina promenade, I noticed the place was buzzing with Sunday strollers, joggers and roller skaters. After finishing my tea I summoned up the courage to join them (the strollers that is) as I certainly needed to stretch my legs. I walked around the marina and discovered a Yacht Club where I found the latest weather map pinned on the notice board. I studied the map and found, to my surprise, that a high pressure system was going to dominate over this part of the Bay for the coming days. That suited me fine.

Surprisingly, later in the evening, I managed to get the forecast from BBC4 and this verified the predictions I had seen earlier today. I went to sleep feeling at peace knowing that I didn't have to worry about fighting any more large waves – at least for now.

Royan - St Gilles Croix de Vie
Monday 8th April 2002

I woke up to a miserable, misty, almost foggy morning and decided to take my time in preparing the boat for departure; but at 07:50 I left the marina. While navigating my way through the narrow entrance channel, I noticed that I had lots of water under the boat this time. At the end of the channel I turned into the main navigation channel of the River Gironde and was assisted by a (just starting) ebb tide that pushed me along, adding 2 knots to my speed.

The main channel ran very close along the beach at Royan but was barely visible through the mist. For a while I sailed just outside the port-hand markers of the buoyed route intended for large shipping. This morning I found myself completely isolated on the water which was great, because I had to cope with several severe fog patches.

The run through the channel turned out to be a lot faster than I had anticipated and I reached Nº2 buoy at the entrance to the river Gironde at 09:28; from here I changed course for my intended destination of Les Sables-d'Olonne, which is only a short distance up the coast from Royan. Strangely, the minute I parted from the coast the fog lifted but the wind started to increase from a north-easterly direction but the waves were minimal and so didn't hamper my progress.

13.35 - passed Ile de Re. However, soon after passing the island it started to get rather choppy and the sea spray presented me with restricted visibility; an hour after passing the north tip of Ile de Re I noticed the sea was littered with something that looked like loads of sticks, but when I moved closer I realised that I was heading directly for a brightly coloured armada of sailing dinghies; from here I couldn't see a way through and going around them looked an impossible task; anyway, I was still some distance away so I decided to carry on for now and not make any decisions until the last minute because past experience has taught me to wait in such circumstances, as sailing boats have a habit of suddenly changing course virtually in front of you, so as usual, be patient!

The waiting paid-off; as when I approached those colourful boats I found that they were tiny sailing dinghies, each having a youngster at the helm, surrounded by dozens of inflatable safety boats; somehow finding a passage through them was easy after all, although I did have to slow down to a mere 3 knots, in order not to swamp them.

This saga delayed me somewhat but in the meantime the weather had become superb with only a little breeze and a flat calm sea, turning this into a perfect afternoon for the sailing dinghies and, of course, me.

You may remember, this morning I had in mind to set sail for Les Sables-d'Olonne but this turned out to be the port for this regatta and I didn't think I would be able to find a place amongst all the boats. Anyway, it was a bit early in the day to stop and now the weather was so brilliant I needed to make hay whilst the sun shone, so I continued the voyage to the next available port along this stretch of coast which looked to be the port of St Gilles Croix-de-Vie; unfortunately, this presented a new problem as this port showed a depth clearance of 3.3 feet at low water and, not knowing the area, I didn't fancy my chances leaving this place in the dark first thing in the morning and felt this was a risk not worth taking so I thought it prudent to anchor in the allocated area outside the breakwater.

I arrived in the approaches to the port of St Gilles Croix-de-Vie at 18:10 and dropped anchor in 18.7 feet of water at a distance of 0.25nm (463metres) from the breakwater and the nearest beach. I didn't mind dropping anchor, especially as the weather turned out to be so pleasant and I thought this might well be the last time on this voyage that I can have the opportunity of enjoying the tranquillity and peace which is surrounding me right now.

What else could you wish for: smooth sea, lovely sunset and a glass of red wine while watching the arrival of the occasional fishing boat; however it did get chilly after sunset and reluctantly I had to run the generator, breaking the peaceful silence.

Anchorage at St Gilles Croix-de-Vie

St Gilles Croix de Vie – Lorient
Tuesday 9th April 2002

The sun had just risen over the hills, slightly reddish mind you which means "Red sky in the morning, sailor's warning" I hope that's wrong for once. Having had a good night's rest I was full of energy and ready to move on to my next destination. After lifting the anchor I turned the boat into the general direction of Lorient which was hopefully going to be my next port of call.

I am afraid that "Red sky in the morning, sailor's warning" was true once again. Although the sky was now a beautifully painted crystal clear blue with the sun having a warm springtime feel to it, the local forecasters told a different story and gave the prediction of a north-easterly force 5 - 7, but this shouldn't interfere with my run and I hope to arrive in Lorient at my calculated time of 19:00.

During the morning the waves had become progressively higher as I moved away from the coast. At around midday I passed the main shipping route into the estuary of the River Loire at Saint Nazaire. South of the La Banche lighthouse I had to change my course sharply into the waves in order to avoid a collision with the gas tanker "Eduard P. J." who came in from my starboard side and therefore had the right of way.

After a long and choppy slog I passed between Belle Ile (Belle Ile Page 323) and the headland of Presqu'ile Quiberon at 16:41.

At 16:50 I passed the port of le Palais when unexpectedly, approaching from behind at great speed, was a coast-guard vessel. She drew up alongside I was told to stop immediately by an officer on the foredeck who indicated that they were ready to board me; minutes later I was swamped by several officers in navy blue overalls, all armed with torches, and whilst one officer was checking my documents another asked permission to look around the boat; of course I had no option other than to say

'Sure, but can I carry-on, I don't want to miss the tide.' The officer taking notes asked,

'How many crew members do you have on board?'

'I am on my own.'

'Where are you bound for?'

'Well, if you are asking for my final destination, that will be somewhere on the south coast of England but tonight, all being well, I hope to moor in Lorient.'

By now I was feeling a bit nervous, well that's a bit of an understatement, because the officers took a hell of a long time and kept walking from the front to the rear of the boat making mysterious noises and one officer asked whether he could see the engine room.

I began to get the feeling that they were looking for drugs and at this stage I thought, thank God I always check the boats I deliver just in case I am carrying something I am not aware of.

After the officers had spent a good half an hour going through the boat they suddenly gathered themselves on the port side and one by one athletically leaped across back onto their cutter saying, 'Bon voyage.' I was dying to ask them what they were looking for but didn't think they would give away that information.

In the meantime the weather had improved between the peninsular and Belle Ile and from here I was able turn directly for the entrance to the river at Lorient, passing the entrance to the river Etel in the distance where some time ago I had picked up a 20 year old commercial wooden built trawler destined for the east coast of England.

18:45 - finally arrived at the entrance buoy of the river Le Blavet to Lorient; but before entering the channel I studied the chart and chose the Passe de Sud channel. Although the channel was clearly marked it did scare me a bit as rocks on either side of the channel were only marked by a stick with a bit on top; most of the rocks were still just below the surface except for a few which revealed their secret locations when the ocean washed over them.

Approach Passe de Sud channel to the river Le Blavet at Lorient

Now let me see, it's now 2 hours after high water and from this moment the tide will drop dramatically, which doesn't give me a lot of room for manoeuvre; I must admit I would not like to enter this area in fog or at night for the first time.

After passing through the narrow and shallow section of the Passe de Sud it all opened up into a massive lagoon with the Citadelle strategically overlooking the entrance, presumably to protect the harbours at the top end of the river. I also noticed the heavy concrete buildings at the far side which undoubtedly were the bunkers for the German U-boats in the last war of 1940-5.

In the distance to starboard, I noticed the shore-line was littered with buildings and to port the marina of Kernevel. The marina mainly consisted of a very heavy wooden pontoon for keeping the waves at bay during stormy conditions.

I called on my VHF channel 9 and was soon guided by the Marinario to the inside of the heavy pontoon where I secured the boat near the marina office. The Marinario strongly suggested that I tie the boat up securely as they were expecting severe weather overnight and tomorrow. Well that's a bit of luck, I thought.

Yes, the Marinario was totally correct, the weather deteriorated overnight and even this big heavy boat was thrown about like a cork on the water.

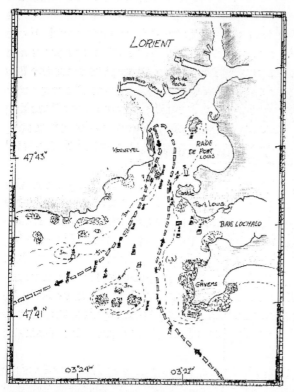

That same day I spent most of my time on board because I was told that the town was a fair distance away from the marina and I needed to keep an eye on the vessel - well, that's my excuse anyway!

The second day I ventured out and walked the "fair distance" into the town. This walk to the town centre turned out to be a short marathon and took me well over 1½ hours but I didn't have anything better to do and it was far better than battling against strong winds and heavy seas!

Belle Ile

Passing Belle Ile reminds me of the first time I visited the place many years ago. Finding this route via the island was a Godsend and Belle Ile became a most important and strategic stop-over with the smaller boats I had to deliver as, understandably, I had become rather nervous crossing this notorious stretch of water with these smaller boats. I stumbled across it one day in March some years ago when I - *bravely!* - left the port of Brest in an attempt to cross the Bay of Biscay in what I can only describe as "mountainous" seas; soon after leaving the sheltered waters of Brest I had found myself looking straight into these transparent massive green walls of water, illuminated by the early morning sun and had thought of that fateful day in February 1974 on the "Christina Claudia".

The seas were so high that I needed to turn away from the oncoming waves; unfortunately because of the direction I wasn't able to return to Brest, and had to let the boat take me into a south-easterly direction, of course it's always more comfortable running with a following sea, and after a while I found that the waves had started to decrease in height although the wind was still very strong.

Being desperate at that time I noticed that the route to Belle Ile was fairly straight forward and without any hazards; also, the Port le Palais, situated on the north side of the island provided fantastic shelter.

Upon my arrival at Port le Palais, I had a strong feeling of safety and tranquillity but most importantly, I was able replenish the fuel and general supplies.

So, from that day forward I would choose to run this diversion route during the winter period for delivering boats with limited fuel range and would never again have to endure those unbelievably long crossings with the smaller boats with the worry of running out of fuel.

Lorient – le Conquet
Saturday 13th April 2002

The weather had calmed down overnight and now we were back into a spring like day once more.

My stay in Lorient had chilled me out but it was now time to make a final move towards home. However, I still had four days sailing ahead of me, providing I didn't encounter any further delays.

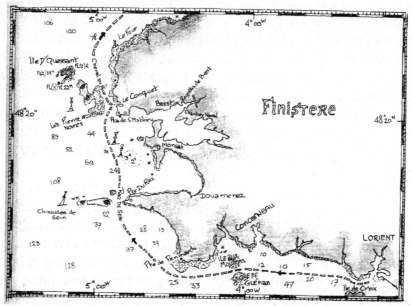

I left the marina at 08:00 and made my way down the outer edge of the main shipping channel and the narrows. Today I needed to take the western passage between Ile aux Moulons on my starboard and Ile de Glènau on my port.

As I have said, the weather was so different today with the sun shining brightly and an offshore wind blowing a moderate force 3 from the north-east, giving me a near flat sea. The day was progressing well and I passed south of Pointe de Penmarc'h headland at 12:48.

The afternoon was pleasant too and because of the strong tide I made good headway towards the famous Raz du Sein, which is a passage between the main headland of Pte du Raz and an outcrop of islands pointing an index finger towards the Americas.

The wind started to increase as I was nearing Raz du Sein and changed into a northerly direction and if this continued I could expect a very, very choppy ride through the passage because the tidal stream would be rushing into the opposite direction of the wind; on the positive side, with the stream running north, it should push me through the passage nicely and yes, as predicted, the wind started to increase to a good force 5, whipping the sea up into a frenzy which tossed the boat about enough for all the cupboard doors to fly open and the contents to be thrown out all over the saloon floor; luckily, this time they were all dry goods which could easily be picked up later.

During this commotion I spotted a sailing mast through the sea spray and it looked as if this sailing boat was on a reciprocal course. I waited until she was closer and found that she was an English flagged yacht making her way into the bay, or at least that was what she was trying to do but she didn't seem to be making any headway; in fact, when I started to monitor her progress on the radar I found that she was slowly moving backwards! Oh, poor souls. According to my calculations they would have to struggle on for another 2 hours before the tide would ease on them.

But on the contrary, I - selfish thinking - was doing well and ran at an unprecedented speed of 14 knots, instead of my usual speed of 8.3 knots; but now, 5 miles after passing Raz du Sein, I found that the waves had started to disappear, although the tidal stream was still running north; I hoped this would continue until I reached my intended destination of le Conquet.

17:53 - passed the Point St Mathieu on the headland at the entrance of the rade of Brest which is also my final approach to La Conquet.

> As I was passing Point St Mathieu it reminded me of a story which I simply can't forget as it was something you wouldn't think could happen to anyone, let alone me! (Page 327)

After passing St Mathieu point and at 18:18 I entered the fishing port of Le Conquet but I couldn't find a buoy to moor onto and the inner harbour would dry out at low water so I moored along the fisherman's quay where I plonked myself alongside two fishing boats, and as it was Saturday I didn't expect any fishing boats to move off first thing on Sunday morning.

Just My Luck
December 1983

It was in that year when I had to deliver a fast Italian 60 foot motor cruiser, built in the seventies. I was familiar with this craft as I had already skippered her several times in the past.

I received from the owner the call in late November asking whether I had time to bring the boat back to the UK from the South of France.

'Sorry, but don't you think it's a little late to start this voyage; you know that the weather in the Atlantic isn't going to be easy.'

But this had fallen on deaf ears, and I don't know why I bothered to state it in the first place!

'Don't worry Bill, I have found two lads who are willing to join you as crew' and he proudly added

'Don tells me he has had experience of crossing the Atlantic on sailing yachts.'

'Ok, but if I can't make Lymington before Christmas then I will have to leave the boat wherever she is and fly back, but unfortunately I wouldn't be able to finish the voyage until after the London and Düsseldorf Boat Shows which will be at the end of January.'

'That's alright but, knowing you, you'll get there in time for Christmas.'

His last remark was rather flattering, but for me to succeed I needed the weather to be favourable all the way and no mishaps with the boat; that seemed to be asking a little too much! Being the person I am, I couldn't say 'no' and thought, Oh well, it won't be too bad, at least I will have the pleasure of two pairs of helping hands. This was a luxury for me as I normally could only afford one, and usually inexperienced crew; having two at my disposal would give me the advantage of running 24/7, as it is known today.

After my usual preparations I collected the money from the owner and joined my crew, Don and Paul, at Heathrow Airport and headed for the port of Vieux Cannes in the south of France.

On the morning of the 1st December 1983 we left Vieux Cannes for Gibraltar. I had set the throttles at 1100 RPM which gave us a steady speed of 9.5 knots, consuming 4.5 litres per nautical mile.

> As a matter of interest, if I cruised at 20 knots the fuel consumption would substantially increase to 9 litres per nm and I learned a long time ago that " fast is slow" and "slow is fast" and... going fast can also be unbelievably stressful on a long run.
>
> There are several reasons for running at displacement speed: it saves excessive structural stress on the boat; you don't pick up so much dirt in the fuel tanks which avoids cleaning fuel filters; longer passages between refuelling points meaning less waiting times in the ports; less stress and tiredness on the body and, as a bonus, saving fuel in the process.

The voyage started off well but the Gulf of Lyon was its usual self, with a gale blowing from the NW which kept us on our toes; having said this, I was still able to sleep for 2 hours at a time. It took 15 hours to cross the Gulf but luckily, the weather started to calm down after the crossing and we arrived 5 days later in Gibraltar, which was well beyond my expectations.

Whilst refuelling the boat (and ourselves) Paul went to make a call from the telephone exchange. He then joined us at the harbour bar where he took a sip of his cold beer, paused for a second or so then dropped a bombshell saying,

'Bill, I have just spoken to my wife and unfortunately she needs me back in England; I also spoke to the owner and he has organized a ticket for me for the 8th December from Lisbon.' Why wasn't I surprised at that!

'Right lads... now that we have this little hiccup, we will have to leave early in the morning so that we get to Lisbon the day after tomorrow, which will be well in time for Paul to catch his flight; that's if the weather plays its part in this too!'

We left the following morning for Lisbon and again we were lucky with the weather and did the run in a record time of 32 hours. On arrival in Belèm we refuelled straight away. Brilliant, I thought, this means we can leave first thing in the morning.

The following morning we dropped Paul off near Lisbon town quay and I said,

'I hope you don't mind, but we need to get going while the weather is good.'

'No, of course not, I am sorry I am not able to continue the voyage to the end.'

I am not sure whether this was the complete truth as Paul had been seasick on several occasions and I suppose the thought of having to cross the Bay was the deciding factor for him leaving and wanting the comfort of his home; anyway, who could blame him.

After dropping Paul off, Don and I departed the port of Belèm and headed for the inshore passage towards Cabo Raso just beyond the bay of Casçais. An hour later we rounded Cabo Raso and we headed straight into 20 foot waves, accompanied by a 25 - 30 knot wind from the same direction. I asked Don, who had the Atlantic passage experience, whether he had seen such conditions on his voyages; he answered, 'yes and worse.'

I suppose this should have made me feel better, as with his experience we had a chance of making Lymington for Christmas. It took a few hours to get used to the motion and the sight of these enormous waves coming towards us but we soon settled down for our long overnight passage to Vigo. Measuring the distance with my dividers over the chart, I calculated that we wouldn't get there much before midday tomorrow - all being well.

As predicted, we arrived the following day. Although I still had plenty of fuel, I thought I would top-up anyway; immediately after we replenished the fuel, water and dry stores, we made the decision to move on because if we lingered we could easily get "cold feet" and stay in port.

Running along the north-west coast of Spain we were accompanied by a small cargo liner which ran parallel to us throughout the night and the following day; in fact she was with us until we reached our destination of Gijon, a port ninety miles east of La Coruña.

During last night I made the decision to run this longer route, hoping to avoid the larger waves which hit the continental shelf and make the long swell

Small cargo liner running parallel overnight

shorter and therefore much higher. I hoped that running towards Gijon may make these waves more manageable.

We arrived in Gijon around 10:00 that morning and after refuelling we plucked up the courage once again - *I am sure this was only because I was determined to get home for Christmas* - and left on our

280 mile crossing to Brest.

The crossing went well, that is... until around midnight when the wind started to pick up big time and registered between 35 – 45 knots; the waves had started to increase to a ridiculous height, but having been at sea for the past 10 days, we had become accustomed to seeing their size, but eventually I was forced to slowdown as the waves started to break with great force over the bow, which in turn seriously restricted our visibility. Unfortunately these conditions continued for the remainder of the night and into the next day; in fact, it had become so hair-raising that looking for the buoy marking the end of the outcrop of islands at Raz de Sein had become extremely difficult; to top it all, the sea spray had reduced the visibility to no more than 1½ nautical miles. We also started to get rogue waves coming from different directions and every time the boat went over one we ended up looking straight into another solid wall of green water, accompanied by a powerful bright silvery-white crest thundering along its top towards us. I kept looking at my watch almost every minute, but it seemed that time had stopped. I had worked out, and seriously believed, that we should have reached our estimated position at the buoy of Chausée de Sein. *Navigating still being done by D.R.*

My mind started to run in circles. I have to see this buoy but I mustn't dither too long in making the decision to change course towards St Mathieu. It was all getting extremely serious; mountainous waves, poor visibility, cold, dog tired and not able to have a hot drink; although I was drinking lots of water I didn't seem to be able to quench this unbelievable thirst and now, of all things, I had to steer the boat by hand as the autopilot, understandably, did not want to play ball in avoiding the rogue waves.

Time was marching-on and now at 16:30 it was beginning to get dark and still we hadn't been able to see the buoy; of course I realized that the speed was fluctuating in these seas, but I felt that something more sinister was going on and we started to ship a hell of a lot more water over the bows; somehow, something just didn't seem right. But what was that? I am sure I just saw a light flash almost directly ahead of us and, simultaneously, Don shouted,

'Bill, did you see that!'

'I think I did Don.'

It looked like we had both seen the lighthouse on the off-lying rocks at the south side of the "Channel du Four" this meant that we were well past the buoy, but I still preferred to wait just a little longer before I made my next decision.

Our progress was extremely slow and it took another 20 minutes before we could make out the identity of the light and yes, as I thought, it was the lighthouse standing on the off-lying rocks at the south-east end of Queasant; it seemed that we had missed the buoy by two miles to our starboard.

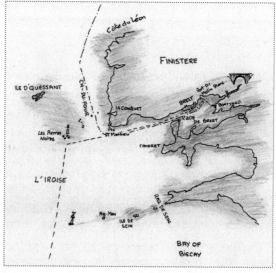

This was unbelievable but with all the bad weather we had encountered we were only a ½ mile off-course which was amazing and I gave a huge sigh of relief. Phew! Now I can change course and head directly for the St Mathieu.

Although totally exhausted, I was well aware that I needed to stay alert as we were about to encounter high beam seas and a strong tidal stream pushing us dangerously close to the rocks and we would have to endure this until we safely passed St Mathieu's point.

'Don, before we change direction, can you check and see that there isn't anything which can be thrown about and damage the boat!'

Don staggered down the stairs, trying to hold on whilst the boat was throwing him violently from side to side, but seconds later he returned to the wheelhouse with a face like a white sheet and with a trembling voice said,

'Bill, there is a lot of water on the floor in the passage way!'

'What do you mean?'

'Well, the water is sloshing back and forth over the carpet.'

The first thought that went through my mind, was whether we had accidently switched on the fresh water pump.

I asked Don to go and check.

We needed to do this as it was not long ago that the owner had replaced all the copper water pipes for plastic hoses and now those hoses had a habit of coming undone with the bouncing and shaking of the boat.

Shortly after he returned and said,

'It's switched off'

'Alright, are the portholes still closed?'

He went back down to check and said,

'Yes Bill, all the portholes are closed and secured, but just to let you know, the water level is still rising!' Thank goodness that the engine room was separated by a water-tight bulkhead.

'Oh..., that's all we need; alright Don, there is nothing we can do other than to proceed carefully towards Brest; luckily, we just have another 15 miles to go.'

It was difficult keeping an accurate course and we were still being thrown about, but we finally reached the shelter of the north shore and soon everything started to calm down. I noticed that the speed, which should have been 7 knots, had dropped down to 5, but the water level in the boat seemed to have stabilised and we weren't taking on any more water; by now all three cabins and two bathrooms were swamped knee-deep in sea water.

I asked Don to check overboard to see whether all three bilge pumps were working. Thankfully they were but we didn't know for how long.

After a strenuous 34 hours at sea (covering 280nm) we finally entered the large port of Brest at 21:30 and I manoeuvred through the naval base into the fishing basin where the fishing fleet had already fully occupied the quayside and the only possible place I could see was alongside a large fishing boat.

Minutes after we secured the boat we were commanded to move to the newly built marina which was just outside the main harbour to port and upriver. I told them, in my very broken French, that we were sinking and needed help and 5 minutes later lots of blue flashing lights lit the quayside and an army of fire brigade officers jumped on board with massive hoses and lots of shouting in all directions; I must say, I didn't have a clue what they were saying but they emptied the boat within 20 minutes and left Don and I with a dirty, damp and extremely cold boat.

After all the blue lights had departed a normal evening silence returned to the port and I said to Don,

'Let's go ashore. I know of a small restaurant across the road where we can warm ourselves and have something to eat and, most importantly, a well-deserved beer. We reminisced whilst having dinner, wondering why the boat was sinking out at sea and not now! Oh well, we are safe, that's the main thing and we will do our investigation tomorrow in daylight.

Early in the morning we were rudely awakened by the crew of the fishing boat who wanted to leave. We repositioned our boat and returned to our bunks but somehow I couldn't fall asleep again.

Later in the morning we went across the road and had a fantastic breakfast. The road side café was fully occupied by lorry drivers who had arrived overnight ready for loading the freshly caught fish. After breakfast we leisurely walked back to the boat where we found several people looking at our bow and pointing. We noticed that they had just discovered the mystery of our sinking.

'What in heavens name is that?' said Don, and then stating the obvious

'That's a hole!'

'I can see that!'

'How did that get there, Bill?'

'I don't know, we'll have to take a closer look.'

We climbed back on board and walked up to the front, laid on the deck and looked over the edge; to my horror I discovered that we had holed the boat near deck level. The hole measured about 50 x 50 cm and peculiarly, it was almost a neatly cut square. I was able to put my hand inside and I could feel the lining of the chain locker. My initial observation was that there wasn't any ventilation between the hull and the chain locker; therefore I assumed that the epoxy paint had held the rotten ply together until now but, with the constant pounding of waves, it had finally given way.

At least we now knew where the water had come from and we just had to find someone who could patch-up the hull. I asked one of the onlookers, in my pigeon French, if he knew where we could get it repaired.

'Yes... over there!' He pointed in the direction across the Elorn River.

'Over on the other side is a Chantier Naval; they will have a shipwright, but you can only get there near high water.'

Instinctively my eyes wandered off into the direction of the slimy green harbour wall to see the state of the tide and I guessed that it was about half-tide so I needed to look in my tide-table to see whether it was rising or falling; as luck would have it the water was on the rise. I thanked the person for the information and we quickly left the commercial port for the boatyard across the river.

We found the shipwright inside a fishing boat.

'Bonjour monsieur, do you have a moment?' and without looking up he replied,

'Oui!'

'Can you please have a look at our boat; we have a hole in the bow and we would like to know whether you can repair it for us?'

'I'll have a look for you, but you'll have to wait until I finish this job.'

Looking at the time I thought, Mmmm… I hope it won't be too long otherwise we'll lose the tide.

Fortunately, 20 minutes later he stood on the wobbly pontoon inspecting the damage at the bow and pulling away all the rotten material bit by bit.

'Ooh là, là.'

He shook his head from side to side and continued

'That's bad!' and emphasized this by letting off a deep sigh.

'I can only do a temporary repair to get you home!'

'That's brilliant. Can you possibly do this for us now?'

'Oui, it will take me about 30 minutes and then you'll be ready to go, but don't get the repair wet for a few hours!'

'Don't worry we won't be going to sea today. We just have to move the boat to the new marina.'

I paid the carpenter, unmoored the boat but I needed to be extremely careful not to hit the bottom on my way out.

Now, you would think this is the end of the story. WRONG! After the ordeal of the past 48 hours we spent the afternoon leisurely putting the boat back together and carrying out my usual checks on the engines and changed the cotton wads fuel filters and I am glad I made that decision because they were nearly clogged-up and I don't think they would have lasted much longer; they certainly wouldn't have made the crossing to England.

We had our dinner in the yacht club and went to bed because we needed to leave early in the morning, on the tide, to reach the open sea at dawn.

I had set the alarm for 03:30 and we departed at 04:00 on the dot. We were lying with the bow facing the wrong way so I needed to swing the boat, almost on the spot, in order to face seaward. As planned we reached the open sea at daybreak and successfully navigated the "Chanel du four" with a following tidal stream; miraculously the sea had become like a mirror, except for the long Atlantic swell left behind from two days ago.

After clearing the last marker in "Chanel du four" I headed directly for Dartmouth, a 13 hour passage. I thought, we had done rather well and it was really unthinkable that this voyage had only taken us 11 days so far.

Passing the Needles towards Spurn point on the south coast of England

The day was unbelievably beautiful; cold, but the sun shone brightly in an almost unblemished blue sky. The sea stayed calm which made me think, shall I, or shan't I, and yes, I did! I made a snap decision about 20 miles off Start Point to change course and head directly for my final destination of Lymington.

I couldn't believe my luck, but everything was going extremely well

337

and it looked like we would reach Spurn Point, on the west side of the Isle of Wight, at 02:00 in the morning.

Then... in the early hours of the morning we hit a wall of thick fog, just after we passed the Needles. I slowly tried to proceed into the Solent but felt too tired, which made me nervous, and thought it better not to continue navigating the channel to Lymington harbour. We had done so well that I wasn't going to take this gamble so close to home so we dropped the anchor in the bay near Spurn Point for the remainder of the night.

We woke at 07:00 only to find that the earlier fog had lifted to a mist with a visibility of ½ a mile, which was good enough for me to enter port.

I slowly navigated into the marina and finally moored along the main wall near the harbourmaster's office. I noticed the harbour master, outside his office, talking to a police officer. We secured the boat and greeted both gentlemen. The officer replied:

'Good morning who's the captain?'

'Good morning sir, I am.'

'Where have you come from?'

I said with a proud voice,

'We came from Cannes in the South of France.'

'Yes, but were you not in Brest the night before last?'

Wow, I was totally perplexed and wondered how on earth he knew that! I hadn't told anyone about us being in Brest and nobody in Brest knew that we were going to Lymington.

'I hesitantly replied,

'Yeeesss!' almost questioning him at the same time.

'How many crew members do you have on board?'

'There are just the two of us'

'Are you sure?'

'Of course I am sure!'

'That is not what I have on my note which says that you have two crew members with you and you left the south of France 12 days ago!'

I thought: Goodness me! In what direction is this conversation going?

Then Don said,

'I think he means Paul!'

'Yes of course!'

I looked at the police officer and could see from the expression on his face that he didn't quite believe me.

'That's right, Officer, Paul went home from Lisbon because the seas didn't agree with him!'

'Captain, would you mind giving me your address and a contact number?'

'Sure'

Closing his note book he said

'That's all for now!'

Don and I cleared the boat and after thanking him we went our separate ways. But I was still unbelievably puzzled by the whole affair.

A few days went by when the doorbell rang at home and I found two police officers standing at the door. I let the officers into the house and they asked me some more questions about the time we were in Brest. I told them all I knew whilst they made further notes; I became more and more curious and asked the officer what all the questioning was about.

'Sorry sir, but we are still investigating at the moment and we can't tell you anything for now.'

Weeks went by then the phone rang.

'Hello?'

'It's the Yorkshire Police, Sir. Sorry to bother you again but I am pleased to let you know that we have eliminated you from our enquiries!'

'Sorry…, I didn't even know I formed part of your enquiries?'

'You did sir, but the case is now closed.'

'Can you please tell me what it was all about?'

'Yes, the day you left Brest, which we believe was at around 04:00, you left a dead body behind which was apparently lodged under your bathing platform; but the case is now solved and it turned out that this person was involved in industrial espionage and had been thrown off the bridge into the river a little upstream from where you were that night.'

I put the phone down and with a huge sigh of relief said 'Darling, you are not going to believe this …' Just my Luck…'

Home Safely

Three days after my departure from Le Conquet with overnight stays in Dartmouth and Yarmouth, on the Isle of Wight, I arrived at my ultimate destination of Port Solent at the top end of Portsmouth harbour on the thirty-fifth day of this epic voyage.

As I have come to expect, in my life as a professional delivery skipper, my arrival was unannounced and without a welcoming party to greet me; that is, except for the resident swans who were more interested in getting a bit of lunch and some fresh water from me.

I switched off the engines for the very last time and thought, thank you Lord for getting me home safely once again.